GREY DATA ANALYTICS FOR MANAGEMENT AND SOCIAL SCIENCES

(*With Excel Implementation*)

R. RAJESH
Assistant Professor
Operations Management and Decision Sciences
IIM Tiruchirappalli, Tiruchirappalli, India

PHI Learning Private Limited
Delhi-110092
2025

In fond memory of ***Shri Asoke K. Ghosh*** *(October 1942 – February 2024), Founder Chairman and Managing Director of PHI Learning, whose vision endlessly inspires.*

The Legacy Continues. . . .

Published by Pushpita Ghosh, PHI Learning Private Limited, Rimjhim House, 111, Patparganj Industrial Estate, Delhi-110092 and Printed by Syndicate Binders, A-20, Hosiery Complex, Noida, Phase-II Extension, Noida-201305 (N.C.R. Delhi).

₹595.00

GREY DATA ANALYTICS FOR MANAGEMENT AND SOCIAL SCIENCES
R. Rajesh

ISBN-978-93-5443-969-8 (Print Book)
ISBN-978-93-5443-847-9 (e-Book)

To

my son "Agastya Raj" aka "Appu"

Contents

Foreword

by Prof. Sifeng Liu

Data analysis and decision-making are essentially important for the social sciences and management domains. In the present era of Big-data, managers and scientists attempt to incorporate as much information as possible to improve the exactitude of decisions. Although inputting more data into any decision-making model does not necessitate or guarantee better results, the availability and access to large data can help managers to choose the right data for making the right decisions. Most often in social sciences and in management, the decision-maker encounters problems with the completeness of information, prior to application of any data analysis or decision-making models. Generally, small and incomplete datasets are regarded as not suitable for put in to any data analysis or decision-making models. Grey theory was proposed by Deng Julong to address the problems with incompleteness of information, where one of the basic assumptions in the formulation of the theory is that the completeness of information is absolute and temporary. Since the inception of the theory, it has found vast applications to various domains in natural sciences, engineering sciences, agricultural sciences, and economics.

Also, grey theory has wide applications in management and social sciences domains, where only limited explorations are made by data scientists in this domain. Also considering the Indian context, the research in this domain has wide scope and is much unexplored. Rajesh has been working since the time of his doctoral thesis works, to develop the gaps connecting mathematical sciences, social sciences, and management. He has explored and experimented several possibilities and applications of various grey-based models, such as the *grey relational analysis, grey prediction, grey clustering, grey programming, grey target decision-making, grey incidence analysis*, and other several combined grey-based models. As the Editor in Chief of the journal, *Grey Systems: Theory and Application*, I am extremely glad to write a foreword for the book "*Grey Data Analytics for Management and Social Sciences*", where the book is typically focused on the applications to aid management and social science practitioners. A case-based reasoning approach is followed throughout the chapters, to demonstrate the implementation of various grey-based methodologies. Also, Excel-based calculations provided for implementation can significantly benefit any undergraduate, postgraduate, or doctoral students in the social sciences and management domains.

Prof. Sifeng Liu, PhD, Fellow of the MSCA Actions,
Honorary Fellow of WOSC Distinguished Professor of
Northwestern Polytechnical University
Director of Center for Grey Systems Studies, NPU
The founding Editor of Grey Systems: Theory and Application and the
Editor-in Chief of The Journal of Grey Systems
The founding president of International Association of Grey Systems and
Uncertainty Analysis and the founding president of
Grey System Society of China
127 Youyi West Road, Xi'an, China, zip code 710072
E-mail: sfliu@nwpu.edu.cn

Foreword

***by* Prof. Jeffrey Yi-Lin Forrest**

With the advancement of AI (artificial intelligence) technology and that of systems science, management science, in particular, and social science, in general, have been experiencing a paradigm shift. What is most noticeable about this shift is the increasing amounts of scholarly efforts devoted to the study of big data to uncover insights and hidden opportunities. In the front of real-life applications, the practitioners of management and social sciences have become more heavily dependent on data analysis and data-driven decision-making. Large datasets are incorporated with various decision-making models to support decision-makers to develop their action plans with greatly improved efficiency.

For the general managerial or social scenario, input data of improved quality tends to produce enhanced quality output. However, no matter how the quality of input data is increased, there are always intrinsic uncertainties with the data due to various humanly uncontrollable reasons, such as the physiological limitations of humans, the concept of data, and the models adopted. For related details, please consult with my recent monographs: *Systemic Principles of Applied Economic Philosophies I: Producers, Consumers and the Firm* and *Systemic Principles of Applied Economic Philosophies II: Value, Decision & Large-Scale Business Forces*, published by Springer in 2024.

With such realization in place, it is found that many decision-making situations in social sciences, in general, and management, in particular, suffer from the availability of exact information for making decisions of expected quality. To deal with such situations successfully, grey systems theory becomes readily available due to its capability to handle the vagueness and incompleteness that inherently exist with any dataset.

Because one of the foundational principles of grey systems theory is to make a maximized use of the information available, the grey theory has been widely applied in various domains of natural science, social sciences and management, ever since the initial proposal of the theory by Deng Julong in 1982. Particular to domains of management and social sciences, this theory has benefited both researchers and practitioners by assimilating available information into data analysis and decision-making models without the required clarity and brevity.

As a scholar who has been on board since the early stages of the development of grey systems theory, I appreciate the efforts of Rajesh in bringing forward applications of this theory to domains of management in particular and social sciences in general. I hope that many researchers in India and from around the world will be motivated to adopt grey-theory-based methodologies in their researches and resolutions of practical problems, after studying Rajesh's book, entitled "Grey Data Analytics for Management and Social Sciences".

The beauty of this book is its case-by-case-based reasoning approach for demonstration and its Excel based implementation. Other than detailing several grey-theory-based models, the book introduces many advanced applications. I believe that the book will significantly help researchers, postgraduate students, as well as undergraduate students, to develop their own frontiers in the domains of social sciences and management.

Prof. Jeffrey Yi-Lin Forrest
Professor, Department of Accounting Economics,
Slippery Rock University, PA, USA
Founding President—International Institute for General Systems Studies (IIGSS)
Co-founder (Institute for Grey Systems Studies,
Nanjing University of Aeronautics and Astronautics)
Founder: IEEE International Conference on Grey Systems and Intelligent Services

Preface

Grey Systems theory has been introduced in the early 1980s, where a control problem of the grey systems was presented by Prof. Deng Julong. Later, in the late 1980s, he extended the theory and outlined multiple methodologies that grey system theory can offer to deal with the uncertainties in particular with information. This became a starting point in the direction of researches related to grey numbers and the associated methodologies. Later, renowned researchers like Prof. Sifeng Liu, Prof. Yi Lin Forrest, and Prof. Naiming Xie have largely expanded the domain of knowledge and applications of Grey Systems. Considering the present context, several researchers are working on the theory and the related applications in various domains including engineering, social sciences, natural sciences, biological sciences, economics, as well as in management sciences. These applications are spread over a wide arena of domains in grey systems analysis; including incidence analysis applications, decision-making applications, clustering applications, prediction applications, programming applications, and lately the causal modelling applications. Also, grey-based methodologies are used in combination with other methods for solving and addressing situations with uncertainties in data, particularly for vague, incomplete, or small datasets.

Although we can see applications of grey systems theory in business, management and the social sciences, most of these are extended in particular to decision-making or related models. Considering the wide scope of grey systems theory to bridge the gap between mathematical sciences and management or social sciences, the idea of the book is emerged. This book is essentially outlined to familiarize the applications of grey systems theory to management and social science students, researchers, faculties, and practitioners. With clear demonstration of case problems for implementation of each method, users can relate to their business or social science situations and thereby get benefited from the implementation aspects. Also, it is expected that the Excel demonstration with formulas can make the task easy and the understanding clearer for users. An online Excel calculation (featuring multiple sheets) for the implementation of all the methodologies mentioned in the textbook is available for users, which can be accessed and downloaded along with the textbook. Hopefully the author believes that the book can significantly benefit a larger audience of graduate, postgraduate, and doctoral students in the management and social sciences domains.

R. Rajesh

Acknowledgements

I am deeply grateful to Prof. Sifeng Liu and Prof. Jeffrey Yi-Lin Forrest for writing the foreword for this book. Their book, *Grey Information: Theory and Practical Applications*, has inspired numerous researchers, including myself, to explore this field and apply various grey systems-based methodologies to many practical problems in the management and the social sciences domains.

R. Rajesh

CHAPTER 1

Grey Information

1.1 INTRODUCTION TO GREY THEORY

Grey theory was first introduced by Deng in 1982 and was further developed by him in 1989. The theory has been widely used in the quantification of uncertain systems and is regarded as a mathematical approach to modelling systems with limited information, uncertainty, or vagueness. Methodologies involving grey theory can be used to analyze and predict the behavior of systems exhibiting uncertain and incomplete patterns of data (Liu et al., 2012). The theory is particularly useful when traditional method of statistics, probability, may not be applicable due to unavailability of a precise mathematical model or insufficiency of data. Grey theory has been widely applied by researchers across various domains in economics, finance, engineering, and environmental science, where uncertainty and incompleteness in information appear to be the major challenges. Management and social science researchers often face challenges while handeling data that is often based on judgments, opinions, or surveys, where the information (data) may be incomplete, small, or inconsistent across groups or individuals. Grey theory can offer a wide range of methodologies to cater the needs of data analysis and decision-making for management and social science researchers. This can extend from decision-making to prediction or from clustering to causal modelling.

The data collected by management and social science researchers can be subject to a data cleaning process, prior to application of any grey based methodologies to gain appropriate insights from the data. After that according to the need of the method, proper treatment of the data can be conducted. These processes are generally noted as the strengthening and weakening operators of data sequences, where the behavioral data sequences will shrink when a strengthening operator is applied and the same will expand when a weakening operator is applied. Some of the basic operators will be discussed in the forthcoming chapters. Although grey theory can be employed to be used in a wide array of problems using their typical methodologies to analyze small data, incomplete data, and/or data with uncertainties, we have included some of the selected methodologies using grey theory that can be beneficial to management and social science researchers and practitioners to gain better insights from the data they have. The problems included in this book uses grey based models including the following: grey incidence models, grey decision-making models, grey causal models, grey prediction models, grey programming models, and grey clustering models. These methods can cover a wide variety of situations for uncertain decision-making and forecasting for the management and social science researchers in practice.

Let us further discuss on the important topic of positioning the grey systems theory and their allied methodologies in the spectrum of science and discuss on the typical situations for its application in the areas of uncertain decision-making environments. In control theory, the darkness of colors is used to represent the clarity of information. Here, black indicates unknown information, white indicates completely known information, and grey indicates the information, which is partially known and partially unknown. The four possibilities for incompleteness of information in systems can be as follows;

1. Incompleteness with the information of elements
2. Incompleteness with the structure of information
3. Incompleteness with the boundary of information
4. Incompleteness with the behavior information of movement

Thus, incompleteness in information is considered as the base of grey systems theory. The properties of grey systems are summarized in Liu et al. (2022) and the same are shown in Table 1.1.

Table 1.1 Comparison of properties of grey systems

	Black	**Grey**	**White**
Information	Unknown	Incomplete	Known
Appearance	Dark	Grey	Bright
Process	New	Replace old with new	Old
Property	Chaos	Complexity	Order
Methodology	Negative	Transition	Positive
Attitude	Indulgence	Tolerance	Serenity
Conclusion	No result	Multiple solution	Unique solution

Considering the above properties, the fundamental principles of grey systems were articulated by Prof. Deng Julong and are reiterated by Liu et al. (2022). These principles are as follows;

1. ***Axiom on informational difference:*** This principle exercises that difference indicates the existence of information, where each piece of information must carry some sort of differences. Say, for example, we consider that object A is different from object B, then there is some information about object B that is not true about object A. If there is more content in the piece of a new information, it brings more differences than compared to the earlier version of the information available to us.
2. ***Axiom on non-uniqueness:*** One of the basic law of application of the grey systems theory is the non-uniqueness in solutions. Here, the solution maker is free to approach a problem with flexibility. Hence, by having flexibility, one can become more effective

in reaching his goals. This is generally achieved through non-unique targets, named as the grey targets. Suppose, for example, if a recent graduate is applying for multiple jobs, then the chances of him/her to get at least one job is more, and hence, the chances to succeed improves.

3. ***Axiom on minimal information:*** One of the noticing characteristics of the grey system theory is its capability to make best use of the available minimum information. Grey systems theory is coined to handle uncertain problems with small samples and/or poor information. Thus, making sufficient discovery with the application of minimal amount of information, is the basic logic in thinking considering grey systems theory.
4. ***Axiom on recognition base:*** This axiom reemphasizes the understanding of information that regards information as the base and foundation on which people recognizes and understand. Hence, through complete and deterministic information, people can gain recognition and based on incomplete and non-deterministic information, people can gain grey recognition.
5. ***Axiom on new information priority:*** This axiom posits that the function considering a new piece of information is greater, when compared to a function considering old pieces of information. This clarifies the fact that in grey systems theory, one can apply additional weights on new information to achieve better results in modelling. While when the new information is available, the motivation for the whitenization of grey elements may get strengthened.
6. ***Axiom on absoluteness of greyness:*** This axiom considers that incompleteness of information is absolute. Hence, completeness of information is relative and temporary. While when the original non-determinism has just disappeared, the new non-determinism will emerge soon. Hence, with endless supply of information, human recognition and understanding of the world also become endless. This points to the fact that the greyness of information is absolute and will not disappear.

1.2 COMPARISON WITH OTHER NON-DETERMINISTIC METHODS

Probability theory, fuzzy set theory, and grey systems theory are the three most-often practiced theories and methods utilizing these theories are widely employed in studies involving non-deterministic systems. These theories enable us to make meaningful sense of incompleteness and uncertainties, even though they handle different types and kind of uncertainties. Fuzzy set theory has its application in dealing with recognitive uncertainties, where the characteristics of having a clear intension and unclear extension can hold true. Suppose for the example of "hot water". It is difficult to define an exact range of temperature to characterize water as hot. This points to the fact that while the intension in stating "hot water" is clear, the extensions of the same being unclear. Fuzzy mathematics can best deal with such uncertainties based on pre-assigned membership functions, which are developed based on experiences.

Probability and statistics can study stochastic uncertainties that emphasizes on the statistical patterns in the historical data of a phenomena, by observing the chances for a possible outcome to occur. The base of the theories to produce reliable results is the assumption that large size samples follow certain patterns, termed as distributions. Grey systems theory on alternate was developed to handle small samples and poor information. These typical problems handled by grey systems theory cannot be successfully handled by either probability or statistics. Grey theory has made this possible through coverage of information and generation of series for obtaining more realistic patterns of data. Thus, grey theory and grey numbers are formulated to handle data with clear extensions and unclear intentions. Say for example, considering the fact that the normal body temperature ranges from 36.5°C to 37.5°C. This indicates a grey number with the extensions being clear, but the exact body temperature of a healthy individual may vary within the range. Comparison tables for different theories dealing with uncertainty are provided by Liu et al. (2011) and the same is included as Table 1.2 as follows:

Table 1.2 Comparison table for different theories dealing with uncertainties

Aspects	Grey systems theory	Probability theory	Fuzzy set theory
Objects of study	Poor information uncertainty	Stochastic uncertainty	Cognitive uncertainty
Basic sets	Grey hazy sets	Cantor sets	Fuzzy sets
Methods	Information coverage	Probability distribution	Function of affiliation
Procedure	Grey series generation	Frequency distribution	Marginal sampling
Requirement	Any distribution	Typical distribution	Experience
Emphasis	Intention	Intention	Extension
Objectives	Laws of reality	Laws of statistics	Cognitive expression
Characteristics	Small samples	Large samples	Experience

1.3 CONCLUSION

This chapter covers the basics of grey information and grey theory, where a comparison of the types and kinds of uncertainty that grey theory can deal with are also made. Along with that the major axioms that forms the basis of grey theory and grey information are also covered. A comparison table is included to compare the major theories that can be used to deal with the uncertainties in the data and the information.

REFERENCES

Deng, J. L. (1982). Control problems of grey systems. *Systems and Control Letters,* 1(5), 288–294.

Deng, J. L. (1989). Introduction to grey system theory. *The Journal of Grey System*, 1(1), 1–24.

Liu, S. F., Yang, Y. J. and Forrest, J. (2022). *Grey Systems Analysis*. Springer-Verlag, Berlin.

Liu, S., Fang, Z., Yang, Y. and Forrest, J. (2012). General grey numbers and their operations. *Grey Systems: Theory and Application*, 2(3), 341–349.

Liu, S., Lin, Y., Liu, S. and Lin, Y. (2011). Introduction to grey systems theory. *Grey Systems: Theory and Applications*, Book series: Understanding Complex Systems, 68, 1–18.

CHAPTER 2

Basic Grey Operations

2.1 INTRODUCTION TO GREY NUMBERS

The grey numbers are usually represented as closed intervals and their operations closely resemble those of the interval calculus (Deng, 1989). Grey numbers are defined with clear extensions and unclear intentions, where the boundaries are clear, but the exact value is unclear. Grey numbers are assumed to be continuous in nature, so that it can take any value in between the lower and upper bounds. Although not much discussed, there are discrete grey numbers also in use (Liu et al., 2012, Liu et al., 2022). Grey system theory classifies information in *three* categories, where the *first* one is white with completely certain information, the *second* one is grey with insufficient information and the *third* one is black with unknown information. As the theory of grey systems are concerned mostly with information in the grey category, most of the statistical characteristics of the system may not be clearly identified.

A grey number is defined as a number with a clear upper and lower boundary, wherein the exact position within the boundaries is unknown. A grey number can be indicated as;

$$a^{\pm} = \left[a^{-}, a^{+}\right] = \left\{t \in a^{\pm} \mid a^{-}, < t < a^{+}\right\}, \tag{2.1}$$

where $a^{\pm}$ indicates the grey number, t indicates the information, and a^{-} and a^{+} represent the upper and lower bounds of the information, respectively. As a grey number indicates the range of variance underlying a number, it can be similar to an interval value with same upper and lower limit. The basic operations for grey numbers are discussed in detail as follows;

$$a^{\pm} \otimes b^{\pm} = \left[f^{-}\left(a^{+}, b^{+}, a^{-}, b^{-}\right), f^{+}\left(a^{+}, b^{+}, a^{-}, b^{-}\right)\right], \tag{2.2}$$

where $\otimes$ indicates the generic operator, f^{-} and f^{+}, respectively, indicate the minimum and maximum functions.

2.2 BASIC GREY OPERATIONS

For the specific operations in grey numbers, +, –, ×, ÷, the following equations are presented;

$$a^{\pm} + b^{\pm} = \left[a^{-} + b^{-}, a^{+} + b^{+}\right], \tag{2.3}$$

$$a^{\pm} - b^{\pm} = \left[a^{-} - b^{+}, a^{+} - b^{-}\right], \tag{2.4}$$

$$a^{\pm} \times b^{\pm} = \left[\min\left(a^{-} \times b^{-}, a^{+} \times b^{+}, a^{-} \times b^{+}, a^{+} \times b^{-}\right), \max\left(a^{-} \times b^{-}, a^{+} \times b^{+}, a^{-} \times b^{+}, a^{+} \times b^{-}\right)\right], \tag{2.5}$$

$$\frac{a^{\pm}}{b^{\pm}} = \left[\min\left(\frac{a^{-}}{b^{-}}, \frac{a^{+}}{b^{+}}, \frac{a^{-}}{b^{+}}, \frac{a^{+}}{b^{-}}\right), \max\left(\frac{a^{-}}{b^{-}}, \frac{a^{+}}{b^{+}}, \frac{a^{-}}{b^{+}}, \frac{a^{+}}{b^{-}}\right)\right], \tag{2.6}$$

and

$$b^{\pm -1} = \left[\frac{1}{b^{+}}, \frac{1}{b^{-}}\right] \tag{2.7}$$

For this, we have the basic assumption that $a^{-} \leq a^{+}$, $b^{-} \leq b^{+}$, and b^{-}, $b^{+} \neq 0$.

The significance of the interval of a grey number can be represented using the degree of greyness. The degree of greyness can be expressed as a function of the boundaries of the grey number;

$$g\left(a^{\pm}\right) = f\left(a^{-}, a^{+}\right). \tag{2.8}$$

Suppose that

$$g^{\pm} = \bigcup_{i=1}^{n}\left[a_i^{-}, a_i^{+}\right], \tag{2.9}$$

where $g \in R$ (R be the set of Real numbers), be indicating the union of closed or open intervals, we can assume that g be a grey number represented as $g^{\pm}$.

For any grey number $g^{+} \in R$, if $|g^{+} - g^{-}| = 0$, then, $g^{\pm}$ is called a white number and for any grey number $g^{+} \in R$, if $|g^{+} - g^{-}| = \infty$, then, $g^{\pm}$ is called a black number.

Thus, the grey number $g^{\pm}$ can be a continuous grey number, if $g^{\pm} = [a_1^{-}, a_n^{+}]$, where $a_i^{-} = a_{i-1}^{-}$. $g^{\pm}$ can be considered as a discrete grey number if $g^{\pm} = \{a_1, a_2, \ldots, a_n\}$, where $a_i = a_i^{-} = a_i^{+}$. $g^{\pm}$ can be considered as a mixed grey number if only one or many parts of its interval shrinks to a crisp number.

Here, $g^{\pm} = [a_1^{-}, a_1] \cup [a_1, a_2] \cup [a_2, a_3] \cup \ldots \cup [a_n, a_n^{+}] = [a_1^{-}, a_n^{+}]$ can represent a general grey number. We can assume for a grey number $g^{\pm}$, where $g^{-}, g^{+} \in R$ are the lower and upper limits, then the degree of greyness can be represented as g^{0} as follows:

$$g^{0} = f\left(g^{-}, g^{+}\right), \tag{2.10}$$

where

$$g^{0} \geq 0; \text{ and } g^{0} = 0, \text{ iff } g^{-} = g^{+}.$$

The degree of greyness can be calculated as follows:

$$g^0 = \frac{g^+ - g^-}{g^+ + g^-} \tag{2.11}$$

Hence, the general operations on two grey numbers, $a^\pm = \bigcup_{i=1}^{m}\left[a_i^-, a_i^+\right]$ and $b^\pm = \bigcup_{i=1}^{n}\left[b_i^-, b_i^+\right]$ can be defined as follows;

$$a^\pm \otimes b^\pm = \bigcup_{i=1}^{m}\bigcup_{j=1}^{n}\left[f^-\left(a_i^+, b_j^+, a_i^-, b_j^-\right), f^+\left(a_i^+, b_j^+, a_i^-, b_j^-\right)\right] \tag{2.12}$$

Thus, the operators +,−, ×, ÷ for the general (discrete, continuous, or mixed) grey number can be further represented as follows:

$$a^\pm + b^\pm = \bigcup_{i=1}^{m}\bigcup_{j=1}^{n}\left[a_i^- + b_j^-, a_i^+ + b_j^+\right] \tag{2.13}$$

$$a^\pm - b^\pm = \bigcup_{i=1}^{m}\bigcup_{j=1}^{n}\left[a_i^- - b_j^+, a_i^+ - b_j^-\right] \tag{2.14}$$

$$\begin{aligned} a^\pm \times b^\pm = \bigcup_{i=1}^{m}\bigcup_{j=1}^{n}\Big[&\min\left(a_i^- \times b_j^-, a_i^- \times b_j^+, a_i^+ \times b_j^-, a_i^+ \times b_j^+\right), \\ &\max\left(a_i^- \times b_j^-, a_i^- \times b_j^+, a_i^+ \times b_j^-, a_i^+ \times b_j^+\right)\Big] \end{aligned} \tag{2.15}$$

$$\frac{a^\pm}{b^\pm} = \bigcup_{i=1}^{m}\bigcup_{j=1}^{n}\left[\min\left(\frac{a_i^-}{b_j^-}, \frac{a_i^-}{b_j^+}, \frac{a_i^+}{b_j^-}, \frac{a_i^+}{b_j^+}\right), \max\left(\frac{a_i^-}{b_j^-}, \frac{a_i^-}{b_j^+}, \frac{a_i^+}{b_j^-}, \frac{a_i^+}{b_j^+}\right)\right] \tag{2.16}$$

$$b^{\pm -1} = \bigcup_{j=1}^{n}\left[\frac{1}{b_j^+}, \frac{1}{b_j^-}\right] \tag{2.17}$$

Here, we assume that $a_i^- < a_i^+$ and $b_j^- < b_j^+$. Further considering Equations 2.16 and 2.17, we assume that $b_j^- \neq 0$ and $b_j^+ \neq 0$.

Adding to the basic operators of grey numbers, the other useful operators are the conjunction and disjunction operators. Consider the two grey numbers,

$$a^\pm = \bigcup_{i=1}^{m}\left[a_i^-, a_i^+\right] \quad \text{and} \quad b^\pm = \bigcup_{i=1}^{n}\left[b_i^-, b_i^+\right],$$

we define the conjunction $(a^\pm \vee b^\pm)$ and disjunction $(a^\pm \wedge b^\pm)$ operators as follows;

$$a^\pm \vee b^\pm = \bigcup_{i=1}^{m}\bigcup_{j=1}^{n}\left[a_i^- \vee b_j^-, a_i^+ \vee b_j^+\right] \tag{2.18}$$

$$a^\pm \wedge b^\pm = \bigcup_{i=1}^{m}\bigcup_{j=1}^{n}\left[a_i^- \wedge b_j^-, a_i^+ \wedge b_j^+\right] \tag{2.19}$$

As a grey number is often represented as a set, we can consider the following set operations between grey numbers. Suppose, for the grey numbers

$$a^{\pm} = \bigcup_{i=1}^{m}\left[a_i^-, a_i^+\right] \text{ and } b^{\pm} = \bigcup_{i=1}^{n}\left[b_i^-, b_i^+\right],$$

we can define union $(a^{\pm} \cup b^{\pm})$, intersection $(a^{\pm} \cap b^{\pm})$, and the complement $(\neg a^{\pm})$, are defined as follows:

$$a^{\pm} \cup b^{\pm} = \bigcup_{i=1}^{m}\bigcup_{j=1}^{n}\left\{\left[a_i^-, a_i^+\right] \cup \left[b_j^-, b_j^+\right]\right\} \quad (2.20)$$

$$a^{\pm} \cap b^{\pm} = \bigcup_{i=1}^{m}\bigcup_{j=1}^{n}\left\{\left\{\left[a_i^-, a_i^+\right] \cap \left[b_j^-, b_j^+\right]\right\}\right\} \quad (2.21)$$

$$\neg a^{\pm} = \bigcup_{i=1}^{m}\left\{\left[-\infty, a_i^-\right], \left[a_i^+, \infty\right]\right\} \quad (2.22)$$

In consideration of the operators on general grey numbers (discrete, continuous, or mixed), let us do some sample operations as examples. Suppose that $a^{\pm}$, $b^{\pm}$, and $c^{\pm}$ are three different grey numbers, where $a^{\pm}$ = [25, 60], $b^{\pm}$ = [40,55,60], and $c^{\pm}$ = {[35,45], 50, 60}, we can apply the prior mentioned operators as follows;

$$a^{\pm} + b^{\pm} = \left[[65,100] \cup [80,115] \cup [85,120]\right] = [65,120]$$

$$b^{\pm} + c^{\pm} = [75,85] \cup \{90\} \cup \{100\} \cup [90,100] \cup \{105\} \cup \{115\} \cup [95,105] \cup \{110\} \cup \{120\}$$
$$= \{[75,105],110,115,120\}$$

$$a^{\pm} + c^{\pm} = [60,105] \cup [75,110] \cup [60,120] = [60,120]$$

We have used similar nature of calculation of $a^{\pm} + b^{\pm}$ for obtaining the initial grey bounds of [60, 105].

$$a^{\pm} - b^{\pm} = [-15,20] \cup [-30,5] \cup [-35,0] = [-35,20]$$

$$b^{\pm} - c^{\pm} = [-5,5] \cup \{-10\} \cup \{-20\} \cup [10,20] \cup \{5\} \cup \{-5\} \cup [15,25] \cup \{10\} \cup \{0\}$$
$$= \{-20,-10,0,[-5,25]\}$$

$$a^{\pm} - c^{\pm} = [-20,25] \cup [-25,10] \cup [-35,0] = [-35,25].$$

Considering the multiplication and division operation on general grey numbers, the following sample results are obtained:

$$a^{\pm} \times b^{\pm} = [1000,2400] \cup [1375,3300] \cup [1500,3600] = [1000,3600]$$

$$b^{\pm} \times c^{\pm} = [1400,1800] \cup \{2000\} \cup \{2400\} \cup [1935,2475] \cup \{2750\} \cup \{3300\} \cup [2100,2700]$$
$$\cup \{3000\} \cup \{3600\}$$
$$= \{[1400,2700],2750,3000,3300,3600\}$$

$$a^{\pm} \times c^{\pm} = [875,2700],[1250,3000],[1500,3600] = [875,3600]$$

$$\frac{a^{\pm}}{b^{\pm}} = \left[\frac{25}{40},\frac{60}{40}\right] \cup \left[\frac{25}{55},\frac{60}{55}\right] \cup \left[\frac{25}{60},\frac{60}{60}\right] = \left[\frac{5}{8},\frac{3}{2}\right] \cup \left[\frac{5}{11},\frac{12}{11}\right] \cup \left[\frac{5}{12},\frac{1}{1}\right] = \left[\frac{5}{12},\frac{3}{2}\right]$$

$$\frac{b^{\pm}}{c^{\pm}} = \left[\frac{40}{45},\frac{40}{35}\right] \cup \left\{\frac{40}{50}\right\} \cup \left\{\frac{40}{60}\right\} \cup \left[\frac{55}{45},\frac{55}{35}\right] \cup \left\{\frac{55}{50}\right\} \cup \left\{\frac{55}{60}\right\} \cup \left[\frac{60}{45},\frac{60}{35}\right] \cup \left\{\frac{60}{50}\right\} \cup \left\{\frac{60}{60}\right\}$$

$$= \left[\frac{8}{9},\frac{8}{7}\right] \cup \left\{\frac{4}{5}\right\} \cup \left\{\frac{2}{3}\right\} \cup \left[\frac{11}{9},\frac{11}{7}\right] \cup \left\{\frac{11}{10}\right\} \cup \left\{\frac{11}{12}\right\} \cup \left[\frac{4}{3},\frac{12}{7}\right] \cup \left\{\frac{6}{5}\right\} \cup \left\{\frac{1}{1}\right\}$$

$$= \left\{\frac{2}{3},\frac{4}{5},\left[\frac{8}{9},\frac{12}{7}\right]\right\}$$

$$\frac{a^{\pm}}{c^{\pm}} = \left[\frac{25}{45},\frac{60}{35}\right] \cup \left[\frac{25}{50},\frac{60}{50}\right] \cup \left[\frac{25}{60},\frac{60}{60}\right] = \left[\frac{5}{9},\frac{12}{7}\right] \cup \left[\frac{1}{2},\frac{6}{5}\right] \cup \left[\frac{5}{12},\frac{1}{1}\right] = \left[\frac{5}{12},\frac{12}{7}\right]$$

The inverse operator and the conjunction and disjunction operators can also be employed on grey numbers and the sample calculation is as follows:

$$a^{\pm -1} = \left[\frac{1}{60},\frac{1}{25}\right]; \quad b^{\pm -1} = \left\{\frac{1}{60}\right\} \cup \left\{\frac{1}{55}\right\} \cup \left\{\frac{1}{40}\right\} = \left\{\frac{1}{60},\frac{1}{55},\frac{1}{40}\right\}$$

$$c^{\pm -1} = \left[\frac{1}{45},\frac{1}{35}\right] \cup \left\{\frac{1}{100}\right\} \cup \left\{\frac{1}{80}\right\} = \left\{\frac{1}{100},\frac{1}{80},\left[\frac{1}{45},\frac{1}{35}\right]\right\}$$

$$a^{\pm} \vee b^{\pm} = [40,60] \cup [55,60] \cup \{60\} = [40,60]$$

$$b^{\pm} \vee c^{\pm} = [40,45] \cup \{50\} \cup \{60\} \cup [55,55] \cup \{55\} \cup \{60\} \cup [60,60] \cup \{60\} \cup \{60\}$$

$$= \{[40,45],50,55,60\}$$

$$a^{\pm} \vee c^{\pm} = [35,60] \cup [50,60] \cup [60,60] = [35,60]$$

$$a^{\pm} \wedge b^{\pm} = [25,40] \cup [25,55] \cup [25,60] = [25,60]$$

$$b^{\pm} \wedge c^{\pm} = [35,40] \cup \{40\} \cup \{40\} \cup [35,45] \cup \{50\} \cup \{55\} \cup [35,45] \cup \{50\} \cup \{60\}$$

$$= \{[35,45],50,55,60\}$$

$$a^{\pm} \wedge c^{\pm} = [25,45] \cup [25,50] \cup [25,60] = [25,60]$$

Considering the union, the intersection, and the complement operation on general grey numbers, the following sample results are obtained:

$$a^{\pm} \cup b^{\pm} = [25,60] \cup [25,60] \cup [25,60] = [25,60]$$

$$b^{\pm} \cup c^{\pm} = [35,45] \cup \{40,50\} \cup \{40,60\} \cup \{[35,45],\{55\}\} \cup \{50,55\} \cup \{60,60\}$$

$$\cup \{[35,45],\{60\}\} \cup \{50,60\} \cup \{60\}$$

$$= \{[35,45],50,55,60\}$$

$$a^{\pm} \cup c^{\pm} = [25,60] \cup [25,60] \cup [25,60] = [25,60]$$

$$a^{\pm} \cap b^{\pm} = \{40\} \cup \{55\} \cup \{60\} = \{40,55,60\}$$

$$b^{\pm} \cap c^{\pm} = \{40\} \cup \{60\} = \{40,60\}; \quad a^{\pm} \cap c^{\pm} = [35,45] \cup \{50\} \cup \{60\} = \{[35,45],50,60\}$$

$$\neg a^{\pm} = [-\infty,25) \cup (60,+\infty] = \{[-\infty,25),(60,+\infty]\}$$

$$\neg b^{\pm} = [-\infty,40) \cup (40,+\infty] \cup [-\infty,55) \cup (55,+\infty] \cup [-\infty,60) \cup (60,+\infty]$$
$$= \{[-\infty,40),(40,55),(55,60)(60,+\infty]\}$$

$$\neg c^{\pm} = [-\infty,35) \cup (45,+\infty] \cup [-\infty,50) \cup (50,+\infty] \cup [-\infty,60) \cup (60,+\infty]$$
$$= \{[-\infty,35),(45,50),(50,60)(60,+\infty]\}$$

2.3 CONCLUSION

Sample calculations for the general grey operations are shown above. In the concept of grey numbers, we generally assume that they have known boundaries; but the exact value being unknown considering a continuous interval. Although not much used, there are discrete and mixed grey numbers also. Thus, the grey operations defined must be of generic nature, considering all categories including continuous, discrete, and mixed grey numbers. The concept of extended grey numbers (Yang and Liu, 2011; Yang et al., 2013) can resolve these queries about generalizability of these operators on grey numbers.

REFERENCES

Deng, J.L. (1989). Introduction to grey system theory. *The Journal of Grey System*, 1(1): 1–24.

Liu, S.F., Yang, Y.J. and Forrest, J. (2022). *Grey Systems Analysis*. Springer-Verlag, Berlin.

Liu, S., Fang, Z., Yang, Y. and Forrest, J. (2012). General grey numbers and their operations. *Grey Systems: Theory and Application*, 2(3), 341–349.

Yang, Y. and Liu, S.F. 2011. Reliability of operations of grey numbers using kernels. *Grey Systems: Theory and Application*, 1(1), 57–71.

Yang, Y., Liu, S. and John, R. (2013). Uncertainty representation of grey numbers and grey sets. *IEEE Transactions on Cybernetics*, 44(9): 1508–1517.

CHAPTER 3

Incidence Based Models

3.1 INTRODUCTION

The incidence based methods use the relative closeness between sequences to understand the closeness in the developmental tendencies among various factors or attributes. The incidence analysis is applied on the behavioral sequence of a system. Incidence analysis using grey theory observes and analyses the relative closeness of sequences (Liu et al., 2017). The behavioral sequences of data are analyzed for their degree of closeness, considering the developmental tendencies of their data sequence (Dong et al., 2018).

3.2 GREY INCIDENCE ANALYSIS

Grey incidence analysis is regarded as one among the most prominent application of grey system theory (Deng 1989; Liu et al., 2022). Prior to incidence analysis of the data, it is mandatory to understand the different operators that can be employed on the data sequences to transform these sequences. The initial sequence of data used for analysis can be any behavioral sequence, horizontal sequence, or any time series data. We elaborate some of the basic operators involved to transform the data sequences, as follows:

Let us assume a time series data, where the performance of a factor considering the kth periodical evaluation is $x_i(k)$, we further represent the behavioral time sequence of X_i for the period, $k = 1, 2, \ldots, n$, as follows:

$$X_i = x_i(1), x_i(2), \ldots, x_i(n). \tag{3.1}$$

We employ a sequence operator, A_1 on Equation 3.1, which satisfies the condition,

$$X_i A_1 = x_i(1)a_1, x_i(2)a_1, \ldots, x_i(n)a_1, \tag{3.2}$$

where

$$x_i(k)a_1 = \frac{x_i(k)}{x_i(1)} \forall k = 1,2,\ldots,n. \tag{3.3}$$

Here, we call A_1 as the *initializing* operator, which is having an initial image of X_iA_1.

We employ an operator, A_2 on Equation 3.1, which satisfies the condition,

$$X_i A_2 = x_i(1)a_2, x_i(2)a_2, \ldots, x_i(n)a_2, \tag{3.4}$$

and

$$x_i(k)a_2 = \frac{x_i(k)}{\overline{X_i}}, \tag{3.5}$$

where

$$\overline{X_i} = \frac{1}{n}\sum_{i=1}^{n} x_i(k) \, \forall k = 1,2,\ldots,n. \tag{3.6}$$

Here, we call A_2 as the *averaging* operator, which is having an average image X_iA_2.

We employ an operator, A_3 on Equation 3.1, which satisfies the condition,

$$X_i A_3 = x_i(1)a_3, x_i(2)a_3, \ldots, x_i(n)a_3, \tag{3.7}$$

where

$$x_i(k)a_3 = \frac{x_i(k) - \min_k\{x_i(k)\}}{\max_k\{x_i(k)\} - \min_k\{x_i(k)\}} \quad \forall k = 1, 2, \ldots, n. \tag{3.8}$$

Here, we call A_3 as the *interval* operator, which is having an interval image X_iA_3.

The purpose of the operators A_1, A_2, and A_3 is to convert the behavioral sequence of system to a non-dimensional sequence, which is regarded as the base for conducting the grey incidence analysis.

3.2.1 Step-by-Step Implementation (Grey Incidence Analysis)

We provide step-by-step implementation process for directing the grey incidence analysis for any sequence data, which can be a behavioral time sequence or horizontal sequence of data (Liu et al., 2022; Rajesh, 2024). The initial steps (*Steps 1–6*) are only required, if the researcher wants to employ a primary data for analysis. If secondary data is used to represent a behavioral sequence, then the researcher can start the analysis procedure by assuming the original sequence as and continue the analysis procedure from *step 7*, starting from Equation 3.30.

Step 1: Identify the major factors and sub-factors

The *first* step is to identify the factors and sub-factors that the researcher needs to analyze. This process can take time, as per the requirements of the study. This is particularly done with strong reference to literature and practice. The incidence analysis can basically tell about the highest contributing sub-factors towards the main factors in the system. Say, for consideration, we assume that the study includes '*s*' factors and '*m*' sub-factors. Let us further assume that we are measuring the behavioral time sequence of data. We also assume that the period of evaluation be '*n*'.

Step 2: Obtain the linguistic rating sequences

Suppose that we employ an analyst or an expert for rating the developmental sequences of these factors and sub-factors for a considered period of study. The rating can be made based on real time tangible indicators or based on perceptions of the evaluator based on his/her knowledge of the factor. This can be decided by the researcher based on the needs of the selected study. The analysts can rate the periodical performances of the factors and sub-factors for the period '*j*' using a linguistic scale. Suppose that we follow a seven-point rating scale, this can vary from *EP, VP, P, F, G, VG, EG* indicating *"extremely poor"*, *"very poor"*, *"poor"*, *"fair"*, *"good"*, *"very good"*, and *"extremely good"*, respectively. The rating scale can be a five point or a seven-point scale, as per the choice of the researcher. Also, if the researcher wants to incorporate the weights during the period '*j*' of the factors and sub-factors into analysis, they can incorporate the same using linguistic labels for weights. We can use a five, seven, or nine-point scale for this as well. Considering the seven-point scale, this can vary from *EL, VL, L, M, H, VH, EH* representing *"extremely low"*, *"very low"*, *"medium"*, *"high"*, *"very high"*, and *"extremely high"*, respectively.

Step 3: Linguistic to grey sequence conversion

The ratings collected in linguistic terms need to be converted to grey numbers, representing an upper and lower bound of values. These limits can represent on a number scale, what these linguistic labels indicate or how are the likely spread of labels? Let us assume $y_i(j)$ can indicate the ith factor rated for the jth period, where: $i = 1, 2,\ldots, s$; $j = 1, 2,\ldots, n$ and $x_k\ (j)$ be the kth sub-factor rated for the jth period; $k = 1, 2, \ldots, m$; $j = 1,2, \ldots, n$. The grey values corresponding to the periodic sequence of factors and sub-factors can be represented, respectively, as:

$$\otimes y_i(j) = \left(\underline{\otimes} y_i(j),\ \overline{\otimes} y_i(j)\right), \tag{3.9}$$

$$\otimes x_k(j) = \left(\underline{\otimes} x_k(j),\ \overline{\otimes} x_k(j)\right). \tag{3.10}$$

A sample of the linguistic labels and the grey scale conversion for the ratings and the weights are shown in Table 3.1.

Table 3.1 Linguistic assessment and the associated grey values

Rating of attribute performance		
Linguistic scale	**Linguistic labels**	**Grey values**
Extremely Poor	EP	[0.0–0.2]
Very Poor	VP	[0.2–0.3]
Poor	P	[0.3–0.4]
Fair	F	[0.4–0.6]
Good	G	[0.6–0.7]
Very Good	VG	[0.7–0.8]
Extremely Good	EG	[0.8–1.0]
Weights assigned to attributes		
Linguistic scale	**Linguistic labels**	**Grey values**
Extremely Low	EL	[1–2]
Very Low	VL	[2–3]
Low	L	[3–4]
Medium	M	[5–6]
High	H	[7–8]
Very High	VH	[8–9]
Extremely High	EH	[9–10]

Step 4: Converting weights into grey scores

Executing the conversion to grey values for the weights also, suppose, $w_i(j)$ be the weight assumed for the ith factor for the jth period; i = 1, 2, ..., s; j = 1, 2, ..., n and $v_k(j)$ can be the weight assumed for k^{th} sub-factor for the jth period; k = 1, 2, ..., m; j = 1, 2, ..., n. The converted grey weights can be represented as follows:

$$\otimes w_i(j) = \left(\underline{\otimes} w_i(j),\ \bar{\otimes} w_i(j)\right), \tag{3.11}$$

$$\otimes v_k(j) = \left(\underline{\otimes} v_k(j),\ \bar{\otimes} v_k(j)\right). \tag{3.12}$$

A sample of the conversion scale for weights is also shown in Table 3.1.

Step 5: Compute the grey weighted rating matrix

By multiplying the weights with the ratings of factors, we get the weighted ratings as follows:

$$\otimes \breve{y}_i(j) = \left(\otimes y_i(j) \times \otimes w_i(j)\right). \tag{3.13}$$

This is done by executing the grey multiplication as elaborated in Chapter 2, which is shown below:

$$\begin{aligned}\otimes \breve{y}_i(j) = \Big[&\Big(\min\left(\underline{\otimes} y_i(j) \times \underline{\otimes} w_i(j), \underline{\otimes} y_i(j) \times \bar{\otimes} w_i(j), \bar{\otimes} y_i(j) \times \underline{\otimes} w_i(j), \bar{\otimes} y_i(j) \times \bar{\otimes} w_i(j)\right),\\ &\max\left(\underline{\otimes} y_i(j) \times \underline{\otimes} w_i(j), \underline{\otimes} y_i(j) \times \bar{\otimes} w_i(j), \bar{\otimes} y_i(j) \times \underline{\otimes} w_i(j), \bar{\otimes} y_i(j) \times \bar{\otimes} w_i(j)\right)\Big)\Big]\end{aligned} \tag{3.14}$$

Similarly,

$$\otimes \breve{x}_k(j) = \left(\otimes x_k(j) \times \otimes v_k(j)\right). \tag{3.15}$$

These matrices for factors and sub-factors can be indicated as follows:

$$\breve{Y} = \left[\otimes \breve{y}_{ij}\right], \tag{3.16}$$

and

$$\breve{X} = \left[\otimes \breve{x}_{kj}\right]. \tag{3.17}$$

Step 6: Grey to white score conversion

The grey values can be whitenized using different methods. We can use a *Converting Fuzzy to Crisp Scores* (CFCS) method for this, by executing a three step process as follows:

(i) **Normalization:** The lower bounds of the normalized scores can be obtained as,

$$\underline{\otimes} \dot{y}_{ij} = \left(\underline{\otimes} \breve{y}_{ij} - \min_j \underline{\otimes}\, \breve{y}_{ij}\right) / \Delta_{\min}^{\max}, \tag{3.18}$$

$$\underline{\otimes} \dot{x}_{kj} = \left(\underline{\otimes}\, \breve{x}_{kj} - {}_{j}^{min}\ \underline{\otimes}\, \breve{x}_{kj}\right) / \theta_{\min}^{\max}. \tag{3.19}$$

Similarly, the upper bounds of the normalized scores can be obtained as,

$$\bar{\otimes} \dot{y}_{ij} = \left(\bar{\otimes} \breve{y}_{ij} - \min_j \bar{\otimes} \breve{y}_{ij}\right) / \Delta_{\min}^{\max}, \tag{3.20}$$

$$\bar{\otimes} \dot{x}_{kj} = \left(\bar{\otimes} \breve{x}_{kj} - \min_j \bar{\otimes} \breve{x}_{kj}\right) / \theta_{\min}^{\max}, \tag{3.21}$$

where $$\Delta_{\min}^{\max} = \min_j \overline{\otimes}\breve{y}_{ij} - \min_j \underline{\otimes}\,\breve{y}_{ij}, \tag{3.22}$$

and $$\theta_{\min}^{\max} = \max_j \overline{\otimes}\,\breve{x}_{kj} - \min_j \underline{\otimes}\,\breve{x}_{kj}. \tag{3.23}$$

(ii) **Compute normalized white values**

$$\tilde{y}_{ij} = \left(\frac{\left(\underline{\otimes}\dot{y}_{ij}\left(1-\underline{\otimes}\dot{y}_{ij}\right)\right)+\left(\overline{\otimes}\dot{y}_{ij}\times\overline{\otimes}\dot{y}_{ij}\right)}{\left(1-\underline{\otimes}\dot{y}_{ij}+\overline{\otimes}\dot{y}_{ij}\right)} \right), \tag{3.24}$$

$$\tilde{x}_{kj} = \left(\frac{\left(\underline{\otimes}\dot{x}_{kj}\left(1-\underline{\otimes}\dot{x}_{kj}\right)\right)+\left(\overline{\otimes}\dot{x}_{kj}\times\overline{\otimes}\dot{x}_{kj}\right)}{\left(1-\underline{\otimes}\dot{x}_{kj}+\overline{\otimes}\dot{x}_{kj}\right)} \right). \tag{3.25}$$

(iii) **Obtain the whitenized matrices**

$$\left[y_{ij}\right] = \left(\min \underline{\otimes}\,\breve{y}_{ij} + \left(\tilde{y}_{ij} \times \Delta_{\min}^{\max}\right)\right), \tag{3.26}$$

$$\left[x_{kj}\right] = \left(\min \underline{\otimes}\,\breve{x}_{kj} + \left(\tilde{x}_{kj} \times \theta_{\min}^{\max}\right)\right). \tag{3.27}$$

Hence, the whitenized matrices for the factors and the sub-factors are indicated as follows:

$$Y = \left[y_{ij}\right], \tag{3.28}$$

and $$X = \left[x_{kj}\right]. \tag{3.29}$$

Step 7: Obtain the absolute matrix of grey incidence (AMGI)

Considering Equations 3.28 and 3.29, the behavioral time sequences of the ratings of the weighted factors and sub-factors can be obtained as follows:

$$Y_i = y_i(1),\, y_i(2), \ldots,\, y_i(n);\ i = 1, 2, \ldots, s, \tag{3.30}$$

$$X_k = x_k(1),\, x_k(2), \ldots,\, x_k(n);\ k = 1, 2, \ldots, m. \tag{3.31}$$

The sequences were converted to their zeroing starting points, which are indicated as follows:

$$Y_i^0 = \left(0, y_i^0(1), y_i^0(2), \ldots, y_i^0(n)\right). \tag{3.32}$$

Similarly, $$X_k^0 = \left(0, x_k^0(1), x_k^0(2), \ldots, x_k^0(n)\right). \tag{3.33}$$

The absolute summation operation is conducted to generate the incidence sequences of the original behavioral sequences. Suppose, for the factors Y_i, the absolute summation is obtained as:

$$\left|Y_{si}\right| = \left| \left(\sum_{l=2}^{n-1} y_i^0(l) + \frac{1}{2} y_i^0(n) \right) \right|;\ i = 1, 2, \ldots, s. \tag{3.34}$$

Further suppose, for the sub-factors X_k, the absolute summation is obtained as:

$$|X_{sk}| = \left| \left(\sum_{l=2}^{n-1} x_k^0(l) + \frac{1}{2} x_k^0(n) \right) \right|; \; k = 1, 2, \ldots,. \tag{3.35}$$

Hence,

$$|X_{sk} - Y_{si}| = \left| \left(\sum_{l=2}^{n-1} (x_k^0(l) - y_i^0(l)) + \frac{1}{2}(x_k^0(n) - y_i^0(n)) \right) \right|. \tag{3.36}$$

We can obtain the sequence of the absolute degree of grey incidence as follows:

$$\varepsilon_{ik} = \left[\frac{(1 + |Y_{si}| + |X_{sk}|)}{(1 + |Y_{si}| + |X_{sk}| + |X_{sk} - Y_{si}|)} \right]. \tag{3.37}$$

Later, the absolute matrix of grey incidence (*AMGI*) is developed using the sequence of ε_{ik} as follows:

$$A = [\varepsilon_{ik}]_{s \times m} = \begin{bmatrix} \varepsilon_{11} & \varepsilon_{12} & \cdots & \varepsilon_{1m} \\ \varepsilon_{21} & \varepsilon_{22} & \cdots & \varepsilon_{2m} \\ \vdots & \vdots & \ddots & \vdots \\ \varepsilon_{s1} & \varepsilon_{s2} & \cdots & \varepsilon_{sm} \end{bmatrix}. \tag{3.38}$$

Step 8: Obtain the relative matrix of grey incidence (RMGI)

Initializing operator has been applied on the sequences and the initial image of the factor sequence Y_i and the sub-factor sequence X_k are developed and the same can be represented as:

$$Y_i' = \text{series of} \left\{ \frac{y_i(l)}{y_i(1)} \right\}; \; l = 1, 2, \ldots, n; \; i = 1, 2, \ldots, s. \tag{3.39}$$

Similarly;

$$X_k' = \text{series of} \left\{ \frac{x_k(l)}{x_k(1)} \right\}; \; l = 1, 2, \ldots, n; \; k = 1, 2, \ldots, m. \tag{3.40}$$

The images of zero starting points are constructed for all Y_i', X_k' series, i.e.,

$$Y_i'^0 = y_i'^0(1), y_i'^0(2), \ldots, y_i'^0(n); \; i = 1, 2, \ldots, s. \tag{3.41}$$

Similarly,

$$X_k'^0 = x_k'^0(1), x_k'^0(2), \ldots, x_k'^0(n); \; k = 1, 2, \ldots, m. \tag{3.42}$$

Considering Y_i' and X_k', the absolute summation sequences are computed as,

$$|Y_{si}'| = \left| \left(\sum_{l=2}^{n-1} y_i'^0(l) + \frac{1}{2} y_i'^0(n) \right) \right|; \; i = 1, 2, \ldots, s. \tag{3.43}$$

$$|X_{sk}'| = \left| \left(\sum_{l=2}^{n-1} x_k'^0(l) + \frac{1}{2} x_k'^0(n) \right) \right|; \; k = 1, 2, \ldots, m. \tag{3.44}$$

Hence, $$\left|X'_{sk}-Y'_{si}\right|=\left|\left(\sum_{l=2}^{n-1}(x_k^{'0}(l)-y_i^{'0}(l))+\frac{1}{2}(x_k^{'0}(n)-y_i^{'0}(n)\right)\right|. \quad (3.45)$$

Further to this, we calculate the relative sequence of grey incidence as,

$$\gamma_{ik}=\left[\frac{\left(1+\left|Y'_{si}\right|+\left|X'_{sk}\right|\right)}{\left(1+\left|Y'_{si}\right|+\left|X'_{sk}\right|+\left|X'_{sk}-Y'_{si}\right|\right)}\right]. \quad (3.46)$$

Later, the relative matrix of grey incidence (*RMGI*) is developed using the sequence of γ_{ik} as follows.

$$B=\left[\gamma_{ik}\right]_{s\times m}=\begin{bmatrix}\gamma_{11} & \gamma_{12} & \cdots & \gamma_{1m}\\ \gamma_{21} & \gamma_{22} & \cdots & \gamma_{2m}\\ \vdots & \vdots & \ddots & \vdots\\ \gamma_{s1} & \gamma_{s2} & \cdots & \gamma_{sm}\end{bmatrix}. \quad (3.47)$$

Step 9: Obtain the synthetic matrix of grey incidence (SMGI)

SMGI represents an overall measure of the relationship closeness between sequences; say for example here, the factors and the sub-factor sequences. As such, SMGI is constructed by combining AMGI and RMGI by assigning appropriate weighting. This can be represented as β and is normally assumed to be 0.5 ($\beta \approx 0.5$).

$$C=\beta A+(1-\beta)\times B, \quad (3.48)$$

i.c., $$C=\beta[\varepsilon_{ik}]+(1-\beta)\times[\gamma_{ik}]. \quad (3.49)$$

Thus the matrix of *SMGI* can be presented as follows.

The $$C=\left[\rho_{ik}\right]_{s\times m}=\begin{bmatrix}\rho_{11} & \rho_{12} & \cdots & \rho_{1m}\\ \rho_{21} & \rho_{22} & \cdots & \rho_{2m}\\ \vdots & \vdots & \ddots & \vdots\\ \rho_{s1} & \rho_{s2} & \cdots & \rho_{sm}\end{bmatrix}. \quad (3.50)$$

Step 10: Compute the overall incidence levels of sub-factors

Summing the values of all degree of incidences of a typical sub-factor over a main factor, we can obtain the sub-factor, which is having the highest likenesses to developmental tendencies considering multiple factors. This can be considered as the aggregated degree of influence (*ADG*) for the sub-factors. Based on the ADG values, we can observe the sub-factor, whose sequence has the most closeness in the developmental tendencies considering multiple factors, altogether.

$$ADG = \left(\frac{\sum_{i=1}^{m} \rho_{ik}}{m} \right). \tag{3.51}$$

As the analysis is being grey incidence analysis, there may not be a most favorable sub-factor which is the resultant of the study. Rather, we have the quasi-preferred sub-factors, which is represented using $\succeq$ symbol, say for example, $X_i \succeq X_j \rightarrow X_i$ is *quasi-preferred* to X_j).

3.2.2 Sample Case Problem (Grey Incidence Analysis)

There are several practical problems in social sciences and management that have used grey incidence analysis (Rajesh 2020; 2022). We focus the case of a company XYZ for building resilience in their supply chains through implementing proactive practices of risk management and reactive practices for risk mitigation. For building resilience in supply chains, it is important to understand the major elements (factors) contributing to resilience. The step-wise implementation is discussed below:

Step 1: On a detailed review of literature on resilience and resilient supply chains, we can understand that *collaboration, flexibility,* and *agility* are the three major components of resilience. Here, we consider these as the major factors contributing to resilience. Considering the practices that leads to these major components and that ultimately helps in improving the resilience capabilities, we can see that *risk management, responsiveness, standardization, postponement,* and *visibility* are the major practices contributing to the resilience of supply chains. We consider the first set of elements as the factors and the second set comprising of practices as the sub-factors contributing to the resilience of the supply chain of XYZ.

Step 2: The performances of these factors and the sub-factors are measured for a period of *six* years from 2018 to 2023 and the same are done by a panel of three business analysts of the firm. These ratings include both the performances of these factors and sub-factors over the considered period of the study and the variation in weights assigned to each of these factors and sub-factors during the considered period of the study, considering the strategies and polices implemented during the period of study. We use the linguistic labels as mentioned in Table 3.1 for recording the performance ratings, and the corresponding weightings assigned to the factors and sub-factors and the initial ratings are shown as follows, where we have used F_1, F_2, and F_3 for indicating the factors *collaboration, flexibility,* and *agility* and S_1, S_2, S_3, S_4, and S_5 are used to indicate the sub-factors *risk management, responsiveness, standardization, postponement,* and *visibility*, respectively. The complete calculation is shown as Excel sheet implementation with formulas for the benefit of readers. The initial ratings and the weightings are given as the input in Excel as shown in Table 3.2.

Steps 3 and 4: These linguistic labels indicating the ratings and the weightings, which are recorded are converted to grey scales, as indicated in Table 3.3.

Step 5: The weighted rating matrix is computed based on the values from Table 3.3, applying the matrix multiplication operations shown in Equations 3.14–3.17. The formula implementation in Excel is shown in Table 3.4 and the resulting matrices after applying the grey multiplication operation is shown in Table 3.5.

Table 3.2 Initial ratings and weightings of factors and sub-factors

Rating of factors

	2018	2019	2020	2021	2022	2023
F1	P	G	F	F	VG	VG
F2	VP	P	G	G	EG	EG
F3	G	G	F	VG	VG	EG

Rating of sub-factors

	2018	2019	2020	2021	2022	2023
S1	EP	P	VP	F	F	G
S2	P	P	F	F	G	VG
S3	EP	VP	P	P	F	G
S4	F	F	G	VG	EG	VG
S5	G	F	G	VG	VG	EG

Weights of factors

	2018	2019	2020	2021	2022	2023
F1	L	L	M	H	H	VH
F2	H	H	VH	VH	EH	EH
F3	VL	L	M	M	H	H

Weights of sub-factors

	2018	2019	2020	2021	2022	2023
S1	EL	L	L	M	M	M
S2	VL	L	M	H	H	VH
S3	M	H	VH	VH	EH	VH
S4	H	H	VH	EH	VH	EH
S5	M	M	H	VH	EH	EH

Table 3.3 Linguistic to grey scale conversion

Rating of factors

	2018	2019	2020	2021	2022	2023
F1	0.3	0.6	0.4	0.4	0.7	0.7
	0.4	0.7	0.6	0.6	0.8	0.8
F2	0.2	0.3	0.6	0.6	0.8	0.8
	0.3	0.4	0.7	0.7	1	1
F3	0.6	0.6	0.4	0.7	0.7	0.8
	0.7	0.7	0.6	0.8	0.8	1

Rating of sub-factors

	2018	2019	2020	2021	2022	2023
S1	0	0.3	0.2	0.4	0.4	0.6
	0.2	0.4	0.3	0.6	0.6	0.7
S2	0.3	0.3	0.4	0.4	0.6	0.7
	0.4	0.4	0.6	0.6	0.7	0.8
S3	0	0.2	0.3	0.3	0.4	0.6
	0.2	0.3	0.4	0.4	0.6	0.7
S4	0.4	0.4	0.6	0.7	0.8	0.7
	0.6	0.6	0.7	0.8	1	0.8
S5	0.6	0.4	0.6	0.7	0.7	0.8
	0.7	0.6	0.7	0.8	0.8	1

Weights of factors

	2018	2019	2020	2021	2022	2023
F1	3	3	5	7	7	8
	4	4	6	8	8	9
F2	7	7	8	8	9	9
	8	8	9	9	10	10
F3	2	3	5	5	7	7
	3	4	6	6	8	8

Weights of sub-factors

	2018	2019	2020	2021	2022	2023
S1	1	3	3	5	5	5
	2	4	4	6	6	6
S2	2	3	5	7	7	8
	3	4	6	8	8	9
S3	5	7	8	8	9	8
	6	8	9	9	10	9
S4	7	7	8	9	8	9
	8	8	9	10	9	10
S5	5	5	7	8	9	9
	6	6	8	9	10	10

Table 3.4 Excel formula: Multiplication

E54 | =MIN(E26*E40,E26*E41,E27*E40,E27*E41)

	A	B	C	D	E	F	G	H	I	J
51										
52				Weighted rating (factors)						
53					2018	2019	2020	2021	2022	2023
54				F1	0.9	1.8	2	2.8	4.9	5.6
55					1.6	2.8	3.6	4.8	6.4	7.2
56				F2	1.4	2.1	4.8	4.8	7.2	7.2
57					2.4	3.2	6.3	6.3	10	10
58				F3	1.2	1.8	2	3.5	4.9	5.6
59					2.1	2.8	3.6	4.8	6.4	8
60										
61										

Table 3.5 Weighted rating matrices

Weighted rating (factors)

	2018	2019	2020	2021	2022	2023
F1	0.9	1.8	2	2.8	4.9	5.6
	1.6	2.8	3.6	4.8	6.4	7.2
F2	1.4	2.1	4.8	4.8	7.2	7.2
	2.4	3.2	6.3	6.3	10	10
F3	1.2	1.8	2	3.5	4.9	5.6
	2.1	2.8	3.6	4.8	6.4	8

Weighted rating (sub-factors)

	2018	2019	2020	2021	2022	2023
S1	0	0.9	0.6	2	2	3
	0.4	1.6	1.2	3.6	3.6	4.2
S2	0.6	0.9	2	2.8	4.2	5.6
	1.2	1.6	3.6	4.8	5.6	7.2
S3	0	1.4	2.4	2.4	3.6	4.8
	1.2	2.4	3.6	3.6	6	6.3
S4	2.8	2.8	4.8	6.3	6.4	6.3
	4.8	4.8	6.3	8	9	8
S5	3	2	4.2	5.6	6.3	7.2
	4.2	3.6	5.6	7.2	8	10

Step 6: The process of whitenization is done in three steps and this includes, normalization, calculation of normalized white values, and computing the final white scores following Equations 3.18 – 3.29. The formula implementation in Excel for normalization is shown in Table 3.6 and the final normalized scores are indicated in Table 3.7. Also, the Excel formula implementation and the values obtained after calculating the normalized white scores and the final white scores are respectively indicated in Tables 3.8–3.11.

Table 3.6 Excel formula: Normalization

C69 f_x =(E54-$J69)/$K69

	A	B	C	D	E	F	G	H	I	J	K	L
64												
65				CFCS								
66									MAX(E54:J54)		I70-J69	
67		Normalization (factors)								MIN(E54:J54)		
68	(i)		2018	2019	2020	2021	2022	2023	Max	Min	Δ_{min}^{max}	
69		F1	0	0.142857	0.174603	0.301587	0.634921	0.746032	5.6	0.9	6.3	
70			0	0.190476	0.31746	0.507937	0.761905	0.888889	7.2	1.6		
71		F2	0	0.081395	0.395349	0.395349	0.674419	0.674419	7.2	1.4	8.6	
72			0	0.093023	0.453488	0.453488	0.883721	0.883721	10	2.4		
73		F3	0	0.088235	0.117647	0.338235	0.544118	0.647059	5.6	1.2	6.8	
74			0	0.102941	0.220588	0.397059	0.632353	0.867647	8	2.1		
75												
76												

Table 3.7 Normalized scores

CFCS

Normalization (factors)

Row	A	B	C	D	E	F	G	H	I	J	K
68	(i)		2018	2019	2020	2021	2022	2023	Max	Min	Δ_{min}^{max}
69		F1	0	0.142857	0.174603	0.301587	0.634921	0.746032	5.6	0.9	6.3
70			0	0.190476	0.31746	0.507937	0.761905	0.888889	7.2	1.6	
71		F2	0	0.081395	0.395349	0.395349	0.674419	0.674419	7.2	1.4	8.6
72			0	0.093023	0.453488	0.453488	0.883721	0.883721	10	2.4	
73		F3	0	0.088235	0.117647	0.338235	0.544118	0.647059	5.6	1.2	6.8
74			0	0.102941	0.220588	0.397059	0.632353	0.867647	8	2.1	

Normalization (sub-factors)

Row	M	N	O	P	Q	R	S	T	U	V
68		2018	2019	2020	2021	2022	2023	Max	Min	θ_{min}^{max}
69	S1	0	0.214286	0.142857	0.47619	0.47619	0.714286	3	0	4.2
70		0	0.285714	0.190476	0.761905	0.761905	0.904762	4.2	0.4	
71	S2	0	0.045455	0.212121	0.333333	0.545455	0.757576	5.6	0.6	6.6
72		0	0.060606	0.363636	0.545455	0.666667	0.909091	7.2	1.2	
73	S3	0	0.222222	0.380952	0.380952	0.571429	0.761905	4.8	0	6.3
74		0	0.190476	0.380952	0.380952	0.761905	0.809524	6.3	1.2	
75	S4	0	0	0.322581	0.564516	0.580645	0.564516	6.4	2.8	6.2
76		0	0	0.241935	0.516129	0.677419	0.516129	9	4.8	
77	S5	0.125	0	0.275	0.45	0.5375	0.65	7.2	2	8
78		0.075	0	0.25	0.45	0.55	0.8	10	3.6	

Table 3.8 Excel formula: Normalized white scores

C82 | f_x | =((C69*(1-C69))+(C70*C70))/(1-C69+C70)

	A	B	C	D	E	F	G	H
79								
80	(ii)	Normalized white (factors)						
81			2018	2019	2020	2021	2022	2023
82		F1	0	0.151515	0.214286	0.388471	0.720769	0.857143
83		F2	0	0.082465	0.420266	0.420266	0.82737	0.82737
84		F3	0	0.089727	0.138235	0.360294	0.59539	0.803863
85								

Table 3.9 Normalized white scores

80	(ii)	Normalized white (factors)					
81		2018	2019	2020	2021	2022	2023
82	F1	0	0.151515	0.214286	0.388471	0.720769	0.857143
83	F2	0	0.082465	0.420266	0.420266	0.82737	0.82737
84	F3	0	0.089727	0.138235	0.360294	0.59539	0.803863
85							
86							

Normalized white (sub-factors)						
	2018	2019	2020	2021	2022	2023
S1	0	0.233333	0.151515	0.645503	0.645503	0.859048
S2	0	0.046359	0.259968	0.428788	0.617527	0.877193
S3	0	0.215977	0.380952	0.380952	0.693333	0.798701
S4	0	0	0.301358	0.538272	0.640417	0.538272
S5	0.12105	0	0.26859	0.45	0.54429	0.754348

Table 3.10 Excel formula: Final white scores

C91 | f_x | =$J69+(C82*$K69)

	A	B	C	D	E	F	G	H	I
88									
89	(iii)	Final whitenized (factors)							
90			2018	2019	2020	2021	2022	2023	
91		F1	0.9	1.854545	2.25	3.347368	5.440845	6.3	
92		F2	1.4	2.109195	5.014286	5.014286	8.515385	8.515385	
93		F3	1.2	1.810145	2.14	3.65	5.248649	6.666265	
94									
95									

Table 3.11 Final white scores

(iii)	Final whitenized (factors)						
		2018	2019	2020	2021	2022	2023
	F1	0.9	1.8545	2.25	3.347368	5.440845	6.3
	F2	1.4	2.1092	5.014286	5.014286	8.515385	8.515385
	F3	1.2	1.8101	2.14	3.65	5.248649	6.666265

Final whitenized (sub-factors)						
	2018	2019	2020	2021	2022	2023
S1	0	0.98	0.636364	2.711111	2.711111	3.608
S2	0.6	0.90597	2.315789	3.43	4.675676	6.389474
S3	0	1.36066	2.4	2.4	4.368	5.031818
S4	2.8	2.8	4.668421	6.137288	6.770588	6.137288
S5	2.96842	2	4.148718	5.6	6.354321	8.034783

Step 7: The absolute matrix of grey incidences (AMGI) are calculated following Equations 3.30 – 3.38. The formula implementation in Excel and the calculation of zeroing starting images are shown in Tables 3.12 and 3.13, the formula implementation and the calculation for ADGI are further shown in Tables 3.14 and 3.15, respectively.

Table 3.12 Excel formula: Zeroing starting images

C100 f_x =C91-$C91

	B	C	D	E	F	G	H	I
98	Zeroing start (factors)							
99		2018	2019	2020	2021	2022	2023	$\|Y_{si}\|$
100	F1	0	0.954545	1.35	2.447368	4.540845	5.4	11.99276
101	F2	0	0.709195	3.614286	3.614286	7.115385	7.115385	18.61084
102	F3	0	0.610145	0.94	2.45	4.048649	5.466265	10.78193

Table 3.13 Zeroing starting image matrices

Zeroing start (factors)

	2018	2019	2020	2021	2022	2023	$\|Y_{si}\|$
F1	0	0.954545	1.35	2.447368	4.540845	5.4	11.99276
F2	0	0.709195	3.614286	3.614286	7.115385	7.115385	18.61084
F3	0	0.610145	0.94	2.45	4.048649	5.466265	10.78193

Zeroing start (sub-factors)

	2018	2019	2020	2021	2022	2023	$\|X_{sk}\|$
S1	0	0.98	0.636364	2.711111	2.711111	3.608	8.842586
S2	0	0.30597	1.715789	2.83	4.075676	5.789474	11.82217
S3	0	1.360656	2.4	2.4	4.368	5.031818	13.04456
S4	0	0	1.868421	3.337288	3.970588	3.337288	10.84494
S5	0	-0.96842	1.180297	2.631579	3.3859	5.066362	8.762536

Table 3.14 Excel formula: AMGI

N113 f_x =(1+$I100+$T$100)/(1+$I100+$T$100+N107)

	K–L	M	N	O	P	Q	R
106		$\|X_{sk} - Y_{si}\|$	S1	S2	S3	S4	S5
107	ABS(T$100-$I100) ←	F1	3.150173	0.170587	1.051806	1.147817	3.230223
108		F2	9.768258	6.788672	5.566279	7.765902	9.848308
109		F3	1.93934	1.040246	2.262639	0.063015	2.019391
110							
111		ADGI					
112		ε_{ik}	S1	S2	S3	S4	S5
113		F1	0.87392	0.993173	0.961172	0.954061	0.870716
114		F2	0.744432	0.822387	0.854369	0.796819	0.742337
115		F3	0.914051	0.95779	0.916474	0.997223	0.910503

Table 3.15 AMGI for factors and sub-factors

$\lvert X_{sk} - Y_{si} \rvert$	S1	S2	S3	S4	S5
F1	3.150173	0.170587	1.051806	1.147817	3.230223
F2	9.768258	6.788672	5.566279	7.765902	9.848308
F3	1.93934	1.040246	2.262639	0.063015	2.019391

ADGI

ε_{ik}	S1	S2	S3	S4	S5
F1	0.87392	0.993173	0.961172	0.954061	0.870716
F2	0.744432	0.822387	0.854369	0.796819	0.742337
F3	0.914051	0.95779	0.916474	0.997223	0.910503

Step 8: The relative matrix of grey incidences (RMGI) are calculated following Equations 3.39 – 3.50. The formula implementation in Excel and the computation of zeroing starting images are shown in Tables 3.16 and 3.17, the formula implementation and the calculation for RDGI are further shown in Tables 3.18 and 3.19, respectively.

Table 3.16 Excel formula: Initial and zeroing starting images

C129 =C120-$C120

Initializing operator (factors)

	2018	2019	2020	2021	2022	2023
F1	1	2.060606	2.5	3.719298	6.045383	7
F2	1	1.506568	3.581633	3.581633	6.082418	6.082418
F3	1	1.508454	1.783333	3.041667	4.373874	5.555221

C91/$C91

Zeroing start (factors)

	2018	2019	2020	2021	2022	2023	$\lvert Y_{si} \rvert$
F1	0	1.060606	1.5	2.719298	5.045383	6	13.32529
F2	0	0.506568	2.581633	2.581633	5.082418	5.082418	13.29346
F3	0	0.508454	0.783333	2.041667	3.373874	4.555221	8.984938

Steps 9 amd 10: The synthetic degree of grey incidences is calculated following Equation 3.51 and the synthetic matrix of grey incidences (SMGI) can be constructed. Further, by summing the values of all degree of incidences of a typical sub-factor over a main factor, we obtain the aggregated degree of influence (*ADG*) for the sub-factors, following Equation 3.52. The formula implementation in Excel and the constructed SMGI are shown in Tables 3.20 and 3.21, the formula implementation and the calculation ADG is shown in Table 3.22.

Table 3.17 Initial and zeroing starting image matrices

Initializing operator (factors)

	2018	2019	2020	2021	2022	2023
F1	1	2.060606	2.5	3.719298	6.045383	7
F2	1	1.506568	3.581633	3.581633	6.082418	6.082418
F3	1	1.508454	1.783333	3.041667	4.373874	5.555221

Zeroing start (factors)

	2018	2019	2020	2021	2022	2023	$\lvert Y_{si} \rvert$
F1	0	1.060606	1.5	2.719298	5.045383	6	13.32529
F2	0	0.506568	2.581633	2.581633	5.082418	5.082418	13.29346
F3	0	0.508454	0.783333	2.041667	3.373874	4.555221	8.984938

Initialising operator (sub-factors)

	2018	2019	2020	2021	2022	2023
S1	0	0.98	0.636364	2.711111	2.711111	3.608
S2	1	1.50995	3.859649	5.716667	7.792793	10.64912
S3	0	1.360656	2.4	2.4	4.368	5.031818
S4	1	1	1.667293	2.191889	2.418067	2.191889
S5	1	0.673759	1.397618	1.886525	2.14064	2.706753

Final whitenized (sub-factors)

	2018	2019	2020	2021	2022	2023	$\lvert X_{sk} \rvert$
S1	0	0.98	0.636364	2.711111	2.711111	3.608	8.842586
S2	0	0.50995	2.859649	4.716667	6.792793	9.649123	19.70362
S3	0	1.360656	2.4	2.4	4.368	5.031818	13.04456
S4	0	0	0.667293	1.191889	1.418067	1.191889	3.873193
S5	0	-0.32624	0.397618	0.886525	1.14064	1.706753	2.951918

Table 3.18 Excel formula: RMGI

N142 f_x =(1+$I129+$T$129)/(1+$I129+$T$129+N136)

	K	L	M	N	O	P	Q	R
134								
135			$\lvert X_{sk} - Y_{si} \rvert$	S1	S2	S3	S4	S5
136	ABS(T$129-$I129)		F1	4.482702	6.378333	0.280723	9.452094	10.37337
137			F2	4.450874	6.41016	0.248895	9.420266	10.34154
138			F3	0.142353	10.71868	4.059626	5.111745	6.03302
139								
140			RDGI					
141			γ_{ik}	S1	S2	S3	S4	S5
142			F1	0.83788	0.842149	0.989847	0.658159	0.624841
143			F2	0.83866	0.841361	0.990978	0.658524	0.625129
144			F3	0.992496	0.734734	0.850138	0.730534	0.681968

Table 3.19 RMGI for factors and sub-factors

	M	N	O	P	Q	R
134						
135	$\lvert X_{sk} - Y_{si} \rvert$	S1	S2	S3	S4	S5
136	F1	4.482702	6.378333	0.280723	9.452094	10.37337
137	F2	4.450874	6.41016	0.248895	9.420266	10.34154
138	F3	0.142353	10.71868	4.059626	5.111745	6.03302
139						
140	RDGI					
141	γ_{ik}	S1	S2	S3	S4	S5
142	F1	0.83788	0.842149	0.989847	0.658159	0.624841
143	F2	0.83866	0.841361	0.990978	0.658524	0.625129
144	F3	0.992496	0.734734	0.850138	0.730534	0.681968

Table 3.20 Excel formula: SMGI

N148 f_x =(0.5*N113)+(0.5*N142)

	M	N	O	P	Q	R
145						
146	SMGI					$\beta \approx 0.5$
147	ρ_{ik}	S1	S2	S3	S4	S5
148	F1	0.8559	0.917661	0.97551	0.80611	0.747778
149	F2	0.791546	0.831874	0.922673	0.727672	0.683733
150	F3	0.953273	0.846262	0.883306	0.863878	0.796236
151						

Table 3.21 SMGI for factors and sub-factors

	A	B	C	D	E	F	G	H	I	J	K	L	M	N	O	P	Q	R
145																		
146													SMGI					$\beta \approx 0.5$
147													ρ_{ik}	S1	S2	S3	S4	S5
148													F1	0.8559	0.917661	0.97551	0.80611	0.747778
149													F2	0.791546	0.831874	0.922673	0.727672	0.683733
150													F3	0.953273	0.846262	0.883306	0.863878	0.796236
151																		

Table 3.22 Excel formula and construction of ADG

N151 =SUM(N148:N150)/3

	A	B	C	D	E	F	G	H	I	J	K	L	M	N	O	P	Q	R
145																		
146													SMGI					$\beta \approx 0.5$
147													ρ_{ik}	S1	S2	S3	S4	S5
148													F1	0.8559	0.917661	0.97551	0.80611	0.747778
149													F2	0.791546	0.831874	0.922673	0.727672	0.683733
150													F3	0.953273	0.846262	0.883306	0.863878	0.796236
151													ADG	0.866906	0.865265	0.927163	0.79922	0.742582
152																		

3.3 CONCLUSION

Through implementation of the grey incidence analysis in the forgoing case, we understand that the sub-factors S_3 (*standardization*) and S_1 (*risk management*) are having the highest degree of incidence in their developmental tendencies considering all the factors (*collaboration, flexibility,* and *agility*) combined together. This is an indication that these sub-factors (*standardization* and *risk management*) can play a vital role in improving the resilience of the case firm and its supply chain.

REFERENCES

Deng, J.L. (1989). Introduction to grey system theory. *The Journal of Grey System*, 1(1), 1–24.

Dong, W., Liu, S. and Fang, Z. (2018). On modeling mechanisms and applicable ranges of grey incidence analysis models. *Grey Systems: Theory and Application*, 8(4), 448–461.

Liu, S.F., Yang, Y.J. and Forrest, J. (2022). *Grey Systems Analysis*. Springer-Verlag, Berlin.

Liu, S., Zhang, H. and Yang, Y. (2017). Explanation of terms of grey incidence analysis models. *Grey Systems: Theory and Application*, 7(1), 136–142.

Rajesh, R. (2020). Exploring the sustainability performances of firms using environmental, social, and governance scores. *Journal of Cleaner Production*, 247, 119600.

Rajesh, R. (2022). A novel advanced grey incidence analysis for investigating the level of resilience in supply chains. *Annals of Operations Research*, 308, 441–490.

Rajesh, R. (2024). Analysing psycho-social conditions of people during the COVID-19 pandemic: A case of Kerala. *International Journal of Disaster Risk Reduction*, 103, 104327.

CHAPTER 4

Decision-Making Models

4.1 INTRODUCTION

The decision-making methods using grey theory generally involves problems with multiple criteria for evaluation and multiple alternative solutions available, where the decision-maker can choose among them, the solution which is most suited to the goal or objective of the problem. This chapter includes detailed step-by-step implementation along with demonstration of sample case problems for each of the methodologies. Here, we elaborate and discuss the implementation of grey relational analysis, grey target decision-making models, grey stratified decision-making models, and grey integrated decision analytics and their practical applications. The methodologies are discussed below in detail.

4.2 GREY RELATIONAL ANALYSIS

The first one to discuss amongst the decision-making models using grey theory is the grey relational analysis. It is also one of the most popular multi-criteria decision-making method and has been adopted by several researchers in social sciences and management (Hamzaçebi and Pekkaya, 2011). Grey relational analysis explores the relations between factors in a system (Kuo et al., 2008). Grey relational analysis is a popular decision-making technique, which is widely used for selection and prioritization of alternatives, in case of problems with multiple objectives (Liu et al., 2022). The method has the advantage that both qualitative and quantitative criteria can be incorporated for evaluation (Wei, 2011). Also, the evaluation can include weights of the criteria and the ratings can be made in linguistic labels and can be converted to grey values, later using predefined conversion scales.

4.2.1 Step-by-Step Implementation (Grey Relational Analysis)

The step-wise procedure for selection of the best alternative using the grey relational analysis is detailed as follows.

Step 1: Obtain the possible alternatives

The possible alternatives are listed from the available list. The alternatives that can be a potential choice for selection need to be sorted out. This can help in saving time for the rating experts not to spend their useful time in rating non-potential alternatives and the same can minimize the complexity of the process by reducing the number of possible options for the selection process. Researchers/ practitioners can use various prior evaluation methods or mandatory checklists to remove non-preferable alternatives in the initial phase of the process. After this, let $S_i = \{S_1, S_2, S_3, \ldots, S_m\}$ be representing m set of potential alternatives for the selection process, where $i = 1, 2, 3, \ldots, m$.

Step 2: Identify the attributes for selection

The attributes for the selection of alternatives need to be identified. Let us assume that there are n independent attributes for evaluation of alternatives, we can represent these attributes as follows. *i.e.*, $A_j = \{A_1, A_2, A_3, \ldots, A_n\}$, where $j = 1, 2, 3, \ldots, n$.

Step 3: Linguistic to grey conversion for weights

Suppose that $\otimes W_j = \{\otimes W_1, \otimes W_2, \otimes W_3, \ldots, \otimes W_n\}$ be the attribute weightings assigned in grey numbers for the corresponding linguistic labels. The linguistic labels for assessment can be converted to grey values with a lower bound ($\underline{G}$) and an upper bound ($\overline{G}$). Let us assume that the weightings are assigned by a group of $t(k = 1, 2, 3, \ldots, t)$ experts, then the grey average of the weights can be calculated. Suppose that the group is represented by A_k, $k = 1, 2, 3, \ldots, t$, and the weights assigned by the expert for the attribute j in linguistic labels can be indicated as $\{W_j^1, W_j^2, W_j^3, \ldots, W_j^t\}$, then the grey number corresponding to the same can be indicated as $\{\otimes W_j^1, \otimes W_j^2, \otimes W_j^3, \ldots, \otimes W_j^t\}$. The average weight for the attribute j can be calculated as follows.

$$\otimes W_j = \frac{1}{t}\left[\otimes W_j^1 + \otimes W_j^2 + \otimes W_j^3 + \cdots + \otimes W_j^t\right] \tag{4.1}$$

i.e.,

$$\otimes W_j = \frac{1}{t}\sum_{k=1}^{t}\left(\otimes W_j^k\right) \tag{4.2}$$

where $\otimes W_j^k$ can represent the grey number for the attribute j evaluated by analyst k. This can be represented as follows.

$$\otimes W_j^k = \left[\underline{W}_j^k, \overline{W}_j^k\right] \tag{4.3}$$

Hence, we further modify Equation 4.2 as follows.

$$\otimes W_j = \left[\left(\frac{1}{t}\sum_{k=1}^{t}\left(\underline{W}_j^k\right)\right), \left(\frac{1}{t}\sum_{k=1}^{t}\left(\overline{W}_j^k\right)\right)\right] \tag{4.4}$$

Step 4: Linguistic to grey conversion for attribute ratings

The performance considering attributes j for the alternative i in linguistic scales, which is rated by the expert k can be indicated as, G_{ij}^{k}, $i = 1, 2, 3, \ldots, m$; $j = 1, 2, 3, \ldots, n$; $k = 1, 2, 3, \ldots, t$.

The same can be indicated as a grey number as follows:

$$\otimes G_{ij}^{k} = \left[\underline{G}_{ij}^{k}, \overline{G}_{ij}^{k}\right] \tag{4.5}$$

Further, we can calculate the average of the ratings given by experts as follows.

$$\otimes G_{ij} = \frac{1}{t}\left[\otimes G_{ij}^{\;1} + \otimes G_{ij}^{\;2} + \otimes G_{ij}^{\;3} + \ldots + \otimes G_{ij}^{\;t}\right] \tag{4.6}$$

i.e.,

$$\otimes G_{ij} = \frac{1}{t}\sum_{k=1}^{t}\left(\otimes G_{ij}^{k}\right) \tag{4.7}$$

We can rewrite Equation 4.7 as,

$$\otimes G_{ij} = \left[\left(\frac{1}{t}\sum_{k=1}^{t}\left(\underline{G}_{ij}^{k}\right)\right), \left(\frac{1}{t}\sum_{k=1}^{t}\left(\overline{G}_{ij}^{k}\right)\right)\right] \tag{4.8}$$

Step 5: Formation of the grey decision matrix

We can form a grey decision matrix D from the obtained average grey ratings, $\otimes G_{ij}$, where each of these values indicate an upper bound and a lower bound.

$$D = \begin{bmatrix} \otimes G_{11} & \otimes G_{12} & \cdots & \otimes G_{1n} \\ \otimes G_{21} & \otimes G_{22} & \cdots & \otimes G_{2n} \\ \vdots & \vdots & \ddots & \vdots \\ \otimes G_{m1} & \otimes G_{m2} & \cdots & \otimes G_{mn} \end{bmatrix} \tag{4.9}$$

Step 6: Normalize the matrix

Normalization is conducted to limit the grey number values between 0 and 1. The benefit (maximize) attribute and the cost (minimize) attributes need to be normalized separately. The cost attribute can be normalized as follows.

$$\otimes G_{ij}^{*} = \left[\frac{G_j^{\min}}{\overline{G}_{ij}}, \frac{G_j^{\min}}{\underline{G}_{ij}}\right] \tag{4.10}$$

where,

$$G_j^{\min} = \min_{1 \le i \le m}\left\{\underline{G}_{ij}\right\} \tag{4.11}$$

The benefit attribute can be normalized as,

$$\otimes G_{ij}^{*} = \left[\frac{\underline{G}_{ij}}{G_j^{\max}}, \frac{\overline{G}_{ij}}{G_j^{\max}} \right] \tag{4.12}$$

where,
$$G_j^{\max} = \max_{1 \le i \le m} \left\{ \overline{G}_{ij} \right\} \tag{4.13}$$

The grey decision matrix after normalization can be indicated using D^* as follows:

$$D^{*} = \begin{bmatrix} \otimes G_{11}^{*} & \otimes G_{12}^{*} & \cdots & \otimes G_{1n}^{*} \\ \otimes G_{21}^{*} & \otimes G_{22}^{*} & \cdots & \otimes G_{2n}^{*} \\ \vdots & \vdots & \ddots & \vdots \\ \otimes G_{m1}^{*} & \otimes G_{m2}^{*} & \cdots & \otimes G_{mn}^{*} \end{bmatrix} \tag{4.14}$$

Step 7: Weighted normalized grey matrix

The weighted normalized grey matrix ($\otimes V_{ij}$) can be constructed, where the same is the product of the normalized grey decision matrix ($\otimes G_{ij}^{*}$) and the criteria weights ($\otimes W_j$).

i.e.,
$$\otimes V_{ij} = \left[\left(\otimes G_{ij}^{*} \right) * \left(\otimes W_j \right) \right] \tag{4.15}$$

As both of them are grey numbers, the grey number multiplication operation can be employed, where

$$\otimes V_{ij} = \Big[\left[\min\left(\underline{G}_{ij} * \underline{W}_j, \underline{G}_{ij} * \overline{W}_j, \overline{G}_{ij} * \underline{W}_j, \overline{G}_{ij} * \overline{W}_j \right) \right], \left[\max\left(\underline{G}_{ij} * \underline{W}_j, \underline{G}_{ij} * \overline{W}_j, \overline{G}_{ij} * \underline{W}_j, \overline{G}_{ij} * \overline{W}_j \right) \right] \Big] \tag{4.16}$$

where,
$$\otimes V_{ij} = \left[\underline{V}_{ij}, \overline{V}_{ij} \right] \tag{4.17}$$

Thus, the obtained weighted normalized grey decision matrix can be shown as follows.

$$D^{**} = \begin{bmatrix} \otimes V_{11} & \otimes V_{12} & \cdots & \otimes V_{1n} \\ \otimes V_{21} & \otimes V_{22} & \cdots & \otimes V_{2n} \\ \vdots & \vdots & \ddots & \vdots \\ \otimes V_{m1} & \otimes V_{m2} & \cdots & \otimes V_{mn} \end{bmatrix} \tag{4.18}$$

Step 8: Create an ideal referential set of the alternatives

Considering the possible alternatives taken for evaluation, $S_i = \{S_1, S_2, S_3, \ldots, S_m\}$; $i = 1, 2, 3, \ldots, m$, we can construct an ideal referential set of alternatives, indicated as $S^{\max}$, where

$S^{\max} = \{G_1^{\max}, G_2^{\max}, G_3^{\max}, \ldots, G_n^{\max}\}$, which contains the best performances of the alternatives in each individual criteria. Thus, if the alternative is close to an ideal referential alternative, it is the most preferred alternative, and vice-versa.

$$S^{\max} = \left[\left[\max_{1\le i\le m} \underline{V}_{i1}, \max_{1\le i\le m} \overline{V}_{i1}\right], \left[\max_{1\le i\le m} \underline{V}_{i2}, \max_{1\le i\le m} \overline{V}_{i2}\right], \left[\max_{1\le i\le m} \underline{V}_{i3}, \max_{1\le i\le m} \overline{V}_{i3}\right], \ldots, \left[\max_{1\le i\le m} \underline{V}_{in}, \max_{1\le i\le m} \overline{V}_{in}\right]\right] \tag{4.19}$$

Step 9: Compute grey possibility values

To understand the relative closeness of an alternative to the ideal referential alternative, we can compare the alternative set $S_i = \{S_1, S_2, S_3, \ldots, S_m\}$; $i = 1, 2, 3, \ldots, m,$ to the ideal referential alternative $S^{\max}$. This can be represented using possibility values as shown.

$$P\left(S_i \le S^{\max}\right) = \frac{1}{n}\sum_{j=1}^{n}\left[P(\otimes V_{ij} \le \otimes S_j^{\max}\right] \tag{4.20}$$

These possibility values indicate the possibility that a grey number is less than or equal to another one, which can be calculated as follows,

$$P(S_i \le S^{\max}) = \frac{1}{n}\sum_{j=1}^{n}\left[\frac{\max(0, L_j^* - \max(0, \overline{V}_{ij} - \underline{S}_j^{\max})}{L_j^*}\right] \tag{4.21}$$

The Equation 4.21 can be further expanded as,

$$P(S_i \le S^{\max}) = \frac{1}{n}\left[\left[\frac{\max(0, L_1^* - \max(0, \overline{V}_{i1} - \underline{S}_1^{\max})}{L_1^*}\right] + \left[\frac{\max(0, L_2^* - \max(0, \overline{V}_{i2} - \underline{S}_2^{\max})}{L_2^*}\right] + \left[\frac{\max(0, L_3^* - \max(0, \overline{V}_{i3} - S_3^{\max})}{L_3^*}\right] + \cdots + \left[\frac{\max(0, L_n^* - \max)(0, \overline{V}_{in} - \underline{S}_n^{\max})}{L_n^*}\right]\right] \tag{4.22}$$

Here, L_j^*; $j = \{1, 2, 3, \ldots, n\}$ is indicating the sum of the length of the grey numbers $\otimes V_{ij}$ and $\otimes S_j^{\max}$, where the same can be indicated as,

$$L_j^* = L\left(\otimes V_{ij}\right) + L\left(\otimes S_j^{\max}\right) \tag{4.23}$$

We can calculate the length of a grey number as,

$$L\left(\otimes V_{ij}\right) = \overline{V}_{ij} - \underline{V}_{ij} \tag{4.24}$$

Hence, Equation 4.23 can be further elaborated as follows:

$$L_j^* = \left[\left(\overline{V}_{ij} - \underline{V}_{ij}\right) + \left(\overline{S}_j^{\max} - \underline{S}_j^{\max}\right)\right] \tag{4.25}$$

Step 10: Prioritization of alternatives

After, the possibility values $(P(S_i \le S^{\max}))$ for all the alternatives are calculated, the process of prioritization of alternatives can be performed. Suppose if the calculated grey possibility values are less, then we can assume that the alternative is close to the ideal referential alternative and vice versa.

4.2.2 Sample Case Problem (Grey Relational Analysis)

In connection to the case problem in Section 3.2.2, considered for the company XYZ for building resilience in their supply chains; we can see that resilience being a major aspect that needs to be considered in strategy and policy implementations also. Hence, various partners of the supply chain need to be resilient to major shocks or disruptions. A supply chain is characterized by its upstream suppliers, downstream customers and the internal processes and operations within. As managing the upstream of the supply chain is important, suppliers needs to be robust and resilient (Rajesh and Ravi, 2015). Also, supplier selection problem using grey relational analysis is addressed in literature (Yang and Chen, 2006). Hence, for the case problem for XYZ, we consider the selection of resilient suppliers from a pool of potential supplier base.

Step 1: *Three* analysts for the case firm with experience were selected to identify potential alternative supplier, considering the resilient supplier selection problem. There are *four* potential alternative suppliers considered for the selection process.

Step 2: Further, the selection of attributes in consideration of resilience capabilities is made and *five* attributes were selected for evaluation, which are *quality, cost, flexibility, collaboration,* and *risk awareness*. These attributes are taken in the order of $A_j = \{A_1, A_2, A_3, A_4, A_5\}$, where $j = 1, 2, 3, 4, 5$.

Step 3: The importance of attributes imparting resilience are decided by the analysts as weightings and the same is done in a *five-point* linguistic scale, varying from *Very Low* to *Very High*, representing *Very Low [VL], Low [L], Medium [M], High [H]*, and *Very High [VH]*. Also, based on the past records, the performance of suppliers is recorded on a five-point linguistic scale varying form *Very Poor* to *Very Good*, varying from *Very Poor [VP], Poor [P], Fair [F], Good [G]* and *Very Good [VG]*. The grey numbers associated to these ratings are decided and the conversion scales are shown in Table 4.1. The Excel sheet showing the initial matrices of linguistic ratings of *three* analysts for *four* suppliers considering *five* attributes are shown in Table 4.2.

Steps 4 and 5: The evaluation for assigning weightings for the attributes are conducted and the evaluation in linguistic labels are converted using the conversion scale as mentioned in Table 4.1. By employing Equations 4.1–4.4, the average weights ($\otimes W_j$; $j = 1, 2, 3, 4, 5$) for the attributes are obtained. Excel implementation of this is shown in Table 4.3. These linguistic ratings of suppliers over attributes are also converted to grey values and the average grey ratings ($\otimes G_{ij}$; $i = 1, 2, 3, 4$; $j = 1, 2, 3, 4, 5$) on suppliers' performances are calculated following Equations 4.5–4.8. The grey decision matrix ($D = \otimes G_{ij}$; $i = 1, 2, 3, 4$; $j = 1, 2, 3, 4, 5$) is constructed following Equation 4.9. The Excel calculations for averaging the suppliers' rating on attributes are shown in Table 4.4, further the average ratings are shown in Table 4.5.

Table 4.1 Linguistic labels and the associated grey scales

Rating of attributes	
Linguistic assessment	**Associated grey values**
Very Poor (VP)	[0, 1]
Poor (P)	[1, 3]
Fair (F)	[4, 5]
Good (G)	[6, 9]
Very Good (VG)	[9, 10]
Weights of attributes	
Linguistic assessment	**Associated grey values**
Very Low (VL)	[0.0, 0.1]
Low (L)	[0.1, 0.3]
Medium (M)	[0.4, 0.5]
High (H)	[0.6, 0.9]
Very High (VH)	[0.9, 1.0]

Table 4.2 Initial linguistic labels of rating and weights

	A	B	C	D	E	F	G	H	I	J	K	L
1							Analyst 1					
2	Weights	Analyst 1	Analyst 2	Analyst 3			Ratings	A1	A2	A3	A4	A5
3	A1	H	VH	H			S1	F	VG	G	VG	VP
4	A2	M	M	H			S2	G	P	VG	G	F
5	A3	H	VH	VH			S3	G	G	P	VP	VG
6	A4	M	L	M			S4	VG	P	G	G	F
7	A5	VH	H	VH								
8							Analyst 2					
9							Ratings	A1	A2	A3	A4	A5
10							S1	G	VG	G	G	VP
11							S2	VG	VP	VG	G	G
12							S3	G	VG	P	P	G
13							S4	VG	P	VG	G	P
14												
15							Analyst 3					
16							Ratings	A1	A2	A3	A4	A5
17							S1	G	VG	G	G	P
18							S2	G	VP	G	G	VG
19							S3	VG	G	VP	VP	VG
20							S4	G	VP	G	VG	G
21												

Table 4.3 Excel formula: Initial grey conversion and average of weights

E24	f_x	=AVERAGE(B24:D24)

	A	B	C	D	E	F	G	H	I	J	K	L
21												
22							Analyst 1					
23	Weights	Analyst 1	Analyst 2	Analyst 3	Avg $\otimes W_j$		Ratings	A1	A2	A3	A4	A5
24	A1	0.6	0.9	0.6	0.7		S1	4	9	6	9	0
25		0.9	1	0.9	0.933333			5	10	9	10	1
26	A2	0.4	0.4	0.6	0.466667		S2	6	1	9	6	4
27		0.5	0.5	0.9	0.633333			9	3	10	9	5
28	A3	0.6	0.9	0.9	0.8		S3	6	6	1	0	9
29		0.9	1	1	0.966667			9	9	3	1	10
30	A4	0.4	0.1	0.4	0.3		S4	9	1	6	6	4
31		0.5	0.3	0.5	0.433333			10	3	9	9	5
32	A5	0.9	0.6	0.9	0.8							
33		1	0.9	1	0.966667		Analyst 2					
34							Ratings	A1	A2	A3	A4	A5
35							S1	6	9	6	6	0
36								9	10	9	9	1
37							S2	9	0	9	6	6
38								10	1	10	9	9
39							S3	6	9	1	1	6
40								9	10	3	3	9
41							S4	9	1	9	6	1
42								10	3	10	9	3
43												
44							Analyst 3					
45							Ratings	A1	A2	A3	A4	A5
46							S1	6	9	6	6	1
47								9	10	9	9	3
48							S2	6	0	6	6	9
49								9	1	9	9	10
50							S3	9	6	0	0	9
51								10	9	1	1	10
52							S4	6	0	6	9	6
53								9	1	9	10	9
54												

Step 6: The grey decision matrix is normalized ($D^* = \otimes G_{ij}^*; i = 1, 2, 3, 4; j = 1, 2, 3, 4, 5$) following Equations 4.10–4.13 and the Excel formula for calculation and the final resulting matrices are shown in Tables 4.6 and 4.7, respectively. The values of the average grey weights are also exported here.

Table 4.4 Average of suppliers' performance rating

H57 | f_x =AVERAGE(H24,H35,H46)

	A	B	C	D	E	F	G	H	I	J	K	L
54												
55							Average rating					
56							$\otimes G_{ij}$	A1	A2	A3	A4	A5
57							S1	5.333333	9	6	7	0.333333
58			AVERAGE(H25,H36,H47)					7.666667	10	9	9.333333	1.666667
59							S2	7	0.333333	8	6	6.333333
60								9.333333	1.666667	9.666667	9	8
61							S3	7	7	0.666667	0.333333	8
62								9.333333	9.333333	2.333333	1.666667	9.666667
63							S4	8	0.666667	7	7	3.666667
64								9.666667	2.333333	9.333333	9.333333	5.666667
65			MIN(H57,H59,H61,H63)				G_j^{min}	5.333333	0.333333	0.666667	0.333333	0.333333
66			MAX(H58,H60,H62,H64)				G_j^{max}	9.666667	10	9.666667	9.333333	9.666667
67												

Table 4.5 Average of suppliers' performance rating

54						
55	Average rating					
56	$\otimes G_{ij}$	A1	A2	A3	A4	A5
57	S1	5.333333	9	6	7	0.333333
58		7.666667	10	9	9.333333	1.666667
59	S2	7	0.333333	8	6	6.333333
60		9.333333	1.666667	9.666667	9	8
61	S3	7	7	0.666667	0.333333	8
62		9.333333	9.333333	2.333333	1.666667	9.666667
63	S4	8	0.666667	7	7	3.666667
64		9.666667	2.333333	9.333333	9.333333	5.666667
65	G_j^{min}	5.333333	0.333333	0.666667	0.333333	0.333333
66	G_j^{max}	9.666667	10	9.666667	9.333333	9.666667

Table 4.6 Excel formula: Norma ized suppliers' performance rating

H71 | f_x =H57/H$66

	A	B	C	D	E	F	G	H	I	J	K	L
68												
69							Normalised matrix					
70							$\otimes G_{ij}^{*}$	A1	A2	A3	A4	A5
71							S1	0.551724	0.9	0.62069	0.75	0.034483
72					H58/H$66			0.793103	1	0.931034	1	0.172414
73							S2	0.724138	0.033333	0.827586	0.642857	0.655172
74								0.965517	0.166667	1	0.964286	0.827586
75							S3	0.724138	0.7	0.068966	0.035714	0.827586
76								0.965517	0.933333	0.241379	0.178571	1
77							S4	0.827586	0.066667	0.724138	0.75	0.37931
78								1	0.233333	0.965517	1	0.586207
79							Avg $\otimes W_j$	0.7	0.466667	0.8	0.3	0.8
80								0.933333	0.633333	0.966667	0.433333	0.966667
81												

Table 4.7 Normalized suppliers' performance rating

	A	B	C	D	E	F	G	H	I	J	K	L
68												
69							Normalised matrix					
70							$\otimes G_{ij}^{*}$	A1	A2	A3	A4	A5
71							S1	0.551724	0.9	0.62069	0.75	0.034483
72								0.793103	1	0.931034	1	0.172414
73							S2	0.724138	0.033333	0.827586	0.642857	0.655172
74								0.965517	0.166667	1	0.964286	0.827586
75							S3	0.724138	0.7	0.068966	0.035714	0.827586
76								0.965517	0.933333	0.241379	0.178571	1
77							S4	0.827586	0.066667	0.724138	0.75	0.37931
78								1	0.233333	0.965517	1	0.586207
79							Avg $\otimes W_j$	0.7	0.466667	0.8	0.3	0.8
80								0.933333	0.633333	0.966667	0.433333	0.966667

Step 7: The weighted normalized matrix ($D^{**} = \otimes V_{ij}$; i = 1, 2, 3, 4; j = 1, 2, 3, 4, 5) is constructed following Equations 4.15 – 4.18. The Excel formula for implementation and the final obtained matrix are indicated in Tables 4.8 and 4.9, respectively.

Table 4.8 Excel formula: Weighted normalized suppliers' performance rating

H84 =MIN(H71*H$79,H71*H$80,H72*H$79,H72*H$80)

	A–F	G	H	I	J	K	L
81							
82		Weighted normalised matrix					
83		$\otimes V_{ij}$	A1	A2	A3	A4	A5
84		S1	0.386207	0.42	0.496552	0.225	0.027586
85	MAX(H71*H$79,H71*H$80,H72*H$79,H72*H$80) ←		0.74023	0.633333	0.9	0.433333	0.166667
86		S2	0.506897	0.015556	0.662069	0.192857	0.524138
87			0.901149	0.105556	0.966667	0.417857	0.8
88		S3	0.506897	0.326667	0.055172	0.010714	0.662069
89			0.901149	0.591111	0.233333	0.077381	0.966667
90		S4	0.57931	0.031111	0.57931	0.225	0.303448
91			0.933333	0.147778	0.933333	0.433333	0.566667
92	MAX(H84,H86,H88,H90) ←	IdealS^{max}	0.57931	0.42	0.662069	0.225	0.662069
93	MAX(H85,H87,H89,H91) ←		0.933333	0.633333	0.966667	0.433333	0.966667
94							

Table 4.9 Weighted normalized suppliers' performance rating

	A–F	G	H	I	J	K	L
81							
82		Weighted normalised matrix					
83		$\otimes V_{ij}$	A1	A2	A3	A4	A5
84		S1	0.386207	0.42	0.496552	0.225	0.027586
85			0.74023	0.633333	0.9	0.433333	0.166667
86		S2	0.506897	0.015556	0.662069	0.192857	0.524138
87			0.901149	0.105556	0.966667	0.417857	0.8
88		S3	0.506897	0.326667	0.055172	0.010714	0.662069
89			0.901149	0.591111	0.233333	0.077381	0.966667
90		S4	0.57931	0.031111	0.57931	0.225	0.303448
91			0.933333	0.147778	0.933333	0.433333	0.566667
92		IdealS^{max}	0.57931	0.42	0.662069	0.225	0.662069
93			0.933333	0.633333	0.966667	0.433333	0.966667
94							

Steps 8–10: The ideal referential set of alternative suppliers are established following Equation 4.19. The grey possibility values for supplier selection are calculated following Equations 4.20–4.25. Further, the suppliers are prioritized in the increasing order of their grey possibility values, considering the lower the better approach. The Excel sheet formula and implementation of the calculation of the sum of the lengths of grey numbers, $\otimes V_{ij}$ and $\otimes G_j$ are shown in Table 4.10 and the obtained values are shown in Table 4.11. The Excel sheet formula for the calculation of grey possibility values $P(S_i \leq S^{max})$ and the prioritization and ranking of suppliers are shown in Table 4.12. Further, the final ranking of suppliers is shown in Table 4.13.

Table 4.10 Excel formula: Calculation of the sum of the lengths ($\otimes V_{ij}$, $\otimes G_j$)

H98 | f_x =(H85-H84)+(H$96-H$95)

	A	B	C	D	E	F	G	H	I	J	K	L
94												
95							$\underline{S}_j^{max}$	0.57931	0.42	0.662069	0.225	0.662069
96							$\overline{S}_j^{max}$	0.933333	0.633333	0.966667	0.433333	0.966667
97							L_j^*	A1	A2	A3	A4	A5
98							S1	0.708046	0.426667	0.708046	0.416667	0.443678
99				(H87-H86)+(H$96-H$95) ←			S2	0.748276	0.303333	0.609195	0.433333	0.58046
100							S3	0.748276	0.477778	0.482759	0.275	0.609195
101							S4	0.708046	0.33	0.658621	0.416667	0.567816

Table 4.11 Sum of the lengths of grey numbers ($\otimes V_{ij}$, $\otimes G_j$)

	A	B	C	D	E	F	G	H	I	J	K	L
94												
95							$\underline{S}_j^{max}$	0.57931	0.42	0.662069	0.225	0.662069
96							$\overline{S}_j^{max}$	0.933333	0.633333	0.966667	0.433333	0.966667
97							L_j^*	A1	A2	A3	A4	A5
98							S1	0.708046	0.426667	0.708046	0.416667	0.443678
99							S2	0.748276	0.303333	0.609195	0.433333	0.58046
100							S3	0.748276	0.477778	0.482759	0.275	0.609195
101							S4	0.708046	0.33	0.658621	0.416667	0.567816

Table 4.12 Excel formula: Grey possibility values $P(S_i \leq S^{max})$

H104 | f_x | =(MAX(0,(H98-MAX(0,H85-H$95))))/H98

	A	B	C	D	E	F	G	H	I	J	K	L	M	N	O	P	Q
102																	
103								A1	A2	A3	A4	A5	$P(S_i \leq S^{max})$	Rank			
104							S1	0.772727	0.5	0.663961	0.5	1	0.687338	2	→ SUM(H104:L104)/5		
105		(MAX(0,(H99-MAX(0,H87-H$95))))/H99 ←					S2	0.569892	1	0.5	0.554945	0.762376	0.677443	1			
106							S3	0.569892	0.64186	1	1	0.5	0.742351	4			
107							S4	0.5	1	0.588133	0.5	1	0.717627	3	→ RANK.AVG(M107,M$104:M$107,1)		

Table 4.13 Grey possibility values $P(S_i \leq S^{max})$ and prioritization of suppliers

	A	B	C	D	E	F	G	H	I	J	K	L	M	N
102														
103								A1	A2	A3	A4	A5	$P(S_i \leq S^{max})$	Rank
104							S1	0.772727	0.5	0.663961	0.5	1	0.687338	2
105							S2	0.569892	1	0.5	0.554945	0.762376	0.677443	1
106							S3	0.569892	0.64186	1	1	0.5	0.742351	4
107							S4	0.5	1	0.588133	0.5	1	0.717627	3

Second supplier (S_2) in this case, is the best supplier and third supplier (S_3) comes out to the least preferred choice in terms of their resilient capabilities.

4.3 GREY TARGET DECISION-MAKING

As several decision-making models in literature uses the benefits of grey theory; either as grey-based methods or uses in combination with other multi-criteria decision-making models such as, AHP, TOPSIS, VIKOR, PROMETHEE, ELECTRE, BWM, DEA, etc. (Yan et al., 2015; Thakur and Ramesh, 2017). In most of the combined decision-making models, grey theory is mostly used to handle with the uncertainties in subjective evaluation, where there is conversion of linguistic evaluation labels to grey scales. In grey-based evaluation methods, such as the GRA, the evaluation of the alternatives is also completed using grey numbers, without whitenization of the same. Grey target decision-making model is another grey-based decision-making model, which is generally used when there are contradictory attributes and trade-offs in the evaluation. As we can see, this method is best suited when there are no best solutions, but there are reasonably good solutions based on the choice preferences. Hence, we can represent those solutions as the quasi-preferred solutions. In the decision-making model, the formulation is made in such a way that the target of the decision-making is grey (Luo and Wang 2012). The grey target decision-making model is built based on 13 definitions and 4 underlying theorems (Liu et al., 2022), where to understand them is a prerequisite for formulation of a grey target decision-making model. These definitions and theorems are elaborated below.

4.3.1 Definitions and Theorems

D1. Definition 1:

Let us assume that

$$T = \left\{ t_{ij} = \left(x_i, y_j \right) \mid x_i \in X, y_j \in Y \right\} \tag{4.26}$$

can represent a situation set, where $a_{ij}^{(k)}$ can be the effect value of t_{ij} with objective k and the event and the countermeasure be represented as x_i and y_i, respectively. Suppose that R be the set of all real numbers, then $a^{(k)} : T \to R; t_{ij} \to a_{ij}^{(k)}$ can indicate the effect mapping of T considering objective k.

D2. Definition 2:

Suppose that $a_{ij}^{(k)} = a_{ih}^{(k)}$, then countermeasures y_j and y_h, respective of the same event x_i are assumed to be equivalent considering objective k. The same can be indicated as, $y_j \cong y_h$. Then, the set

$$Y_i^{(k)} = \left\{ y_j \mid y_j \in Y, y_j \cong y_h \right\}, \tag{4.27}$$

can be regarded as the effect equivalence class for the countermeasure y_h for the event x_i and considering the objective k.

D3. Definition 3:

Suppose that for the objective k, the effects represent that the greater value is better. Assume $a_{ij}^{(k)} > a_{ih}^{(k)}$, then the countermeasure y_j is considered superior to the countermeasure y_h, for the event x_i and considering the objective k. This can be denoted as, $y_j \succ y_h$. Hence, the set

$$Y_{ih}^{(k)} = \left\{ y_j \mid y_j \in Y, y_j \succ y_h \right\}, \tag{4.28}$$

can be is indicated as a superior class for the countermeasure y_h for the event x_i and considering the objective k.

D4. Definition 4:

Similar to as said in definition 2, if $a_{ih}^{(k)} = a_{gh}^{(k)}$, the events x_i and x_g may be considered equivalent for the countermeasure y_h considering objective k. This can be denoted as, $x_i \cong x_g$. Further, the set

$$X_h^{(k)} = \left\{ x_i \mid x_i \in X,\ x_i \cong x_g \right\}, \tag{4.29}$$

can be called as the effect equivalence class for the event x_g, and for the countermeasure y_h considering objective k. Further, definition 3 can be extended for the set $X_{gh}^{(k)}$ for superiority.

D5. Definition 5:

Suppose $a_{ij}^{(k)} = a_{gh}^{(k)}$, the situation set, t_{ij} can be regarded as equivalent to the corresponding situation set t_{gh} considering objective k. This is shown as, $t_{ij} \simeq t_{gh}$. Then, the set

$$T^{(k)} = \left\{ t_{ij} \mid t_{ij} \in T, t_{ij} \cong t_{gh} \right\}, \tag{4.30}$$

can be regarded as the effect equivalence class for situation t_{gh} and considering the objective k. Further, for the set $T_{gh}^{(k)}$, the definition 3 for superiority can be regarded true.

D6. Definition 6:

Let $z_1^{(k)}$ and $z_2^{(k)}$ be the upper and lower threshold values of the situational effects considering objective k. Then,

$$T^1 = \left\{ r \mid z_1^{(k)} \le r \le z_2^{(k)} \right\}, \tag{4.31}$$

can be regarded as the grey target of one-dimensional decision-making considering the objective k. Further, $a_{ij}^{(k)} \in [z_1^{(k)}, z_2^{(k)}]$ can be considered as a satisfactory effect considering objective k, where the corresponding desirable situation is t_{ij}, considering objective k and the desirable countermeasure be y_j for the event x_i, considering objective k.

D7. Definition 7:

Suppose $z_1^{(1)}$ and $z_2^{(1)}$ are the threshold values for the situational effects of a typical objective; suppose, objective 1 and $z_1^{(2)}$ and $z_2^{(2)}$ are the threshold values considering another objective, suppose, objective 2, then

$$T^2 = \left\{ r^{(1)}, r^{(2)} \mid z_1^{(1)} \le r^{(1)} \le z_2^{(1)}, z_1^{(2)} \le r^{(2)} \le z_2^{(2)} \right\}, \tag{4.32}$$

can be regarded as the grey target of two-dimensional decision-making. Suppose that the effect vector for the situation t_{ij} can satisfy the condition, $a_{ij} = \left(a_{ij}^{(1)}, a_{ij}^{(2)}\right) \in T^{(2)}$, then we can consider t_{ij} as a desirable situation considering the objectives 1 and 2, where y_j can be regarded as a desirable countermeasure for the event x_i considering the objectives 1 and 2.

D8. Definition 8:

Suppose that there are multiple objectives and let $z_1^{(1)}$ and $z_2^{(1)}$, $z_1^{(2)}$ and $z_2^{(2)}$,..., $z_1^{(t)}$ and $z_2^{(t)}$ represents the threshold for situational effects considering these multiple objectives 1, 2, 3, …, t, respectively; then, we can represent the region of t dimensional Euclidean space as follows:

$$T^t = \left\{ \begin{array}{c} \left(r^{(1)}, r^{(2)}, \ldots, r^{(t)}\right) \mid z_1^{(1)} \le r^{(1)} \le z_2^{(1)}, z_1^{(2)} \le \\ r^{(2)} \le z_2^{(2)}, \ldots, z_1^{(t)} \le r^{(t)} \le z_2^{(t)} \end{array} \right\}. \tag{4.33}$$

T^t can be considered as a grey target of t dimensional decision-making. Suppose that the effect vector for situation t_{ij}, can satisfy the condition; $a_{ij} = (a_{ij}^{(1)}, a_{ij}^{(2)}, \ldots, a_{ij}^{(t)}) \in T^t$, where $a_{ij}^{(k)}$, k = 1, 2, 3, …, t can be the effect value for situation t_{ij} considering objective k, then t_{ij} can be regarded as a desirable situation considering t objectives, which are, objective 1, 2, 3, …, t and y_j can be regarded as a desirable countermeasure for the event x_i considering the multiple objectives, which are indicated as objective 1, 2, 3, …, t.

D9. Definition 9:

Consider the set

$$R^t = \left\{ \begin{array}{c} \left(r^{(1)}, r^{(2)}, \ldots, r^{(t)}\right) \mid \left(r^{(1)} - r_0^{(1)}\right)^2 + \left(r^{(2)} - r_0^{(2)}\right)^2 + \ldots \\ + \left(r^{(t)} - r_0^{(t)}\right)^2 \le R^2 \end{array} \right\}, \tag{4.34}$$

where R^t can be considered as a t dimensional spherical grey target with center $r_0 = \left(r_0^{(1)}, r_0^{(2)}, \ldots, r_0^{(t)}\right)$ and the radius being R. Then, the optimum effect vector can be represented as, $r_0 = \left(r_0^{(1)}, r_0^{(2)}, \ldots, r_0^{(t)}\right)$.

D10. Definition 10:

Suppose, $r_1 = \left(r_1^{(1)}, r_1^{(2)}, \ldots, r_1^{(t)}\right) \in R^t$ then

$$|r_1 - r_0| = \left[\left(r_1^{(1)} - r_0^{(1)}\right)^2 + \left(r_1^{(2)} - r_0^{(2)}\right)^2 + \ldots + \left(r_1^{(t)} - r_0^{(t)}\right)^2\right]^{1/2}, \tag{4.35}$$

can be regarded as the bulls-eye distance for the effect vector r_1.

D11. Definition 11:

Suppose if, t_{ij} and t_{gh} can be two unalike situations and $a_{ij}=\left(a_{ij}^{(1)},a_{ij}^{(2)},\ldots,a_{ij}^{(t)}\right)$ and $a_{gh}=\left(a_{gh}^{(1)},a_{gh}^{(2)},\ldots,a_{gh}^{(t)}\right)$ can represent the effect vectors of t_{ij} and t_{gh}, respectively. Suppose this satisfy, $\left|a_{ij}-r_0\right|\geq\left|a_{gh}-r_0\right|$, then t_{gh} can be regarded as a superior situation to t_{ij}, and the same can be denoted as $t_{gh}\succ t_{ij}$.

D12. Definition 12:

Suppose for any i = 1, 2, 3, …, n and j = 1, 2, 3, …, m, if $a_{ij} \neq r_0$ is true always, then we can conclude that there are no existing optimum situation or any event does not have an optimum countermeasure.

D13. Definition 13:

Further, if there are no existing optimum situation, there exist g and h such that for any i = 1, 2, 3, …, n and j = 1, 2, 3, …, m, where $\left|a_{ij}-r_0\right|\geq\left|a_{gh}-r_0\right|$ is true always. Then, for any $t_{ij}\in T$, where $t_{gh}\succ t_{ij}$, indicating that t_{gh} can be a quasi-optimum situation and x_g be a quasi-optimum event and y_h be a quasi-optimum countermeasure.

The proofs of the below mentioned theorems are elaborated in Liu et al. (2022).

T1. Theorem 1:

Let us assume that $T=\left\{t_{ij}=\left(x_i,y_j\right)\mid x_i\in X,y_j\in Y\right\}\neq\varnothing$ and $A^{(k)}=\left\{a_{ij}^{(k)}\mid t_{ij}\in T\right\}$ can represent the effect set having objective k, then the respective mapping for $a^{(k)}:\left\{T^{(k)}\right\}\to A^{(k)};t^{(k)}\to a_{ij}^{(k)}$ is one-to-one and onto.

T2. Theorem 2:

Assume that $a_{ij}^{(k)}$ is the effect for the situation t_{ij} having objective k, then considering any $t\in T_{ij}^{(k)}$, we can assume t is also desirable. This indicates that if t_{ij} is desirable, then all situations with its effect superior class are also considered as desirable.

T3. Theorem 3:

Consider a t dimensional spherical grey target,

$$R^t=\left\{\left(r^{(1)},r^{(2)},\ldots,r^{(t)}\right)\mid\left(r^{(1)}-r_0^{(1)}\right)^2+\left(r^{(2)}-r_0^{(2)}\right)^2+\cdots+\left(r^{(t)}-r_0^{(t)}\right)^2\leq R^2\right\},$$

where $T=\left\{t_{ij}=\left(x_i,y_j\right)\mid x_i\in X,\ y_j\in Y\right\}$ is the situation set. This indicates that T is an ordered set and the ordering relation is *superiority*.

T4. Theorem 4:

Consider for the situation set $(T,\succ)$, there does always a quasi-optimum situation exist.

4.3.2 Grey Target Decision-Making

Considering the above definitions and the outlined theorems, we can construct a grey target decision-making model for achieving conflicting objectives in practice. The step-wise procedure for the implementation of a grey target decision-making model is elaborated as follows.

Step 1: Selected experts can be employed for rating the performances of alternatives in contradictory attributes. These ratings are on Likert scales, generally varying from 1–7.

Step 2: The weight schemes for the objective contradictions can be suitably assumed. Suppose that objective 1 and objective 2 are having contradictions, a weighting scheme of (0.7, 0.3) indicates that the alternative selection preference goes more in satisfying the first objective.

Step 3: Further, the average of the ratings is calculated. The average of the evaluation scores can be obtained for each alternative and further, the cumulative average scores can be calculated by assuming suitable weight schemes.

Step 4: The cumulative average preference ratings can be used for ranking the alternatives. The same can be conducted for all objective contradictions. This indicates the general inclination of selection of alternatives, when there is an objective contradiction.

Step 5: The effect vectors considering the situations are calculated. These effect vectors indicate the preference of an alternative in view of situations with all objective contradictions. Let us assume a t dimensional grey target having radius R and suppose that $r_{(0)}$ indicates the optimum effect vector.

Step 6: The bulls-eye distances of the effect vectors of every alternative is calculated. These bulls-eye distances indicate the superior nature of the effect vectors. If the distance is closer, the indication is that the alternative is close to the optimum effect vector, and vice-versa.

Step 7: The ranking can be done in the ascending order of bulls-eye distances. Let us assume for a situation t_{ij}, which is superior to a situation t_{gh}; then we can assume the relation $t_{ij} \succ t_{gh}$, which says that situation t_{ij} can be a quasi-preferred situation to t_{gh}.

4.3.3 Sample Case Problem (Grey Target Decision-Making)

We considered the case of implementation of strategies with objective contradictions. The electronic manufacturing company *A* was considered as the case, where strategic preferences for *sustainability* and *resilience* are considered for implementation. As many of the supporting strategies focusing on resilience and sustainability focus are having objective contradictions, any alternative strategic plan must be evaluated for their capability to contribute to resilience and sustainability (Rajesh, 2021). The *five* alternative strategies (AS) with weighting schemes varying from (0.1, 0.9), (0.3, 0.7), (0.5, 0.5), (0.7, 0.3), and (0.9, 0.1) were considered for evaluation, where these weights indicate the strategic preference towards sustainability and resilience focuses. We have observed *three* objective contradictions among sustainability and resilience in practice. These strategic objective contradictions (OC) are *efficiency* and *flexibility*

(OC1); *adaptability* and *competency* (OC2); and *resource conservation* and *redundancy* (OC3).

Step 1: We have considered the ratings of *three* supply chain analysts for *five* alternatives towards *three* of the objective contradictions among sustainability and resilience.

Step 2: We consider and observe the strategic preference of the company over *five* alternative weighting schemes of the *three* objective contradictions. These ratings are observed on Likert scales varying from 1-7, where 1 indicates a least preferred choice and 7 indicates most preferred choice. The initial matrices are shown in Table 4.14.

Table 4.14 Initial matrices of ratings for objective contradictions

	A	B	C	D	E	F	G	H
1								
2	OC1		Sustainability	Resilience	Analyst 1	Analyst 2	Analyst 3	Average
3		AS1	0.1	0.9	2	1	2	1.666667
4		AS2	0.3	0.7	3	3	4	3.333333
5		AS3	0.5	0.5	4	4	5	4.333333
6		AS4	0.7	0.3	5	5	4	4.666667
7		AS5	0.9	0.1	4	3	3	3.333333
8								
9	OC2		Sustainability	Resilience	Analyst 1	Analyst 2	Analyst 3	Average
10		AS1	0.1	0.9	1	2	2	1.666667
11		AS2	0.3	0.7	3	3	4	3.333333
12		AS3	0.5	0.5	5	4	5	4.666667
13		AS4	0.7	0.3	6	5	6	5.666667
14		AS5	0.9	0.1	5	6	5	5.333333
15								
16	OC3		Sustainability	Resilience	Analyst 1	Analyst 2	Analyst 3	Average
17		AS1	0.1	0.9	1	1	2	1.333333
18		AS2	0.3	0.7	3	3	4	3.333333
19		AS3	0.5	0.5	5	5	6	5.333333
20		AS4	0.7	0.3	6	7	5	6
21		AS5	0.9	0.1	5	4	5	4.666667

Step 3: The average of the ratings was calculated and we assume an equal weighting for the scores of all analysts. This is also shown in Table 4.14.

Step 4: The average ratings were obtained and the *five* alternatives were ranked for all the *three* objective contradictions. These preference ranks are indicative of the choice preference of the firm considering the objective contradictions. The Excel formula for the average and the ranking order is illustrated in Table 4.15.

Table 4.15 Excel formula: Ranking order of alternative strategies

I3 | f_x =RANK(H3,H$3:H$7,0)

	A	B	C	D	E	F	G	H	I	J	K
1											
2	OC1		Sustainability	Resilience	Analyst 1	Analyst 2	Analyst 3	Average	Order	$\left(r^{(i)} - r_0^{(i)}\right)^2$	
3		AS1	0.1	0.9	2	1	2	1.666667	5	16	
4		AS2	0.3	0.7	3	3	4	3.333333	3	4	
5		AS3	0.5	0.5	4	4	5	4.333333	2	1	AVERAGE(E5:G5)
6		AS4	0.7	0.3	5	5	4	4.666667	1	0	
7		AS5	0.9	0.1	4	3	3	3.333333	3	4	
8											
9	OC2		Sustainability	Resilience	Analyst 1	Analyst 2	Analyst 3	Average			
10		AS1	0.1	0.9	1	2	2	1.666667	5	16	
11		AS2	0.3	0.7	3	3	4	3.333333	4	9	
12		AS3	0.5	0.5	5	4	5	4.666667	3	4	
13		AS4	0.7	0.3	6	5	6	5.666667	1	0	
14		AS5	0.9	0.1	5	6	5	5.333333	2	1	
15											
16	OC3		Sustainability	Resilience	Analyst 1	Analyst 2	Analyst 3	Average			
17		AS1	0.1	0.9	1	1	2	1.333333	5	16	
18		AS2	0.3	0.7	3	3	4	3.333333	4	9	
19		AS3	0.5	0.5	5	5	6	5.333333	2	1	
20		AS4	0.7	0.3	6	7	5	6	1	0	
21		AS5	0.9	0.1	5	4	5	4.666667	3	4	

Step 5: Further, the effect vectors of *five* alternative schemes were calculated. This indicates the choice preference of the firm over each alternative. Thus, each element in Table 4.15 shows the effect vector of a typical alternative.

Step 6: The superiority of the effect vectors is calculated based on the bulls-eye distances of all effect vectors. The Excel formula and calculation for the bulls-eye distances are represented in Table 4.16.

Step 7: The alternative choices indicating the weighting schemes were ranked in the increasing order of the bulls-eye distances. We follow a quasi-preference style for the alternatives, where the alternatives can be assumed more preferable to others and not in an exact rank order. The final ranking order for alternative strategies are indicated in Table 4.17. The ranking order is as follows; $AS4 \succ AS3 \succ AS5 \succ AS2 \succ AS1$.

4.4 GREY STRATIFIED DECISION-MAKING

Decision-making situations are often complex and a selection or choice is often not made in a single round of evaluation. Also, the decision-making situations can have multiple objectives. Grey stratified decision-making (GSDM) model can be beneficial to such situations, where these models have the flexibility to assign different layers, thereby making it able to accommodate different dimensions and multiple objectives in a decision-making situation (Liu et al., 2022). Hence, a GSDM model can help in assorting the alternatives in strata and thereby helping the decision-makers to have a structured and organized decision-making process. The GSDM model can be implemented in layers, where the basic model consists of *two* layers.

4.4.1. Step-wise Implementation (Grey Stratified Decision-Making)

Suppose that we consider the GSDM model, which is to be implemented in *two* layers. The detailed step-wise implementation procedure for a *two* layer GSDM model can be elaborated below:

Step 1: The criteria and the alternatives for the selection process can be finalized for evaluation, suppose that $A = \{a_1, a_2, \ldots, a_n\}$ is indicating the criteria for evaluation and $B = \{b_1, b_2, \ldots, b_n\}$ be the decision units for evaluation, or we can say as the alternatives. The evaluation of the alternative with respect to a criteria can be indicated as x_{ij}; $i = 1, 2, 3, \ldots, n$; $j = 1, 2, 3, \ldots, m$. This indicates the evaluation of an alternative i, considering the criterion j.

Step 2: We can assign different grey classes to initially categorize the alternatives into. Suppose, we have four grey classes, where this vary from *best, acceptable, basically acceptable, and not acceptable*. The evaluation of an alternatives can be indicated using $f_k(.)$, where $k = 1, 2, 3, \ldots, s$, indicate the grey classes, we assume here as $s = 4$ (*best*, *acceptable*, *basically acceptable*, and *not acceptable*). This gives flexibility for the decision-makers to select only the alternatives in the higher classes for further evaluation in the next level.

Step 3: Assume the whitenization weight function as, θ_i, $i = 1, 2, 3, \ldots, n$, which satisfies the

Table 4.16 Excel formula: Bulls eye distances

N3 =RANK(M3,M$3:M$7,1)

	A	B	C	D	E	F	G	H	I	J	K	L	M	N	O	P
1																
2	OC1		Sustainab	Resilience	Analyst 1	Analyst 2	Analyst 3	Average	Order	$\left(r^{(i)} - r_0^{(i)}\right)^2$		Bulls-eye distance		Rank		
3		AS1	0.1	0.9	2	1	2	1.666667	5	16	(I3-1)^2	AS1	6.928203	5		
4		AS2	0.3	0.7	3	3	4	3.333333	3	4		AS2	4.690416	4		
5		AS3	0.5	0.5	4	4	5	4.333333	2	1	AVERAGE(E5:G5)	AS3	2.44949	2		
6		AS4	0.7	0.3	5	5	4	4.666667	1	0		AS4	0	1		
7		AS5	0.9	0.1	4	3	3	3.333333	3	4	RANK(H7,H$3:H$7,0)	AS5	3	3	SQRT(J7+J14+J21)	
8																
9	OC2		Sustainab	Resilience	Analyst 1	Analyst 2	Analyst 3	Average								
10		AS1	0.1	0.9	1	2	2	1.666667	5	16						
11		AS2	0.3	0.7	3	3	4	3.333333	4	9						
12		AS3	0.5	0.5	5	4	5	4.666667	3	4						
13		AS4	0.7	0.3	6	5	6	5.666667	1	0						
14		AS5	0.9	0.1	5	6	5	5.333333	2	1						
15																
16	OC3		Sustainab	Resilience	Analyst 1	Analyst 2	Analyst 3	Average								
17		AS1	0.1	0.9	1	1	2	1.333333	5	16						
18		AS2	0.3	0.7	3	3	4	3.333333	4	9						
19		AS3	0.5	0.5	5	5	6	5.333333	2	1						
20		AS4	0.7	0.3	6	7	5	6	1	0						
21		AS5	0.9	0.1	5	4	5	4.666667	3	4						

Table 4.17 Final ranking order for alternative strategies

	A	B	C	D	E	F	G	H	I	J	K	L	M	N
1														
2	OC1		Sustainability	Resilience	Analyst 1	Analyst 2	Analyst 3	Average	Order	$\left(r^{(i)} - r_0^{(i)}\right)^2$		Bulls-eye distance		Rank
3		AS1	0.1	0.9	2	1	2	1.666667	5	16		AS1	6.928203	5
4		AS2	0.3	0.7	3	3	4	3.333333	3	4		AS2	4.690416	4
5		AS3	0.5	0.5	4	4	5	4.333333	2	1		AS3	2.44949	2
6		AS4	0.7	0.3	5	5	4	4.666667	1	0		AS4	0	1
7		AS5	0.9	0.1	4	3	3	3.333333	3	4		AS5	3	3
8														
9	OC2		Sustainability	Resilience	Analyst 1	Analyst 2	Analyst 3	Average						
10		AS1	0.1	0.9	1	2	2	1.666667	5	16				
11		AS2	0.3	0.7	3	3	4	3.333333	4	9				
12		AS3	0.5	0.5	5	4	5	4.666667	3	4				
13		AS4	0.7	0.3	6	5	5	5.666667	1	0				
14		AS5	0.9	0.1	5	6	5	5.333333	2	1				
15														
16	OC3		Sustainability	Resilience	Analyst 1	Analyst 2	Analyst 3	Average						
17		AS1	0.1	0.9	1	1	2	1.333333	5	16				
18		AS2	0.3	0.7	3	3	4	3.333333	4	9				
19		AS3	0.5	0.5	5	5	5	5.333333	2	1				
20		AS4	0.7	0.3	6	7	5	6	1	0				
21		AS5	0.9	0.1	5	4	5	4.666667	3	4				

condition $\sum_{1=1}^{n} \theta_i = 1$. Then,

$$\sigma_j^k = \frac{\sum_{i=1}^{n} f^k(x_{ij}) \times \theta_i}{\sum_{k=1}^{s} \sum_{i=1}^{n} f^k(x_{ij}) \times \theta_i}, \tag{4.36}$$

where $i = 1, 2, 3, \ldots, n$; $j = 1, 2, 3, \ldots, m$; $k = 1, 2, 3, \ldots, s$ can be regarded as the decision coefficient that the alternative i belonging to the grey class j. Thus,

$$\sigma_j = \sigma_j^1, \sigma_j^2, \ldots, \sigma_j^s, \tag{4.37}$$

for $j = 1, 2, 3, \ldots, m$ is considered as the vector of the decision coefficient of alternative j. Suppose that $\max_{1 \le k \le s}\{\sigma_j^k\} = \sigma_j^{k*}$, then we consider that the alternative j belongs to the class k_*.

Step 4: Consider the layer 2 of the evaluation process, we assume that $B = (b_1, b_2, \ldots, b_m\}$ be the set of alternatives for further evaluation. We consider these as the events and $C = (c_1, c_2, \ldots, c_p\}$ are the set of countermeasures. Thus, we form individual sets of the events and the countermeasures, which are regarded as a situation set, indicated as below,

$$S = B \times C = \left\{s_{jl} = \left(b_j, c_l\right) | b_j \in B, c_l \in C\right\}, \tag{4.38}$$

where $j = 1, 2, 3, \ldots, m$; $l = 1, 2, 3, \ldots, p$,

Here, S indicates the situation set.

Step 5: Further, we can assume that there are q objectives and for each objective r, we obtain the observational effects, which is indicated as, $u_{jl}^{(r)}, j = 1, 2, 3, \ldots, m$; $l = 1, 2, 3, \ldots, p$; $r = 1, 2, 3, \ldots, q$. The observational effects can be assigned to classes. Here, we can assign three classes, the first one can be an *upper effect measure*, where the preferable value is the higher one of the effect and thus, the observational effect $\gamma_{jl}^{(r)}$ can be obtained as follows.

$$\gamma_{jl}^{(r)} = \frac{u_{jl}^{(r)}}{\max_j \max_l \left\{u_{jl}^{(r)}\right\}} \tag{4.39}$$

The *lower effect measure* is the second category of observation effect calculated, where the lower value of the effect is preferred. Hence, the observational effect $\gamma_{jl}^{(r)}$ can be computed as follows.

$$\gamma_{jl}^{(r)} = \frac{\min_j \min_l \left\{u_{jl}^{(r)}\right\}}{u_{jl}^{(r)}} \tag{4.40}$$

The third category being the *moderate effect measure*, where a moderate value of the observational effect is preferred. Let us assume that $u_{j0l0}^{(r)}$ be a fixed moderate value with objective r, then the moderate observational effect can be computed as follows.

$$\gamma_{jl}^{(r)} = \frac{u_{j0l0}^{(r)}}{u_{j0l0}^{(r)} + \left| u_{jl}^{(r)} - u_{j0l0}^{(r)} \right|} \tag{4.41}$$

The obtained values of the observational effects can be indicated in the form of a matrix as shown below.

$$\beta^{(r)} = \left[\gamma_{jl}^{(r)}\right]_{m \times p} = \begin{bmatrix} \gamma_{11}^{(r)} & \cdots & \gamma_{1p}^{(r)} \\ \vdots & \ddots & \vdots \\ \gamma_{m1}^{(r)} & \cdots & \gamma_{mp}^{(r)} \end{bmatrix}, \tag{4.42}$$

where $$\gamma_{jl} = \gamma_{jl}^{(1)}, \gamma_{jl}^{(1)}, \ldots, \gamma_{jl}^{(q)} \tag{4.43}$$

γ_{jl} is indicating the uniform effect measures of a situation s_{jl}. The decision-weights can be assumed using any methods, based on the preference of the decision-maker. If the decision weight for the objective r, represented as $\varnothing_r$ satisfy the condition,

$$\sum_{r=1}^{q} \varnothing_r = 1, \tag{4.44}$$

then $$\gamma'_{jl} = \gamma_{jl}^{(r)} \times \varnothing_r. \tag{4.45}$$

γ'_{jl} represents the synthetic measure of the effect of the situation s_{jl} and the matrix indicating these values can be represented as follows.

$$\beta' = \left[\gamma'_{jl}\right]_{m \times p} = \begin{bmatrix} \gamma'_{11} & \cdots & \gamma'_{1p} \\ \vdots & \ddots & \vdots \\ \gamma'_{m1} & \cdots & \gamma'_{mp} \end{bmatrix} \tag{4.46}$$

Suppose that $\max\limits_{1 \le l \le p} \{\gamma'_{jl}\} = \gamma'_{jl0}$, then c_{l0} can be regarded as the optimum countermeasure considering the event b_j. Further if, $\max\limits_{1 \le l \le p} \{\gamma'_{jl}\} = \gamma'_{i0l}$, then b_{j0} may be assumed as an optimum event consistent to the countermeasure c_l.

Lastly, if $\max\limits_{1 \le i \le m} \max\limits_{1 \le l \le p} \{\gamma'_{jl}\} = \gamma'_{j0l0}$, then s_{j0l0} may be considered as an optimum situation, for the observational effects.

4.4.2 Sample Case Problem (Grey Stratified Decision-Making)

We have further looked into the supplier selection problem, as mentioned in Section 4.2.2. The case company XYZ as mentioned prior wishes to improve their resilience capabilities by selecting the proper supplier who can support their mission. They assume that various partners of the supply chain also need to be resilient to disruptions. Hence, for the same case problem for XYZ mentioned prior, we consider the selection of resilient suppliers, from a pool of potential supplier base by using the GSDM model. As we see that GSDM models are prior applied to supplier selection problems (Luo and Wang, 2012; Rajesh and Aljabhan, 2022). As resilience being the primary objective, we have conducted a layer 1 (strata) of evaluation for their resilience capabilities and then if they qualify for the same, we further evaluate them for the supplier selection process. The step-wise implementation of the model is detailed as follows;

Step 1: We select *three* analysts for the case firm with experience to identify potential alternative supplier, considering the resilient supplier selection problem. There are *four* potential alternative suppliers considered for the selection process. Further, the selection of attributes in consideration of resilience capabilities is made and *five* attributes were selected for evaluation, which are *quality, cost, flexibility, collaboration*, and *risk awareness.*

Step 2: As *collaboration* and *risk awareness* are considered as the resilience attributes and all the other *three* attributes, *quality, cost,* and *flexibility* are regarded as the primary performance attributes, we conduct an initial evaluation (layer 1) of the suppliers for their capabilities considering *collaboration* and *risk awareness.* Later, the layer 2 of evaluation is proceeded considering the suppliers' capabilities on *quality, cost,* and *flexibility.* The *four* alternative suppliers selected were evaluated by the analysts through brainstorming and have rated the suppliers out of 100, considering the data from their publically reported information and their past performances. The scores obtained for *four* suppliers, considering their capabilities for *collaboration* and *risk awareness* are shown in Table 4.18. Also, the grey classes used in Layer 1 of evaluation are shown in Table 4.18.

Table 4.18 Average suppliers' ratings on social sustainability factors

	A	B	C	D	E
1	**Layer 1**		**Supplier Rating**		
2	**Attributes**	**Supplier 1**	**Supplier 2**	**Supplier 3**	**Supplier 4**
3	**Collaboration**	73	79	56	55
4	**Risk awareness**	62	53	76	68
5					
6					
7	f1	Best			
8	f2	Acceptable			
9	f3	Basically acceptable			
10	f4	Not acceptable			

Step 3: The whitenization weight functions are constructed based on Equations 4.36 and 4.37. We further define the grey classes and the decision coefficient for the supplier i belongs to the grey class j is recorded. The grey classes are indicated in Equations 4.47–4.50 and the whitenization weight functions are presented in Figure 4.1. The decision coefficients for the *four* suppliers are calculated and a classification scheme for the suppliers are made, which are

consisting of four classes; *best, acceptable, basically acceptable,* and *not acceptable*. We have proceeded with further evaluation of the suppliers in layer 2, only if the suppliers fall in any of the first *three* classes, in order.

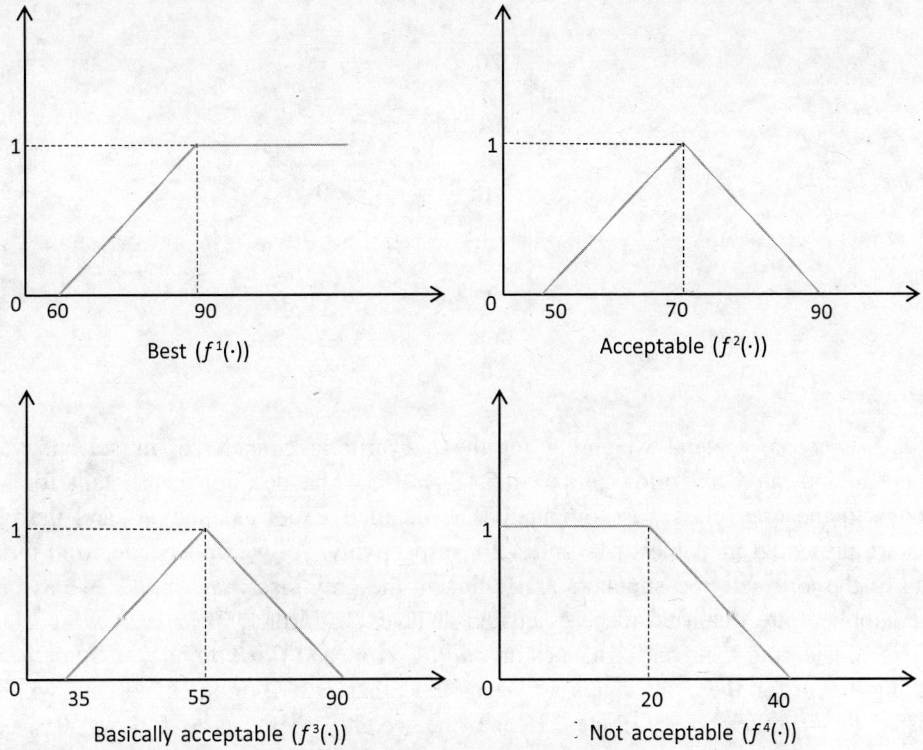

Figure 4.1 Grey classes and the whitenization weight functions.

$$f^1(x) = \begin{cases} 0; & x < 60 \\ \dfrac{x-60}{30}; & 60 \le x \le 90\,; \\ 1; & x > 90 \end{cases} \tag{4.47}$$

$$f^2(x) = \begin{cases} 0; & x < 50 \\ \dfrac{x-50}{20}; & 50 \le x \le 70 \\ \dfrac{90-x}{20}; & 70 < x \le 90 \\ 0; & x > 90 \end{cases}\;; \tag{4.48}$$

$$f^3(x) = \begin{cases} 0; & x < 35 \\ \dfrac{x-35}{20}; & 35 \le x \le 55 \\ \dfrac{75-x}{20}; & 55 < x \le 75 \\ 0; & x > 75 \end{cases}; \tag{4.49}$$

$$f^4(x) = \begin{cases} 0; & x < 0 \\ 1; & 0 \le x \le 20 \\ \dfrac{40-x}{20}; & 20 < x \le 40 \\ 0; & x > 40 \end{cases} \tag{4.50}$$

Step 4: We consider equal weighting for the *two* criteria considered for selection and the weights are indicated as follows; $\theta_1 = 0.5$, $\theta_2 = 0.5$. The decision coefficient for supplier *i* belongs to the grey class *j* is computed. The detailed Excel calculations and the obtained results are presented in Tables 4.19 and 4.20, respectively. As we understand from the results that all of the *four* selected suppliers are falling in the grey class; *acceptable*, we assume that all the suppliers are qualified to be evaluated at layer 2. Further, in layer 2, we evaluate the suppliers considering their performances on *quality, cost,* and *flexibility*. We assume a variable weighting $(\varnothing_r)$ for these attributes as we assume that *cost* is more important, while when compared to the other *two* attributes. Hence, the weight scheme is as follows; 0.3, 0.4, and 0.3, respectively.

The performances of suppliers in quality, *cost,* and *flexibility* are measured and we create a situation set of each supplier with a primary performance attribute (*quality, cost, flexibility*). The considered situation set (Ex: Supplier 1, flexibility) is considered for finding its effects considering two objectives, the *delivery strategy* and the *return strategy*. The observational effects from the analysts are presented in Table 4.21. The observational effects are normalized, considering in mind that the attributes; *quality* and *flexibility* are benefit attributes and *cost* is a non-beneficial attribute. Considering the layer 2 of the evaluation, the detailed Excel sheet implementation and the final results are presented in Tables 4.22 and 4.23, respectively. The observational effects of situations are calculated following Equations 4.38 to 4.43, the results of the same are shown in Table 4.20. Considering the combined effects based on all objectives, we can see that *Supplier 1* may be a best choice and *Supplier 2* be the least preferred choice, as per the results from the GSDM model implementation.

Table 4.19 Excel formula: Layer 1 of evaluation in GSDM

K6 =MAX(G6:J6)

	A	B	C	D	E	F	G	H	I	J	K	L	M	N	O	P	Q	R	S
1	**Layer 1**		**Supplier Rating**					**Supplier 1**							**Supplier 2**				
2	**Attributes**	**Supplier 1**	**Supplier 2**	**Supplier 3**	**Supplier 4**	**Weights**	**f1**	**f2**	**f3**	**f4**			**Weights**	**f1**	**f2**	**f3**	**f4**		
3	**Collaboration**	73	79	56	55	0.5	0.433333	0.85	0.1	0	SUM(G5:J5)		0.5	0.633333	0.55	0	0		
4	**Risk awareness**	62	53	76	68	0.5	0.066667	0.6	0.65	0			0.5	0	0.15	0.9	0		
5						**Sum**	0.25	0.725	0.375	0	1.35	**Sum**	**Sum**	0.316667	0.35	0.45	0	1.116667	**Sum**
6						**Sigma 1k**	0.185185	0.53703704	0.27777778	0	0.537037037	**Max**	**Sigma 2k**	0.283582	0.3134328	0.402985	0	0.402985	**Max**
7	f1	Best						**Sig 1, k=2**								**Sig 2, k=3**			
8	f2	Acceptable						Acceptable								Basically acceptable			
9	f3	Basically acceptable																	
10	f4	Not acceptable						**Supplier 3**							**Supplier 4**				
11						**Weights**	**f1**	**f2**	**f3**	**f4**			**Weights**	**f1**	**f2**	**f3**	**f4**		
12						0.5	0	0.3	0.95	0			0.5	0	0.25	1	0		
13						0.5	0.533333	0.7	0	0			0.5	0.266667	0.9	0.35	0		
14						**Sum**	0.266667	0.5	0.475	0	1.241666667	**Sum**	**Sum**	0.133333	0.575	0.675	0	1.383333	**Sum**
15						**Sigma 3k**	0.214765	0.40268456	0.38255034	0	0.402684564	**Max**	**Sigma 4k**	0.107383	0.4630872	0.543624	0	0.543624	**Max**
16								**Sig 3, k=2**								**Sig 4, k=3**			
17								Acceptable								Basically acceptable			
18									IF(E3<35,0,IF(33>75,0,IF(B3<55, ((B3-35)/20), ((75-B3)/20))))										
19							IF(B3<60,0,IF(B3>90,1,((B3-60)/30)))												
20										IF(B3<0,0,IF(B3>40,0,IF(B3<20,1, ((40-B3)/20))))									
21								IF(B3<50,0,IF(B3>90,0,IF(B3<70, ((B3-50)/20), ((90-B3)/20))))											

Table 4.20 Layer 1 of evaluation in GSDM

K25

	A	B	C	D	E	F	G	H	I	J	K	L	M	N	O	P	Q	R	S
1	**Layer 1**		**Supplier Rating**					**Supplier 1**							**Supplier 2**				
2	**Attributes**	**Supplier 1**	**Supplier 2**	**Supplier 3**	**Supplier 4**	**Weights**	f1	f2	f3	f4			**Weights**	f1	f2	f3	f4		
3	**Collaboration**	73	79	56	55	0.5	0.433333	0.85	0.1	0			0.5	0.633333	0.55	0	0		
4	**Risk awareness**	62	53	76	68	0.5	0.066667	0.6	0.65	0			0.5	0	0.15	0.9	0		
5						**Sum**	0.25	0.725	0.375	0	1.35	**Sum**		0.316667	0.35	0.45	0	1.116667	**Sum**
6		Sigma 1	Sigma 2	Sigma 3	Sigma 4	**Sigma 1k**	0.185185	0.53703704	0.27777778	0	0.537037037	**Max**	sigma 2k	0.283582	0.3134328	0.402985	0	0.402985	**Max**
7								**Sig 1, k=2**								**Sig 2, k=3**			
8	f1	Best						Acceptable								Basically acceptable			
9	f2	Acceptable																	
10	f3	Basically acceptable						**Supplier 3**							**Supplier 4**				
11	f4	Not acceptable				**Weights**	f1	f2	f3	f4			**Weights**	f1	f2	f3	f4		
12						0.5	0	0.3	0.95	0			0.5	0	0.25	1	0		
13						0.5	0.533333	0.7	0	0			0.5	0.266667	0.9	0.35	0		
14						**Sum**	0.266667	0.5	0.475	0	1.241666667	**Sum**	**Sum**	0.133333	0.575	0.675	0	1.383333	**Sum**
15						**Sigma 3k**	0.214765	0.40268456	0.38255034	0	0.402684564	**Max**	**Sigma 4k**	0.107383	0.4630872	0.543624	0	0.543624	**Max**
16								**Sig 3, k=2**								**Sig 4, k=3**			
17								Acceptable								Basically acceptable			

Table 4.21 Observational effects from analysts

E27 =MAX(C25:E26)

	A	B	C	D	E	F
22		Layer 2		Observational effects		
23		Objectives		Quality		
24		U(1)	Supplier 1	Supplier 2	Supplier 3	Supplier 4
25		Delivery Strategy	73	70	77	72
26		Return Strategy	67	74	71	68
27				Max	77	
28						
29		Objectives		Cost		
30						
31		U(2)	Supplier 1	Supplier 2	Supplier 3	Supplier 4
32		Delivery Strategy	91	83	84	86
33		Return Strategy	71	78	79	80
34				Min	71	
35						
36		Objectives		Flexibility		
37						
38		U(3)	Supplier 1	Supplier 2	Supplier 3	Supplier 4
39		Delivery Strategy	79	65	79	80
40		Return Strategy	77	65	71	68
41				Max	79	

Table 4.22 Excel formula: Layer 2 of evaluation in GSDM

F64 =MAX(C64:E64)

	A	B	C	D	E	F	G
43				Quality			
44		Weights	0.3	0.3	0.3		
45		U(1)	Supplier 1	Supplier 2	Supplier 3		
46		Delivery Strategy	0.9480519	0.909090909	1	C25/$E$27	
47		Return Strategy	0.8701299	0.961038961	0.9220779		
48							
49				Cost			
50		Weights	0.4	0.4	0.4		
51		U(2)	Supplier 1	Supplier 2	Supplier 3		
52		Delivery Strategy	0.7802198	0.855421687	0.8452381	$E$34/C32	
53		Return Strategy	1	0.91025641	0.8987342		
54							
55				Flexibility			
56		Weights	0.3	0.3	0.3		
57		U(3)	Supplier 1	Supplier 2	Supplier 3		
58		Delivery Strategy	1	0.82278481	1	C39/$E$41	
59		Return Strategy	0.9746835	0.82278481	0.8987342		
60							
61		rij	Supplier 1	Supplier 2	Supplier 3	Max	
62		Delivery Strategy	0.8965035	0.86173139	0.9380952	0.938095238	Supplier 3
63		Return Strategy	0.953444	0.899249695	0.9057373	0.953444024	Supplier 1
64		Average	0.9249738	0.880490543	0.9219163	0.92497376	Supplier 1
65						Overall Best	Supplier 1
66			(C46*C$44+C52*C$50+C58*C$56)			MAX(C62:E62)	
67							
68				AVERAGE(D62:D63)			

Table 4.23 Layer 2 of evaluation in GSDM

K25

	A	B	C	D	E	F	G
43				Quality			
44		Weights	0.3	0.3	0.3		
45		U(1)	Supplier 1	Supplier 2	Supplier 3		
46		Delivery Strategy	0.9480519	0.909090909	1		
47		Return Strategy	0.8701299	0.961038961	0.9220779		
48							
49				Cost			
50		Weights	0.4	0.4	0.4		
51		U(2)	Supplier 1	Supplier 2	Supplier 3		
52		Delivery Strategy	0.7802198	0.855421687	0.8452381		
53		Return Strategy	1	0.91025641	0.8987342		
54							
55				Flexibility			
56		Weights	0.3	0.3	0.3		
57		U(3)	Supplier 1	Supplier 2	Supplier 3		
58		Delivery Strategy	1	0.82278481	1		
59		Return Strategy	0.9746835	0.82278481	0.8987342		
60							
61		rij	Supplier 1	Supplier 2	Supplier 3	Max	
62		Delivery Strategy	0.8965035	0.86173139	0.9380952	0.938095238	Supplier 3
63		Return Strategy	0.953444	0.899249695	0.9057373	0.953444024	Supplier 1
64		Average	0.9249738	0.880490543	0.9219163	0.92497376	Supplier 1
65						Overall Best	Supplier 1

4.5 GREY INTEGRATED DECISION ANALYTICS

Grey integrated decision analytics (GIDA) model being a new entrant into the series of decision-making methods that utilizes grey theory. GIDA is a simple and comprehensive multi-criteria decision-making (MCDM) model, which can determine the weights of the criteria, along with the evaluation of alternatives (Rajesh, 2024). Determining the weights of the criteria is a significant task in many of the multi-criteria decision-making methods, where most of these methods rely on Analytic Hierarchy Process (AHP) or other methods to determine the weights of the criteria for evaluation. As many of the weight determining methods have the limitation regarding the number of criteria and the check for consistency, subjective evaluation of weights of criteria based on expert opinions are also considered, while evaluating alternatives in many multi-criteria decision-making methods.

4.5.1 Implementation of the Model

The model can be used particularly for group decision-making situations. We elaborate the *eight* step procedure for implementing GIDA, which is shown as,

Step 1: The *first* step is to select and finalize the attributes to be considered for the selection process. Along with that, the alternatives to be evaluated also need to be determined. There can be a pre-screening for the alternatives, so as to reduce the number of alternatives to be considered for the final evaluation.

Step 2: After selecting the attributes for the selection process, the relative weightings among the attributes needs to be determined. This can be through the process of pair-wise comparisons. Often *five* point or a *seven* point Likert scale is used for this purpose. This comparison resembles to that of the Analytical Hierarchy Process, where a *nine*-point scale is used instead. Suppose, if a factor A compared to B is five times more important, then the pair-wise comparison value of importance can be marked as 5. It is also apparent that B is five times less important A, which can be indicated using 1/5.

Step 3: Experts can be employed for performing the pair-wise comparison among attributes. The values are normalized in Step 2 and an upper triangular matrix is constructed based on these pair-wise comparisons. Suppose that there are n such responses, we can take the average of all responses. Let us assume that A_{ij}^{k} represents the rating of the kth respondent, on comparing factor, i to j, then the average rating can be indicated as follows,

$$A = \frac{\sum_{k=1}^{m} A_{ij}^{k}}{n}. \tag{4.51}$$

Step 4: Suppose that the matrix of the average of the rating is indicated by matrix A. We can determine the critical, ideal and most-typical values of the level of importance, where the critical value represents the least value of importance for a particular factor A, while when compared to any random factor B. Similarly, the ideal value indicates the highest value of importance, and the most typical value indicates the most likely value (often calculated as the median of the values) of the level of importance of a factor A, while when compared to any random factor B.

Step 5: Further, we calculate the normalized whitenized weights for the attributes. Whitenization can be performed using

$$w = \frac{w_c + 4 \times w_t + w_i}{6},$$

where w_c is indicating the critical value, w_i shows the ideal value, and w_t represents the most typical value. We can assign a higher weighting for the most typical value, as it is the most preferable value of importance that A can have, when compared to any random factor B. The critical and the ideal values are given equal weightings, while executing the whitenization process. Further, the final whitenized weights are normalized by diving individual weights by the sum of the weights. We can assume that there are m attributes considered and w_j may represent the whitenized weights for each of these attributes j. Thus, we can obtain the normalized weights as follows.

$$w_j' = \frac{w_j}{\sum_{j=1}^{m} w_j}. \tag{4.52}$$

Step 6: We have to further define the events, outcomes, and also the objectives of the study. The event can be the decision problem; the outcome can be the alternative for selection; the event-outcome pair is referred to as a situation. Say, for example, the (selection problem, alternative 1) can be referred to as situation 1, and so on and let $s_{11} = (a_1, b_1)$ can indicate this situation. Let us assume that there are m attributes and n objectives associated with the study. The selection problem can be framed for each of the objectives and the relative ranking of the alternatives can be determined, following *step 7*.

Step 7: Further, the ranking of situation sets is made considering the objectives. We can evaluate each situation set with respect to objectives; suppose if a typical situation s_{11} is evaluated considering objective 1, the effects can be calculated. Let $u_{11}^{(1)}$ be the corresponding effect and for other objectives also, the effects are calculated as follows, $u_{11}^{(2)}, u_{11}^{(3)}, \ldots, u_{11}^{(m)}$. The situations are then ranked based on these effects, where a larger effect will receive a higher rank. These effect rankings can be made with the help of expert ratings or a survey, where the sum of the ranks of the effects can be calculated in consideration of a particular situation. Suppose that $u_{11}^{(1i)}$ represents the effect of a situation s_{11}, where the *event 1* and *outcome 1* are employed; and the considered objective being *objective 1*, which is evaluated by the ith expert. The sum of the ranks can be calculated as $\sum_i u_{11}^{(1i)}$.

Step 8: The aggregated ranks can be obtained by arranging the rank sum in the increasing order. Say for example, the least rank sum will be assigned 1, and so on. Suppose if the rank sum appears to be the same for two alternatives, then same rank can be assigned to them. Suppose if the rank sum is 25, 27, 27, and 30; *rank 1, rank 2, rank 2*, and *rank 4* can be indicated, respectively. Thus, the ranking can be completed for all alternatives.

Step 9: The distance from an ideal referential alternative is to be calculated further. This can be denoted as the bulls-eye distances from the optimum effect vector. Suppose that the rankings obtained for the effects $u_{11}^{(1)}, u_{11}^{(2)}, u_{11}^{(3)}, \ldots, u_{11}^{(m)}$ are represented as $r_1, r_2, \ldots, r_m$, respectively and the optimum effect vector can be represented as;

$$r_0 = \left(r_0^{(1)}, r_0^{(2)}, \ldots, r_0^{(m)}\right). \tag{4.53}$$

The calculation of bulls-eye distances can be made as follows;

$$\left|r_1 - r_0\right| = \left[w_1' \times \left(r_1^{(1)} - r_0^{(1)}\right)^2 + w_2' \times \left(r_1^{(2)} - r_0^{(2)}\right)^2 + \cdots + w_m' \times \left(r_1^{(m)} - r_0^{(m)}\right)^2\right]^{1/2}, \tag{4.54}$$

here $w_1', w_2', \ldots, w_m'$ can indicate the whitenized normalized weights as shown in step 5.

Step 10: The alternatives are ranked based on the bulls-eye distances, which are calculated from the optimum effect vector. Suppose that the alternative is close to the optimum effect vector, then the bulls-eye distances are small and vice-versa. The alternatives are thus ranked in the increasing order of their bulls-eye distances.

4.5.2 Sample Case Problem (Grey Integrated Decision Analytics)

We further revisit the case of resilient supplier selection problem, where capabilities of risk mitigation and collaboration are considered to be important along with other primary performance factors for the selection of suppliers. As the case firm XYZ demands the capability to adapt and respond during the time of a crisis, it is important for the supplier also to be resilient to react to disruptions. The problem of resilient supplier selection is revisited with *four* potential alternative suppliers considered for the evaluation process and there are *five* criteria for evaluation, where *two* of them belong to the criteria considered for ensuring the resilience capabilities of suppliers. Here *collaboration* and *risk awareness* are considered as the criteria for evaluation, along with which we consider the primary performance attributes namely, *quality, cost,* and *flexibility* for the evaluation process. We have re-arranged the order of evaluation by considering the primary performance attributes first, which is indicated as follows; *quality, cost, flexibility, collaboration,* and *risk awareness.* We consider the ratings from *three* analysts for obtaining the importance relations of criteria and also the performance of the *four* potential suppliers, considering the above *five* criteria is evaluated. Hence, we obtain two evaluation matrices from each analyst, where the *first* one indicates the pair-wise evaluation of importance relations among criteria and the *second* one represents the performance evaluation of suppliers considering the criteria. The step-wise implementation of the GIDA methodology is explained below.

Step 1 and 2: The criteria for evaluation and the alternatives are finalized and we conduct a pairwise comparison of attributes, considering their relative importance (first factor over the second) on a Likert scale of 1 to 7, varying from equal to very high importance. Also, inverse of the values was assigned, if the second attribute seems to be more important than the first. The input matrices gotten from the evaluation of *three* analysts are shown in Table 4.24.

Table 4.24 Pair-wise comparison among the criteria by analysts

	A	B	C	D	E	F
1						
2	**Analyst 1**	**Quality**	**Cost**	**Flexibility**	**Collaboration**	**Risk awareness**
3	Quality	1	1	3	4	3
4	Cost	1	1	2	2	3
5	Flexibility	0.33333333	0.5	1	3	2
6	Collaboration	0.25	0.5	0.33333333	1	1
7	Risk awareness	0.33333333	0.333333	0.5	1	1
8						
9	**Analyst 2**	**Quality**	**Cost**	**Flexibility**	**Collaboration**	**Risk awareness**
10	Quality	1	2	3	3	3
11	Cost	0.5	1	2	2	2
12	Flexibility	0.33333333	0.5	1	3	2
13	Collaboration	0.33333333	0.5	0.33333333	1	1
14	Risk awareness	0.33333333	0.5	0.5	1	1
15						
16	**Analyst 3**	**Quality**	**Cost**	**Flexibility**	**Collaboration**	**Risk awareness**
17	Quality	1	2	3	3	3
18	Cost	0.5	1	2	2	5
19	Flexibility	0.33333333	0.5	1	3	2
20	Collaboration	0.33333333	0.5	0.33333333	1	1
21	Risk awareness	0.33333333	0.2	0.5	1	1

Step 3: We record the critical, ideal, and the most typical value of pair-wise importance among attributes. We have *three* evaluation matrices corresponding to *three* analysts and the average of the pairwise comparison of ratings is observed. The highest, lowest and the median of the values in each row are recorded as the ideal, critical, and the most typical values, considering the importance that a factor play in a system. Say, for example, the importance of the attribute *quality* over the other *four* attributes were recorded, where we see that the ideal value is 3.333, the critical value being 1, and the most typical value appears to be 3. The Excel calculations for the same are shown in Table 4.25. Also, the final calculated scores are shown in Table 4.26.

Table 4.25 Excel formula: The average scores, critical, ideal, and the most typical values

K24 | f_x =ROUND(J24/$J$29,3)

	A	B	C	D	E	F	G	H	I	J	K
22											
23	**Average**	**Quality**	**Cost**	**Flexibility**	**Collaboration**	**Risk awareness**	**Critical**	**Ideal**	**Typical**	**Whit Weight**	**Norm Weight**
24	Quality	1	1.667	3	3.333	3	1	3.333	3	2.889	0.308
25	Cost	0.667	1	2	2	3.333	0.667	3.333	2	2.667	0.284
26	Flexibility	0.333	0.5	1	3	2	0.333	3	1	2.222	0.237
27	Collaboration	0.306	0.5	0.333	1	1	0.306	1	0.5	0.801	0.085
28	Risk awareness	0.333	0.344	0.5	1	1	0.333	1	0.5	0.806	0.086
29		ROUND(AVERAGE(B17,B10,B3),3)							**Total**	9.385	
30								MAX(B24:F24)	MEDIAN(B24:F24)		
31							MIN(B24:F24)			ROUND((G24+4*H24+I24)/6,3)	

Table 4.26 The average scores, critical, ideal, and the most typical values

	A	B	C	D	E	F	G	H	I	J	K
22											
23	**Average**	**Quality**	**Cost**	**Flexibility**	**Collaboration**	**Risk awareness**	**Critical**	**Ideal**	**Typical**	**Whit Weight**	**Norm Weight**
24	Quality	1	1.667	3	3.333	3	1	3.333	3	2.889	0.308
25	Cost	0.667	1	2	2	3.333	0.667	3.333	2	2.667	0.284
26	Flexibility	0.333	0.5	1	3	2	0.333	3	1	2.222	0.237
27	Collaboration	0.306	0.5	0.333	1	1	0.306	1	0.5	0.801	0.085
28	Risk awareness	0.333	0.344	0.5	1	1	0.333	1	0.5	0.806	0.086
29									Total	9.385	

Step 4 and 5: The whitenized and the normalized whitenized weights are obtained from the ideal, critical, and the most typical values, following Equations 4.47 and 4.48, respectively. The values are also shown in Tables 4.25 and 4.26. For understanding, the whitenized and the normalized whitenized weights for the attribute *Quality* is gotten as 2.889 and 0.308, respectively.

Step 6: We further define the events, outcomes, and the objectives for the selection problem. The event can be the problem of resilient supplier selection (RSS) itself and the outcomes corresponds to *four* available alternative suppliers. The situation sets consisting of pairs of event-outcome can be indicated as follows: s_{11} = (*RSS, Supplier* 1), s_{12} = (*RSS, Supplier* 2), …, s_{14} = (*RSS, Supplier* 4). Since we consider *five* criteria for evaluation, there are *five* objectives for the study. Hence, the selection of suppliers based on only some particular criteria can be considered as one objective.

Step 7: The ranking of all situations are made, where we consider in mind one objective at a time and the effects are recorded by analyst rating. Suppose for example considering the ranking from first analyst, we can see that Supplier 3 performs best in Quality criteria and can be given rank 1, in consideration of the *first* objective of satiating *Quality*. Similarly, all other suppliers can be ranked based on their situational effects. Three analysts were involved in ranking the same and the suppliers' ranks based on situational effects are done for all *five* objectives (criteria). These situational effects based on analyst's rankings are shown in Table 4.27.

Table 4.27 Analysts' ranking of situational effects considering objectives

	A	B	C	D	E	F
29						
30	**Event = supplier selection**					
31	**Outcome = (supplier 1, ..., 4)**					
32	**Situation = (attribute 1, ..., 5)**					
33						
34	**Analyst 1**	**Quality**	**Cost**	**Flexibility**	**Collaboration**	**Risk awareness**
35	Supplier 1	5	4	5	5	3
36	Supplier 2	2	6	3	3	6
37	Supplier 3	1	2	1	4	5
38	Supplier 4	3	3	2	1	1
39						
40	**Analyst 2**	**Quality**	**Cost**	**Flexibility**	**Collaboration**	**Risk awareness**
41	Supplier 1	6	5	4	5	3
42	Supplier 2	2	6	5	4	6
43	Supplier 3	1	2	1	3	5
44	Supplier 4	3	4	2	1	2
45						
46	**Analyst 3**	**Quality**	**Cost**	**Flexibility**	**Collaboration**	**Risk awareness**
47	Supplier 1	5	6	4	5	2
48	Supplier 2	2	5	5	2	6
49	Supplier 3	1	2	2	4	5
50	Supplier 4	3	4	1	1	3

Step 8: As the evaluation corresponds to rankings from three different analysts, the aggregation of responses is conducted by adding the responses (ranks), where the sum of ranks is used as a measure, instead of taking average. The supplier alternative with the lowest rank sum is assigned further as rank 1 and so on. The Excel calculations for the consolidated ranks are shown in Table 4.28.

Table 4.28 Excel formula: Rank sum and the consolidated ranks for suppliers

B59 | *fx* =RANK(B53, B$53:B$56,1)

	A	B	C	D	E	F	G
51							
52	**Rank Sum**	**Quality**	**Cost**	**Flexibility**	**Collaboration**	**Risk awareness**	
53	Supplier 1	16	15	13	15	8	SUM(B47+B41+B35)
54	Supplier 2	6	17	13	9	18	
55	Supplier 3	3	6	4	11	15	
56	Supplier 4	9	11	5	3	6	
57							
58	**Consolidated (Rank)**	**Quality**	**Cost**	**Flexibility**	**Collaboration**	**Risk awareness**	**r(0)**
59	Supplier 1	4	3	3	4	2	1
60	Supplier 2	2	4	3	2	4	1
61	Supplier 3	1	1	1	3	3	1
62	Supplier 4	3	2	2	1	1	1

Step 9: We consider an ideal referential supplier, where the supplier is assumed to have secured rank 1 in all the considered objective (criteria), where the optimum effect vector is r_0 = (1, 1, 1, 1, 1, 1, 1). The bulls-eye distances are calculated from the optimum effect vector or from the ideal referential supplier for further ranking the suppliers. The normalized weights determined for the criteria, as in Step 5 were also considered, while calculating the bulls-eye distances. The Excel calculations for the bulls-eye distances are shown in Table 4.29. Further, the final bulls-eye distances are shown in Table 4.30.

Step 10: The suppliers are then ranked in the increasing order of bulls-eye distances, where the supplier who is closer to the ideal referential supplier will be having the lowest bulls-eye distances calculated. The final rankings are also shown in Tables 4.29 and 4.30. Considering the case problem, we can see that *Supplier 3* can be regarded a best supplier and *Supplier 1* can be regarded as a least preferred choice, as per results obtained from implementing the GIDA methodology.

Table 4.29 Excel formula: Bulls-eye distances and suppliers' ranking

I67 | f_x =RANK(H67,H$67:H$70,1)

	A	B	C	D	E	F	G	H	I	J
64										
65	**Criteria weights**	0.308	0.284	0.237	0.085	0.086	K24 to K28			
66	**Bulls eye distances**	**Quality**	**Cost**	**Flexibility**	**Collaboration**	**Risk awareness**	**sum**	**Bulls eye dist**	**Rank**	
67	Supplier 1	9	4	4	9	1	5.707	2.389	4	
68	Supplier 2	1	9	4	1	9	4.671	2.161	3	
69	Supplier 3	0	0	0	4	4	0.684	0.827	1	
70	Supplier 4	4	1	1	0	0	1.753	1.324	2	
71		(B59-$G59)^2					SUM(B67*B$65+C67*C$65+D67*D$65+E67*E$65+F67*F$65)			
72										
73								ROUND(SQRT(G67),3)		

Table 4.30 Bulls-eye distances and suppliers' ranking

	A	B	C	D	E	F	G	H	I
64									
65	**Criteria weights**	0.308	0.284	0.237	0.085	0.086			
66	**Bulls eye distances**	**Quality**	**Cost**	**Flexibility**	**Collaboration**	**Risk awareness**	**sum**	**Bulls eye dist**	**Rank**
67	Supplier 1	9	4	4	9	1	5.707	2.389	4
68	Supplier 2	1	9	4	1	9	4.671	2.161	3
69	Supplier 3	0	0	0	4	4	0.684	0.827	1
70	Supplier 4	4	1	1	0	0	1.753	1.324	2

4.6 CONCLUSION

The decision-making models using grey theory are broadly discussed in this chapter. Also, practical implementation of various methodologies is shown. Researchers / practitioners can utilize these methods either as standalone or in combination with other methods according to the need of their research problem. Broadly, we discuss in detail regarding the implementation of grey relational analysis, grey target decision-making models, grey stratified decision-making models, and grey integrated decision analytics and their practical applications.

REFERENCES

Hamzaçebi, C. and Pekkaya, M. (2011). Determining of stock investments with grey relational analysis. *Expert Systems with Applications*, 38(8), 9186–9195.

Kuo, Y., Yang, T. and Huang, G.W. (2008). The use of grey relational analysis in solving multiple attribute decision-making problems. *Computers & Industrial Engineering*, 55(1), 80–93.

Liu, S.F., Yang, Y.J. and Forrest, J. (2022). *Grey Systems Analysis*. Springer-Verlag, Berlin.

Luo, D. and Wang, X. (2012). The multi-attribute grey target decision method for attribute value within three-parameter interval grey number. *Applied Mathematical Modelling*, 36(5), 1957–1963.

Rajesh, R. (2021). Optimal trade-offs in decision-making for sustainability and resilience in manufacturing supply chains. *Journal of Cleaner Production*, 313, 127596.

Rajesh, R. (2024). Grey models for data analysis and decision-making in uncertainty during pandemics. *International Journal of Disaster Risk Reduction*, 104881.

Rajesh, R. and Aljabhan, B. (2022). A novel grey stratified decision-making (GSDM) model for social sustainability-based supplier selection. *IEEE Transactions on Computational Social Systems*, 11(1), 531–545.

Rajesh, R. and Ravi, V. (2015). Supplier selection in resilient supply chains: a grey relational analysis approach. *Journal of Cleaner Production*, 86, 343–359.

Thakur, V. and Ramesh, A. (2017). Healthcare waste disposal strategy selection using grey-AHP approach. *Benchmarking: An International Journal*, 24(3), 735–749.

Wei, G. (2011). Grey relational analysis model for dynamic hybrid multiple attribute decision-making. *Knowledge-Based Systems*, 24(5), 672–679.

Yan, S., Liu, S., Liu, J. and Wu, L. (2015). Dynamic grey target decision-making method with grey numbers based on existing state and future development trend of alternatives. *Journal of Intelligent and Fuzzy Systems*, 28(5), 2159–2168.

Yang, C.C. and Chen, B.S. (2006). Supplier selection using combined analytical hierarchy process and grey relational analysis. *Journal of Manufacturing Technology Management*, 17(7), 926–941.

CHAPTER 5

Causal/Influence Models

5.1 INTRODUCTION

Causal, often referred to as influence modelling, which are a new addition of techniques to the arena of grey systems analysis, where the factors with most influential power and the factors which are getting more influenced can be separated (Rajesh, 2023a; 2024a). The common influence analysis techniques that involve multiple criteria can be the Cause and Effect Analysis (CEA), the Interpretive Structural Modelling (ISM), the Total Interpretive Structural Modelling (TISM), and the Decision-Making through Trial and Evaluation Laboratory (DEMATEL) methods. As such these methods have its own limitations, where the CEA method cannot quantify the causes and effects and the ISM/ TISM methods have the limitation of separating the important cause-effect pairs and have the difficulty in incorporating large number of responses; whereas, the DEMATEL methodology has the limitation that it cannot create a hierarchical model, as well as it is difficult to incorporate large number of responses (Singh et al., 2023). Also, none of these methods can work on problems, where the causal relations can vary when there are multiple objectives in a causal modelling situation (Singh et al., 2024).

5.2 GREY CAUSAL MODELLING

The Grey Causal Modelling (GCM) and the Grey Influence Analysis (GINA) techniques have been added to the group of grey based analysis techniques, which can address some of the limitations of the aforementioned conventional causal modelling techniques. GCM considers four of the major elements in a causal modelling situation, such as; the *events*, the *outcomes*, the *objectives*, and the *effects*. These aforementioned elements can cover a complex causal modelling situation (Yash and Rajesh, 2024). Suppose that there are n identified parameters/ factors in a system, which can be indicated as follows:

$$A = \{a_i\} = \{a_1, a_2, \ldots, a_n\}, \tag{5.1}$$

Let us further construct a situation set by considering the Cartesian product of the set with itself.

$$s_{ij} = A \times A = \{a_i, a_j\} \forall i = 1, 2, \ldots, n; j = 1, 2, \ldots, n; i \neq j \tag{5.2}$$

Let B be representing the influence relation matrix that represents the influence of a factor a_i over a_j, which can be indicated as follows:

$$B = \begin{array}{c|cccc} & a_1 & a_2 & \cdots & a_n \\ \hline a_1 & 1 & - & - & - \\ a_2 & - & 1 & - & - \\ \vdots & \vdots & \vdots & \ddots & \vdots \\ a_n & - & - & - & 1 \end{array}, \tag{5.3}$$

A five or seven point Likert scale can be used for rating the level of influences, where 1 designates the lowest value and 7 designates the highest. The relationship matrices can be constructed based on expert responses or any survey based study. Further, we can calculate the average or the weighted average of the responses. We can calculate the row sum of the elements in the matrix and the same can be represented as r_i and the sum of the column elements can be indicated as c_j. We can calculate $r_i + c_j \ \forall i = 1, 2, \ldots, n; \ j = 1, 2, \ldots, n; \ i = j$ will indicate the overall importance that the factor can create in the system, whether it is influencing or getting influenced by other factors. Subsequently, the value $r_i - c_j \ \forall i = 1, 2, \ldots, n; \ j = 1, 2, \ldots, n; \ i \neq j$ indicates the causal or consequence nature of a factor. Various combinations of cause, consequence can be constructed based on the $r_i - c_j$ values. If the value of $r_i - c_j$ appears to be positive, the factor is causal in nature and if the same is negative, the factor is more of consequence by nature. In GCM, these cause, consequence sets can be referred to as a situation set of an event and an outcome. Hence, the corresponding situation set can be represented as follows:

$$s_{ij} = \{event, outcome\} = (a_i, a_j) \forall i = 1, 2, \ldots, n; \ j = 1, 2, \ldots, n; \ i \neq j. \tag{5.4}$$

We can assume that there are m objectives for the study and for the kth objective, we may construct a situation set, where the situation set can be indicated as follows:

$$s_{ij}^{(k)} = \left(a_i^{(k)}, a_j^{(k)}\right) \forall k = 1, 2, \ldots, m; \ i = 1, 2, \ldots, n; \ j = 1, 2, \ldots, n; \ i \neq j. \tag{5.5}$$

For every such situation set comprising of an event, an outcome, an objective, we can calculate the effects. These effects can be indicated as $u_{ij}^{(k)}$. Let us consider the effects for the objective 1 and the event 1.

For each of the situation set consisting of the *event*, the *outcome*, and the *objective*, we calculate the *effect*, which are represented as, $u_{ij}^{(k)}$. Say for example, considering the objective 1 and the event 1, the set of effects can be represented by the set,

$$u_{1j}^{(1)} = \left\{u_{11}^{(1)}, u_{12}^{(1)}, \ldots, u_{1n}^{(1)}\right\}. \tag{5.6}$$

The matrix representing the effects for any situation $s_{ij}^{(k)}$ can be indicated as shown below:

$$u_{ij}^{(k)} = \begin{bmatrix} u_{11}^{(1)} & u_{12}^{(1)} & \vdots & u_{1n}^{(1)} \\ u_{21}^{(1)} & u_{22}^{(1)} & \vdots & u_{2n}^{(1)} \\ \vdots & \vdots & \vdots & \vdots \\ u_{n1}^{(1)} & u_{n2}^{(1)} & \vdots & u_{nn}^{(1)} \\ u_{11}^{(2)} & u_{12}^{(2)} & \vdots & u_{1n}^{(2)} \\ u_{21}^{(2)} & u_{22}^{(2)} & \vdots & u_{2n}^{(2)} \\ \vdots & \vdots & \vdots & \vdots \\ u_{n1}^{(m)} & u_{n2}^{(m)} & \vdots & u_{nn}^{(m)} \\ & & \vdots & \end{bmatrix} \tag{5.7}$$

The definitions and theorems as proposed by Liu et al. (2022) for the target decision-making model using grey theory has been extended to causal modelling situations and the same can be elaborated as follows:

5.2.1 Definitions and Theorems

D1. Definition 1:

Let us consider

$$S = \left\{ s_{ij} = (a_i, a_j);\ i = 1, 2, \ldots, n;\ j = 1, 2, \ldots, n;\ i \neq j;\ a_i, ba_j \in A \right\}, \tag{5.8}$$

as a situation set of causal modelling with an event and the respective outcome, where $u_{ij}^{(k)}$ be the effect vector for the situation s_{ij} having objective k. Let us assume that a_i and a_j be the respective event and its outcome. Considering set of real numbers R, the effect mapping of S with objective k can be indicated as follows: $u^{(k)} : S \rightarrow R; s_{ij} \rightarrow u_{ij}^{(k)}$.

D2. Definition 2:

Suppose that the effects $u_{ij}^{(k)}$ and $u_{ih}^{(k)}$ are equal, then we further assume that the outcomes a_j and a_h are considered equivalent for the event a_i having objective k. The same can be indicated as $a_j \cong a_h$. Then, the effect equivalence class for the outcome a_h, considering the event a_i having objective k, can be represented using the set $A_i^{(k)}$ as follows:

$$A_i^{(k)} = \left\{ a_j \mid a_j \in A, a_j \cong a_h \right\}, \tag{5.9}$$

D3. Definition 3:

Suppose the considered objective k signifies the effect where a greater value is considered as preferable ($u_{ij}^{(k)} > u_{ih}^{(k)}$), then considering the outcomes, a_j is considered superior to a_h, considering the event a_i having objective k. This can be indicated as $a_j \succ a_h$ and the set indicating a superior class outcome for a_h considering the event a_i and the objective k can be represented as follows:

$$A_{ih}^{(k)} = \left\{ a_j \mid a_j \in A, a_j \succ a_h \right\} \tag{5.10}$$

D4. Definition 4:

Suppose, if the situation $u_{ih}^{(k)}$ is equal to $u_{gh}^{(k)}$, then the events a_i and a_g can be considered equivalent for the outcome a_h having objective k, which can be indicated as $a_i \cong a_g$. Then, the set indicating effect equivalence class of the event a_g considering the outcome a_h having objective k can be represented as follows:

$$A_h^{(k)} = \left\{ a_i \mid a_i \in A, a_i \cong a_g \right\}, \tag{5.11}$$

This is an extension of definition 2. Also, the definition 3 for superiority can also be applicable to the set $A_{gh}^{(k)}$.

D5. Definition 5:

Further to this, if the effects $u_{ij}^{(k)}$ and $u_{gh}^{(k)}$ are equal, then the respective situation set s_{ij} can be regarded as equivalent to the situation set s_{gh}, having objective k and this can be indicated as $s_{ij} \cong s_{gh}$. Then, the set indicating the effect equivalence class of situation s_{gh} having objective k can be shown as follows:

$$S^{(k)} = \left\{ s_{ij} \mid s_{ij} \in S, s_{ij} \cong s_{gh} \right\}, \tag{5.12}$$

Also, the definition 3 for superiority can be applied for the set $S_{gh}^{(k)}$

D6. Definition 6:

Assuming that $d_1^{(k)}$ and $d_2^{(k)}$ be indicating the upper and lower threshold values considering the situational effects with objective k. Then, the grey target of one-dimensional causal model having objective k can be represented as follows:

$$S^1 = \left\{ r \mid d_1^{(k)} \le r \le d_2^{(k)} \right\}, \tag{5.13}$$

Then, $u_{ij}^{(k)} \in \left[d_1^{(k)}, d_2^{(k)} \right]$ can be regarded as a satisfactory effect having objective k and the respective desirable situation can be indicated as s_{ij}, having objective k; where the desirable outcome is a_j, the desirable event is a_i.

D7. Definition 7:

Suppose that $d_1^{(1)}$ and $d_2^{(1)}$ be indicating the threshold values of the situational effects, considering any particular objective, say *objective 1* and $d_1^{(2)}$ and $d_2^{(2)}$ be representing the threshold value of the situational effects for another objective, say *objective* 2, then, the grey target of two-dimensional causal model can be indicated as follows:

$$S^2 = \left\{ r^{(1)}, r^{(2)} \mid d_1^{(1)} \le r^{(1)} \le d_2^{(1)}, d_1^{(2)} \le r^{(2)} \le d_2^{(2)} \right\}, \tag{5.14}$$

Suppose that the effect vector for the situation s_{ij} satisfies the effect,

$$u_{ij} = \left(u_{ij}^{(1)}, u_{ij}^{(2)} \right) \in S^2, \tag{5.15}$$

then, we can consider s_{ij} to be desirable situation considering both the objectives, objective 1 and 2. Also, we can interpret that a_j be a desirable outcome considering the event a_i, where the objectives being objective 1 and 2.

D8. Definition 8:

Consider the threshold for the situational effects for multiple objectives, where the objectives being objective 1, 2, 3, …, s be indicated as $d_1^{(1)}$ and $d_2^{(1)}$, $d_1^{(2)}$ and $d_2^{(2)}$,…, $d_1^{(s)}$ and $d_2^{(s)}$. Then, the s dimensional Euclidean space can be represented as follows:

$$S^s = \left\{(r^{(1)}, r^{(2)}, \ldots, r^{(s)}) \mid d_1^{(1)} \le r^{(1)} \le d_2^{(1)}, d_1^{(2)} \le r^{(2)} \le d_2^{(2)}, \ldots, d_1^{(s)} \le r^{(s)} \le d_2^{(s)}\right\}, \quad (5.16)$$

This can be referred to as a grey target of s dimensional causal model and if the effect vector for the situation s_{ij} can satisfy the effect condition;

$$u_{ij} = \left(u_{ij}^{(1)}, u_{ij}^{(2)}, \ldots, u_{ij}^{(s)}\right) \in S^s, \quad (5.17)$$

here, $u_{ij}^{(k)}$, $k = 1, 2, 3, \ldots, s$ is indicating the effect value of situation s_{ij} considering the objective k. We can consider that s_{ij} be a desirable situation having s objectives, represented as objective 1, 2, 3, …, s and a_j and a_i be indicating the respective desirable outcome and the event, for the objectives indicated as objective 1, 2, 3, …, s.

D9. Definition 9:

We can further define a set indicating the s dimensional spherical grey target, with center as follows:

$$r_0 = \left(r_0^{(1)}, r_0^{(2)}, \ldots, r_0^{(s)}\right) \quad (5.18)$$

$$R^s = \left\{(r^{(1)}, r^{(2)}, \ldots, r^{(s)}) \mid (r^{(1)} - r_0^{(1)})^2 + (r^{(2)} - r_0^{(2)})^2 + \cdots + (r^{(s)} - r_0^{(s)})^2 \le R^2\right\}, \quad (5.19)$$

The optimum effect vector can be indicated as $r_0 = (r_0^{(1)}, r_0^{(2)}, \ldots, r_0^{(s)})$ and the radius be R.

D10. Definition 10:

The bulls-eye distances of the effect vector r_1, where

$$r_1 = \left(r_1^{(1)}, r_1^{(2)}, \ldots, r_1^{(s)}\right) \in R^s, \quad (5.20)$$

can be represented as follows:

$$|r_1 - r_0| = \left[(r_1^{(1)} - r_0^{(1)})^2 + (r_1^{(2)} - r_0^{(2)})^2 + \cdots + (r_1^{(t)} - r_0^{(s)})^2\right]^{1/2}. \quad (5.21)$$

D11. Definition 11:

Let us assume that u_{ij} and u_{gh} be indicating the effect vectors for the situations s_{ij} and s_{gh}, respectively, which can be indicated as follows:

$$u_{ij} = \left(u_{ij}^{(1)}, u_{ij}^{(2)}, \ldots, u_{ij}^{(s)}\right), \quad (5.22)$$

and

$$u_{gh} = \left(u_{gh}^{(1)}, u_{gh}^{(2)}, \ldots, u_{gh}^{(s)}\right), \quad (5.23)$$

Then, s_{gh} can be regarded as a superior situation, when compared to s_{ij}, if it satisfies the condition, $|u_{ij} - r_0|>|u_{gh} - r_0|$ and the same can be indicated as $s_{gh} \succ s_{ij}$.

D12. Definition 12:

Consider for any value of $i = 1, 2, 3, \ldots, n$ and $j = 1, 2, 3, \ldots, n$, suppose that $u_{ij} \neq r_0$ remains true always, then there are no solutions that can be regarded as optimal. Hence, we can assume that the events do not have any optimum outcomes.

D13. Definition 13:

Consider that there are no optimum situations, but there exist g and h such that for $i = 1, 2, 3, \ldots, n$ and $j = 1, 2, 3, \ldots, n$, where $|a_{ij} - r_0| \geq |a_{gh} - r_0|$ remains true. In this case, for any situation satisfying $s_{ij} \in S$, $s_{gh} \succ s_{ij}$, the quasi optimum situation can be s_{gh}, where the quasi optimum event and outcome being a_g and a_h, respectively.

The theorems considered for the GCM are built on the similar grounds of that of the decision-making model, the grey target decision-making model. The base of these theorems can be found in Liu et al. (2022). Here, the idea of the *situations*, *objectives* and its *effects* are taken into consideration for demonstrating a grey causal modelling situation.

T1. Theorem 1:

Let $U^{(k)} = \{u_{ij}^{(k)} \mid s_{ij} \in S\}$ be considered as the effect set for the situation $S = (s_{ij} = (a_i, a_j); i = 1, 2, \ldots, n; j = 1, 2, \ldots, n; i \neq j; a_i, a_j \in A) \neq \varnothing$ having objective k; Then, the considered mapping $u^{(k)} : \{S^{(k)}\} \to U^{(k)}; s^{(k)} \to u_{ij}^{(k)}$ will be one-to-one and onto.

T2. Theorem 2:

Consider for a situation s_{ij} having objective k, where the effect being $u_{ij}^{(k)}$. Suppose for any $s \in S_{ij}^{(k)}$, s is considered as desirable. This indicates that if s_{ij} is regarded as a desirable situation, then all situations in its effect superior class can also be regarded as desirable situations.

T3. Theorem 3:

Let

$$R^s = \{(r^{(1)}, r^{(2)}, \ldots, r^{(s)}) \mid (r^{(1)} - r_0^{(1)})^2 + (r^{(2)} - r_0^{(2)})^2 + \ldots + (r^{(s)} - r_0^{(s)})^2 \leq R^2\}$$

be representing an s dimensional spherical grey target, considering the situation set $S = \{s_{ij} = (a_i, a_j); i = 1, 2, \ldots, n;\ j = 1, 2, \ldots, n; i \neq j; a_i, a_j \in A\}$; then, we can consider that S can be an ordered set with the ordering relation as *superiority.*

T4. Theorem 4:

Considering the situation set $(S, \succ)$, there always exist a quasi-optimum situation.

5.2.2 Grey Target of Causal Modelling

Considering a situation of relative optimization, the grey target of causal modelling is a region having desirable effects, which is similar to that of a grey target of decision-making (Luo and Wang, 2012). As we see, finding an absolute best in a cause and consequence situation can be challenging. Hence, we may use the GCM to find a quasi-optimal solution, which can be regarded as a satisfactory optimum solution. The grey target of causal modelling can be reduced until it reaches a point in the causal model, which can be considered as the best effect and the situation corresponding to it can be regarded as a best situation representing the best consequence for an event. Let us assume that R^s be representing a s-dimensional spherical grey target having center r_0 and the radius being R. Here, r_0 indicates the optimum effect vector and thereafter, the bulls eye distances can be calculated using Equations 5.20 and 5.21. The bulls eye distances are indicators of the superiority of the effect vector r_1. Suppose that u_{ij} and u_{gh} are the effect vectors considering the two situations s_{ij} and s_{gh}, respectively as shown in Equations 5.22 and 5.23. The situation s_{gh} can be considered equivalent to situation $s_{ij}(s_{gh} \approx s_{ij})$, if $|u_{ij} - r_0| = |u_{gh} - r_0|$. For the sake of calculation, we may assume the center of the grey target of causal modelling by applying transformation to the effect vectors and the 2-norm of the effect vectors can be regarded as the bulls-eye distance in causal modelling.

5.2.3 Sample Case Problem (Grey Causal Modelling)

We consider the problem of improving the resilience capabilities of the firm XYZ. We have considered the problem of supplier selection using multiple grey based methodologies in the previous chapter. As resilience is becoming an essential problem, it is essential that the drivers of risks needs to be addressed to improve the level of resilience capabilities. But while checking the drivers of risks, it is seen that these drivers are interlinked and a cause-consequence relation exist among them. Hence, addressing the causal driver can fix some of the problems with the effect drivers too. As these cause-consequence relations can also vary with different objectives, the problem transforms to a complex causal modelling situation. Grey Causal Modelling (GCM) can be best used in such situations. The step-wise implementation of the same are elaborated as follows.

Step 1: In the *first* phase of the study, we have identified *ten* drivers of risks considering the case of XYZ and is generally applicable to a manufacturing environment. These identified drivers of risks are names as follows: *forecast errors* (A_1), *bullwhips* (A_2), *cost of capacity* (A_3), *supply failure* (A_4), *fluctuating exchange rates* (A_5), *product obsolescence* (A_6), *integration related issues* (A_7), *inventory costs* (A_8), *inflexibility* (A_9), *and vertical integrations* (A_{10}).

Step 2: A group of three analysts were employed to rate the influence of a factor over the other in Likert scales varying from 1–7. As there are ten factors taken for analysis, there is need to evaluate (10 × 10) – 10 = 90 number of influence relations. This is indicated in Table 5.1. Further to this, we calculate the r_i and the c_j values corresponding to row and column sum and $r_i - c_j \, \forall i = j$ are calculated. Based on the sign of the $r_i - c_j$ values, the cause and consequence factors are separated. If the value is positive, we can group them as causal and if the same appears negative, we can group them under consequences. We see that the drivers A_3, A_5, A_7, and A_9 appear to be in the category of causal factors, whereas the factors A_1, A_2, A_4, A_6, A_8, and A_{10} appear in the consequence factors. The Excel formula for calculation of the same are shown in Table 5.2 and the final values are presented in Table 5.3.

Step 3: We further consider three objectives, where the *first* is to be *cost effective* (k = 1), *second* one is to be *more productive* (k = 2), and the *third* one is to be *more flexible* (k = 3). As we have *three* objectives, we can construct (4(*event*) × 6(*outcome*) × 3(*objectives*)) = 72

Table 5.1 Average influence relation matrix

	A	B	C	D	E	F	G	H	I	J	K
1	Factors	A1	A2	A3	A4	A5	A6	A7	A8	A9	A10
2	A1	1	7	3	5	1	5	4	6	5	4
3	A2	5	1	4	5	1	3	4	2	3	6
4	A3	3	4	1		7	6	5	2	3	6
5	A4	1	3	4	1	3	5	3	2	1	1
6	A5	6	4	5	6	1	7	5	6	3	2
7	A6	5	1	2	3	4	1	4	3	5	6
8	A7	7	6	5	5	4	3	1	7	3	4
9	A8	1	3	5	2	3	4	5	1	5	6
10	A9	7	4	3	3	3	2	1	6	1	7
11	A10	6	4	3	6	5	5	4	3	1	1

Table 5.2 Excel formula: Event and outcome separation of factors

M15 | =L15-B25

	A	B	C	D	E	F	G	H	I	J	K	L	M	N	O
14	Factors	A1	A2	A3	A4	A5	A6	A7	A8	A9	A10	Ri	Ri + Cj	Factors	
15	A1	1	7	3	5	1	5	4	6	5	4	41	-1	A1	SUM(B15:K15)
16	A2	5	1	4	5	1	3	4	2	3	6	34	-3	A2	L16-C25
17	A3	3	4	1		7	6	5	2	3	6	37	2	A3	
18	A4	1	3	4	1	3	5	3	2	1	1	24	-12	A4	
19	A5	6	4	5	6	1	7	5	6	3	2	45	13	A5	
20	A6	5	1	2	3	4	1	4	3	5	6	34	-7	A6	
21	A7	7	6	5	5	4	3	1	7	3	4	45	9	A7	
22	A8	1	3	5	2	3	4	5	1	5	6	35	-3	A8	
23	A9	7	4	3	3	3	2	1	6	1	7	37	7	A9	
24	A10	6	4	3	6	5	5	4	3	1	1	38	-5	A10	
25	Cj	42	37	35	36	32	41	36	38	30	43				SUM(K15:K24)

Table 5.3 Event and outcome separation of factors

	A	B	C	D	E	F	G	H	I	J	K	L	M	N
14	Factors	A1	A2	A3	A4	A5	A6	A7	A8	A9	A10	Ri	Ri + Cj	Factors
15	A1	1	7	3	5	1	5	4	6	5	4	41	-1	A1
16	A2	5	1	4	5	1	3	4	2	3	6	34	-3	A2
17	A3	3	4	1		7	6	5	2	3	6	37	2	A3
18	A4	1	3	4	1	3	5	3	2	1	1	24	-12	A4
19	A5	6	4	5	6	1	7	5	6	3	2	45	13	A5
20	A6	5	1	2	3	4	1	4	3	5	6	34	-7	A6
21	A7	7	6	5	5	4	3	1	7	3	4	45	9	A7
22	A8	1	3	5	2	3	4	5	1	5	6	35	-3	A8
23	A9	7	4	3	3	3	2	1	6	1	7	37	7	A9
24	A10	6	4	3	6	5	5	4	3	1	1	38	-5	A10
25	Cj	42	37	35	36	32	41	36	38	30	43			

situation sets, where each set is representing a combination of a cause and consequence, which is indicated as a pair of event and outcome, considering each objective. The representation of the event-outcome pairs for every objectives is shown in Table 5.4, where the rows indicate the events, the columns indicate the outcomes, and the relations for each of the objectives is read from the event to outcome.

Table 5.4 Situation sets and the respective event-outcome combinations

	A	B	C	D	E	F	G
27	**Sij (1)**						
28	***k=1***	**A1**	**A2**	**A4**	**A6**	**A8**	**A10**
29	**A3**	S11 (1)	S12 (1)	S13 (1)	S14 (1)	S15 (1)	S16 (1)
30	**A5**	S21 (1)	S22 (1)	S23 (1)	S24 (1)	S25 (1)	S26 (1)
31	**A7**	S31 (1)	S32 (1)	S33 (1)	S34 (1)	S35 (1)	S36 (1)
32	**A9**	S41 (1)	S42 (1)	S43 (1)	S44 (1)	S45 (1)	S46 (1)
33	**Sij (2)**						
34	***k=1***	**A1**	**A2**	**A4**	**A6**	**A8**	**A10**
35	**A3**	S11 (2)	S12 (2)	S13 (2)	S14 (2)	S15 (2)	S16 (2)
36	**A5**	S21 (2)	S22 (2)	S23 (2)	S24 (2)	S25 (2)	S26 (2)
37	**A7**	S31 (2)	S32 (2)	S33 (2)	S34 (2)	S35 (2)	S36 (2)
38	**A9**	S41 (2)	S42 (2)	S43 (2)	S44 (2)	S45 (2)	S46 (2)
39	**Sij (3)**						
40	***k=1***	**A1**	**A2**	**A4**	**A6**	**A8**	**A10**
41	**A3**	S11 (3)	S12 (3)	S13 (3)	S14 (3)	S15 (3)	S16 (3)
42	**A5**	S21 (3)	S22 (3)	S23 (3)	S24 (3)	S25 (3)	S26 (3)
43	**A7**	S31 (3)	S32 (3)	S33 (3)	S34 (3)	S35 (3)	S36 (3)
44	**A9**	S41 (3)	S42 (3)	S43 (3)	S44 (3)	S45 (3)	S46 (3)

Step 4: Considering the *second* phase of the study, the cause-consequence (event-outcome) relations were ranked by experts considering different objectives. As we have presently *four* events, *six* outcomes, and *three* objectives, the event-outcome pairs are ranked from 1 to 6, based on their effects. These rankings are also made by the group of *three* analysts, where 1 is indicating the highest ranked effect and 6 is indicating a lowest ranked effect. The rankings based on effects for different objectives are shown in Table 5.5. The effect vectors corresponding to each and every situation are calculated based on Equations 5.18 to 5.23 and the bulls-eye distances are calculated from the optimum effect vector. The Excel sheet formula and implementation of the same are shown in Table 5.6.

Table 5.5 Ranking of situations for objectives

	A	B	C	D	E	F	G
46	**k=1**	A1	A2	A4	A6	A8	A10
47	A3	6	3	1	2	4	5
48	A5	4	5	2	3	6	1
49	A7	3	4	5	6	2	1
50	A9	2	1	3	4	6	5
51							
52	**k=2**	A1	A2	A4	A6	A8	A10
53	A3	4	5	3	2	1	6
54	A5	2	1	6	3	4	5
55	A7	2	3	4	1	6	5
56	A9	3	4	5	1	6	2
57							
58	**k=3**	A1	A2	A4	A6	A8	A10
59	A3	6	4	3	1	2	5
60	A5	5	4	2	3	1	6
61	A7	3	4	6	5	2	1
62	A9	2	1	3	6	4	5

Step 5: The effects are arranged in the descending order of bulls-eye distances and the corresponding situations are noted. Then, the magnitude of the effects, m_{ij} values are calculated and the situation sets are further represented in *four* regions (quarters) considering the effects, where the upper bound value (i_{UB}) of m_{ij} for all the regions are also calculated, following Equations 5.24 and 5.25.

$$m_{ij} = \left(\frac{1}{|u_{ij} - r_0|} \right) \times 10; \; |u_{ij} - r_0| > 0 \quad \text{and} \quad m_{ij} = \delta; \; |u_{ij} - r_0| = 0, \tag{5.24}$$

where δ is a small value.

$$i_{UB} = |u_{ij} - r_0|_{\min} + i \times \left(\frac{|u_{ij} - r_0|_{\max} - |u_{ij} - r_0|_{min}}{4} \right); \; i = 1, 2, 3, 4. \tag{5.25}$$

Further, the magnitude plots are constructed, where the calculated values of the magnitude of effects were used. We can see that the upper bound values of the regions 4, 3, 2, 1 respectively are 2.981, 4.548, 6.115, and 7.682. The magnitude of the effects is plotted in the magnitude plot as shown in Figure 5.1. The magnitude plot represents the situations in *four* regions, based on the effects. The size of the circle is an indication of the magnitude and from the magnitude plot. The Excel calculations for the magnitude of effects are shown in Table 5.7 and the final values are presented in Table 5.8.

Step 6: We further construct the causal magnitude table, where the events in the first region are given a weighting of 4, a value of 3 is assigned for the events in the second region, further

Table 5.6 Excel formula: Bulls eye distances of effect vectors

F65 =ROUND(SQRT((C65-1)^2+(D65-1)^2+(E65-1)^2),3)

	A	B	C	D	E	F
64	Sl. No.	Effects	uij (1)	uij (2)	uij (3)	mod(uij - r(0))
65	1	u11	6	4	6	7.681
66	2	u12	3	5	4	5.385
67	3	u13	1	3	3	2.828
68	4	u14	2	2	1	1.414
69	5	u15	4	1	2	3.162
70	6	u16	5	6	5	7.55
71	7	u21	4	2	5	5.099
72	8	u22	5	1	4	5
73	9	u23	2	6	2	5.196
74	10	u24	3	3	3	3.464
75	11	u25	6	4	1	5.831
76	12	u26	1	5	6	6.403
77	13	u31	3	2	3	3
78	14	u32	4	3	4	4.69
79	15	u33	5	4	6	7.071
80	16	u34	6	1	5	6.403
81	17	u35	2	6	2	5.196
82	18	u36	1	5	1	4
83	19	u41	2	3	2	2.449
84	20	u42	1	4	1	3
85	21	u43	3	5	3	4.899
86	22	u44	4	1	6	5.831
87	23	u45	6	6	4	7.681
88	24	u46	5	2	5	5.745

the third and fourth regions are, respectively, assigned with a weighting of 2 and 1. The sum of the row elements for all the events are calculated and the Pareto principle is applied to the factors, where the top 20% of the events are regarded as the major causal events that can create 80% of the effects. As we have 10 factors considered for the study, the top two factors can be regarded as critical causal factors. The causal magnitude table and the calculation are presented in Table 5.9. A round off to a higher integer can be made on executing this. Thus, the decisive causal factors considering the study are *cost of capacity* (A_3) and *inflexibility* (A_9), while interpreting the results of the GCM model implementation for the case.

Table 5.7 Excel formula: Magnitude plot construction

G114 | =ROUND((1/F114)*10,3)

	A	B	C	D	E	F	G	H	I	J	K	L	M	N
90	**Ranks**	**Effects**	**u11 (1)**	**u11 (2)**	**u11 (3)**	**u11 -r(0)**	**Magnitude**	**Situation**						
91	1	u14	2	2	1	1.414	7.072	(A3, A6)	ROUND(SQRT((C91-1)^2+(D91-1)^2+(E91-1)^2),3)					
92	2	u41	2	3	2	2.449	4.083	(A9, A1)	ROUND((1/F92)*10,3)					
93	3	u13	1	3	3	2.828	3.536	(A3, A4)						
94	4	u31	3	2	3	3	3.333	(A7, A1)						
95	5	u42	1	4	1	3	3.333	(A9, A2)						
96	6	u15	4	1	2	3.162	3.163	(A3, A8)						
97	7	u24	3	3	3	3.464	2.887	(A5, A6)						
98	8	u36	1	5	1	4	2.5	(A7, A10)						
99	9	u32	4	3	4	4.69	2.132	(A7, A2)						
100	10	u43	3	5	3	4.899	2.041	(A9, A4)		**UB-LB/4**	1.567		ROUND((7.681-1.414)/4,3)	
101	11	u22	5	1	4	5	2	(A5, A2)		**1st**	2.981		1.414+1*$K$100	
102	12	u21	4	2	5	5.099	1.961	(A7, A1)		**2nd**	4.548		1.414+2*$K$100	
103	13	u23	2	6	2	5.196	1.925	(A5, A4)		**3rd**	6.115		1.414+3*$K$100	
104	14	u35	2	6	2	5.196	1.925	(A7, A8)		**4th**	7.682		1.414+4*$K$100	
105	15	u12	3	5	4	5.385	1.857	(A3, A2)						
106	16	u46	5	2	5	5.745	1.741	(A9, A10)						
107	17	u25	6	4	1	5.831	1.715	(A5, A8)						
108	18	u44	4	1	6	5.831	1.715	(A9, A6)						
109	19	u26	1	5	6	6.403	1.562	(A5, A10)						
110	20	u34	6	1	5	6.403	1.562	(A7, A6)						
111	21	u33	5	4	6	7.071	1.414	(A7, A4)						
112	22	u16	5	6	5	7.55	1.325	(A3, A10)						
113	23	u11	6	4	6	7.681	1.302	(A3, A1)						
114	24	u45	6	6	4	7.681	1.302	(A9, A8)						

Table 5.8 Magnitude plot construction

	A	B	C	D	E	F	G	H	I	J	K
90	**Ranks**	**Effects**	**u11 (1)**	**u11 (2)**	**u11 (3)**	**u11 -r(0)**	**Magnitude**	**Situation**		**UB-LB/4**	1.567
91	1	u14	2	2	1	1.414	7.072	(A3, A6)		**1st**	2.981
92	2	u41	2	3	2	2.449	4.083	(A9, A1)		**2nd**	4.548
93	3	u13	1	3	3	2.828	3.536	(A3, A4)		**3rd**	6.115
94	4	u31	3	2	3	3	3.333	(A7, A1)		**4th**	7.682
95	5	u42	1	4	1	3	3.333	(A9, A2)			
96	6	u15	4	1	2	3.162	3.163	(A3, A8)			
97	7	u24	3	3	3	3.464	2.887	(A5, A6)			
98	8	u36	1	5	1	4	2.5	(A7, A10)			
99	9	u32	4	3	4	4.69	2.132	(A7, A2)			
100	10	u43	3	5	3	4.899	2.041	(A9, A4)			
101	11	u22	5	1	4	5	2	(A5, A2)			
102	12	u21	4	2	5	5.099	1.961	(A7, A1)			
103	13	u23	2	6	2	5.196	1.925	(A5, A4)			
104	14	u35	2	6	2	5.196	1.925	(A7, A8)			
105	15	u12	3	5	4	5.385	1.857	(A3, A2)			
106	16	u46	5	2	5	5.745	1.741	(A9, A10)			
107	17	u25	6	4	1	5.831	1.715	(A5, A8)			
108	18	u44	4	1	6	5.831	1.715	(A9, A6)			
109	19	u26	1	5	6	6.403	1.562	(A5, A10)			
110	20	u34	6	1	5	6.403	1.562	(A7, A6)			
111	21	u33	5	4	6	7.071	1.414	(A7, A4)			
112	22	u16	5	6	5	7.55	1.325	(A3, A10)			
113	23	u11	6	4	6	7.681	1.302	(A3, A1)			
114	24	u45	6	6	4	7.681	1.302	(A9, A8)			

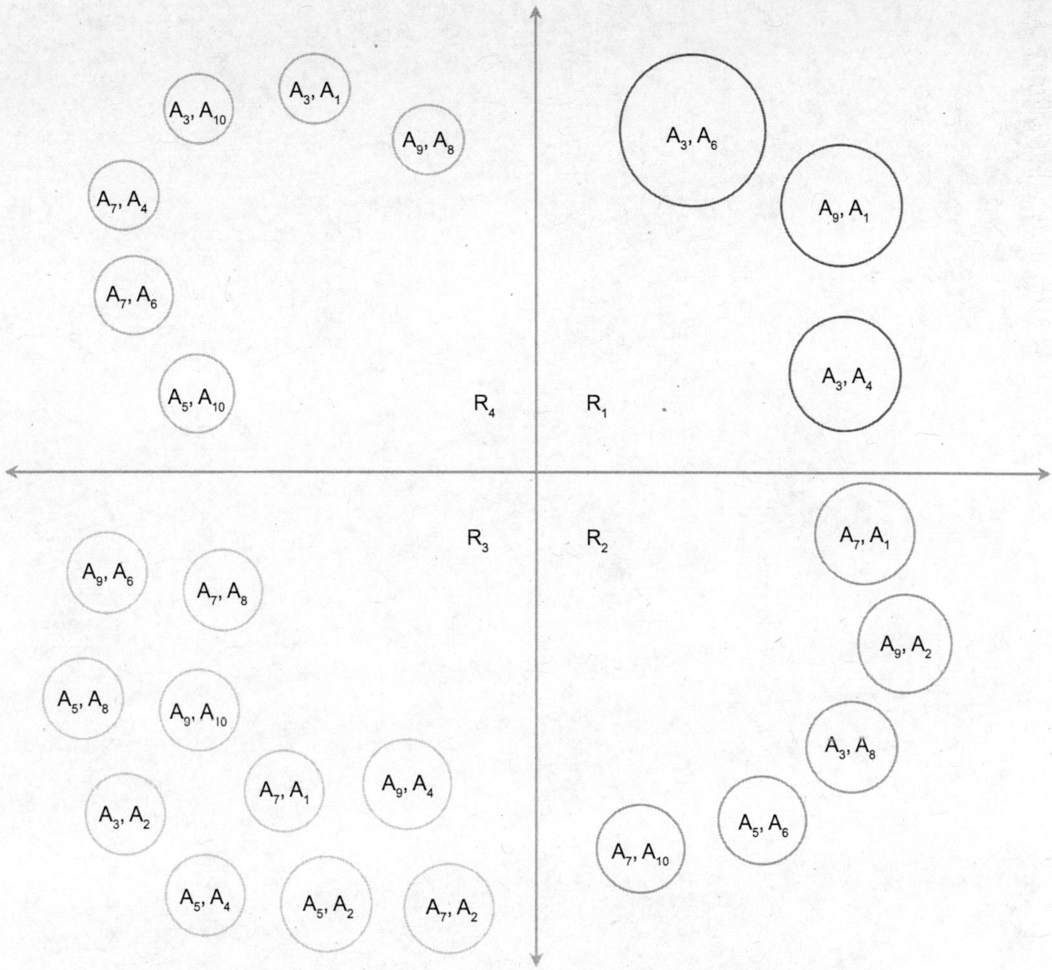

Figure 5.1 Magnitude plot for cause-consequence (event-outcome) relations.

5.3 GREY INFLUENCE ANALYSIS

Grey Influence Analysis (GINA) is prosed as another new addition to the category of grey based methods, where the applicability is with causal/influence modelling situations (Rajesh, 2023b, 2023c, 2024b). The methodology has the advantage of consolidating a large number of responses, which can be used as the input and is particularly used, when the study is survey-based or expert response-based. The methodology uses grey theory and is categorized as a causal/influence modelling technique (Singh et al., 2024; Kumar et al., 2024; Chouhan et al., 2025; Sharma et al., 2025). The technique is based on grey theory (Deng, 1989) and input-output models (Liu et al., 2022) and is mainly helpful to understand and quantify the relations among factors or attributes identified in a study. The definitions for the same are basically the extension of the definitions of grey input-output models and the proofs for the same are presented in 'Grey Systems Analysis' by Liu et al. (2022). The definitions, which forms the basis of grey influence analysis are elaborated in the following section.

Table 5.9 Causal magnitude table

L119 | f_x =SUM(B119:K119)

	A	B	C	D	E	F	G	H	I	J	K	L
116	**Factors**	**A1**	**A2**	**A3**	**A4**	**A5**	**A6**	**A7**	**A8**	**A9**	**A10**	**Sum**
117	**A1**											
118	**A2**											
119	**A3**	1	2		4		4		3		1	15
120	**A4**											
121	**A5**		2		2		3		2		1	10
122	**A6**											
123	**A7**	3	2		1		1		2		3	12
124	**A8**											
125	**A9**	4	3		2		2		1		2	14
126	**A10**											

5.3.1 Definitions

D1. Definition 1

Let us assume that the influence of a particular i^{th} factor over the jth factor be measured in grey scales and the same is represented as $\otimes x_{ij}$, $i, j = 1,2,3,\ldots,n$. Then, the influence matrix can be further represented as:

$$X(\otimes) = \left[\otimes x_{ij}\right]_{n\times n} = \begin{bmatrix} \otimes x_{11} & \cdots & \otimes x_{1n} \\ \vdots & \ddots & \vdots \\ \otimes x_{n1} & \cdots & \otimes x_{nn} \end{bmatrix}. \tag{5.26}$$

D2. Definition 2

The influence measured as above can be indicated as $\otimes x_{ij}$; i, j = 1, 2, 3,…,n. Then, the sum of influence that a factor j creates in the system can be represented using $\otimes x_j$. Further the direct influence coefficient, which is indicated as $\otimes a_{ij}$ can be calculated using the following;

$$\otimes a_{ij} = \frac{\otimes x_{ij}}{\otimes x_j};\ i, j = 1,2,3,\ldots,n, \tag{5.27}$$

The direct influence coefficient represents the degree of influence of a factor j over i, which shows how closely they are related, considering the level of influences.

D3. Definition 3

The matrix indicating the direct influence coefficients ($\otimes a_{ij}$) are constructed, which can be called as the direct influence coefficient matrix, as indicated below:

$$A(\otimes) = \left[\otimes a_{ij}\right]_{n\times n} = \begin{bmatrix} \otimes a_{11} & \cdots & \otimes a_{1n} \\ \vdots & \ddots & \vdots \\ \otimes a_{n1} & \cdots & \otimes a_{nn} \end{bmatrix}. \tag{5.28}$$

D4. Definition 4

The complete influence coefficient matrix can be further constructed as follows:

$$B(\otimes) = \left((I - A(\otimes))^{-1} - I\right), \tag{5.29}$$

Here, I is indicating the identity matrix having the same dimension of matrix A. The degree of grey relationships among factors can be represented in the form of a matrix B, which can be represented as follows:

$$B(\otimes) = \left[\otimes b_{ij}\right]_{n\times n} = \begin{bmatrix} \otimes b_{11} & \cdots & \otimes b_{1n} \\ \vdots & \ddots & \vdots \\ \otimes b_{n1} & \cdots & \otimes b_{nn} \end{bmatrix}. \tag{5.30}$$

D5. Definition 5

If the complete influence coefficient can be represented and calculated using $B(\otimes) = ((I - A(\otimes))^{-1} - I)$, then the grey responsibility coefficient for the ith factor can be calculated as follows:

$$u_i(\otimes) = \frac{\sum_{j=1}^{n} b_{ij}(\otimes)}{\frac{1}{n}\sum_{i=1}^{n}\sum_{j=1}^{n} b_{ij}(\otimes)} \tag{5.31}$$

D6. Definition 6

Further to this, if the complete influence coefficient can be represented and calculated using $B(\otimes) = ((I - A(\otimes))^{-1} - I)$, then the grey influence coefficient for the jth factor can be calculated as:

$$v_j(\otimes) = \frac{\sum_{i=1}^{n} b_{ij}(\otimes)}{\frac{1}{n}\sum_{i=1}^{n}\sum_{j=1}^{n} b_{ij}(\otimes)}. \tag{5.32}$$

D7. Definition 7

The indication of the level of influence of a factor i over other factors in the system is characterized by the grey responsibility coefficient and the indication of the level of influence that a factor j can receive from other factors in the system is depicted by the grey influence coefficient. Further, the grey importance coefficients can be an indicator of the measure of how a particular factor is important to the system either as influencing or being influenced by other factors. This can be indicated as follows:

$$t_{ij}(\otimes) = u_i(\otimes) + v_j(\otimes) \forall i = j. \tag{5.33}$$

5.3.2 Steps in GINA Evaluation

The detailed step-wise implementation of the GINA model is discussed below:

Step 1: Ascertain the attributes

The first step for the implementation of the GINA approach is the identification of factors or attributes under consideration pertaining to the system. The process can be decided based on the requirement of the topic, which can include literature review, expert interviews, brainstorming, surveys, or various combination of the same.

Step 2: Collect the influence ratings

Further, the influence relations among the identified factors or attributes under consideration needs to be recorded and collected. This can be through a survey based or expert response based data collection process. The direct influence of the particular factor over another factor is recorded in linguistic labels that often varies from varying from *Very High* to *Very Low* considering a five point Likert scale, in detail includes *Very High*, *High*, *Medium*, *Low*, and *Very Low* or we may use a seven point Likert scale instead.

Step 3: Cleaning the responses

This is one of the important steps in the implementation of the GINA methodology, where the responses are to be cleaned, so that any incomplete and biased responses are removed. This process can be either conducted manually or by using any appropriate tools. The purpose is to endure the validity and reliability of the findings.

Step 4: Conversion to grey scales

The influence relations as observed in linguistic labels are converted to grey scales using a previously determined conversion table. For each of the linguistic labels, a grey number with a lower bound and an upper bound value is assigned. Let us assume that the grey number $\otimes x_{ij}$ indicate the influence of a particular factor i over j, then we can represent $\otimes x_{ij}$ as:

$$\otimes x_{ij} = \left(\underline{\otimes} x_{ij}, \overline{\otimes} x_{ij}\right) \tag{5.34}$$

Step 5: Aggregating the grey influences

The responses corresponding to influence relations, which are represented in grey numbers, are aggregated using the grey number addition operator (Deng, 1989). Further, the matrix representing the cumulative influence relations are obtained. The addition or aggregation operation is preferred so as to minimalize the data loss, while if the average influence relations are calculated. We can further assume that there are n valid responses collected from the survey or expert evaluations. The aggregated value of these influence relations can be calculated using Equation 5.35 as follows:

$$\sum_{l=1}^{n} \otimes x_{ij}^{l} = \left(\sum_{l=1}^{n} \underline{\otimes} x_{ij}^{l}, \sum_{l=1}^{n} \overline{\otimes} x_{ij}^{l}\right), \tag{5.35}$$

here l is representing an index that can vary from 1, 2, 3, …, n.

Step 6: Grey value whitenization

The aggregated grey influence scores are whitenized using three models—the critical, the ideal, and the most typical model. In the *critical model whitenization*, the lower bounds of the aggregate influences are considered as the crisp values, where in the *ideal model whitenization*, the upper bounds of the aggregate influences are considered as the crisp values. The critical and ideal models indicate the minimum and maximum level of influence of a factor over the other, respectively. The third model being the *most typical model whitenization*, where we consider the average of the lower bound and the upper bound as the crisp score for further calculation.

Step 7: Obtain the direct influence coefficients

We can further calculate the direct influence coefficients using Equations 5.27 and 5.28, where three crisp values (k = 1, 2, 3) are calculated that corresponds to the *critical*, *ideal*, and the *most typical* model whitenization. These whitenized scores are represented using Equation 5.36,

$$a_{ij}^{k} = \frac{x_{ij}^{k}}{x_{j}^{k}};\ i, j = 1, 2, 3, \ldots, n;\ k = 1, 2, 3. \tag{5.36}$$

Further, we calculate the direct influence coefficient matrices having values a_{ij}^{k}, which is indicated using Equation 5.37 as follows:

$$A^{k} = \left[a_{ij}^{k}\right]_{n\times n} = \begin{bmatrix} a_{11}^{k} & \cdots & a_{1n}^{k} \\ \vdots & \ddots & \vdots \\ a_{n1}^{k} & \cdots & a_{nn}^{k} \end{bmatrix};\ k = 1, 2, 3. \tag{5.37}$$

Step 8: Observe the complete influence coefficients

The complete influence coefficient matrices are further observed based on Equations 5.29 and 5.30 and these matrices can be represented using Equations 5.38 and 5.39.

$$B^k = \left((I - A^k)^{-1} - I\right), \tag{5.38}$$

here I is showing the identity matrix, which is having the same dimension of A^k and further we can indicate the matrices of B^k as follows:

$$B^k = \left[b_{ij}^k\right]_{n\times n} = \begin{bmatrix} b_{11}^k & \cdots & b_{1n}^k \\ \vdots & \ddots & \vdots \\ b_{n1}^k & \cdots & b_{nn}^k \end{bmatrix}; \; k = 1, 2, 3. \tag{5.39}$$

Step 9: Estimate the grey responsibility and influence coefficients

We can further calculate the grey responsibility and influence coefficients based on Equations 5.31 and 5.32, respectively. These are shown in Equations 5.40 and 5.41, where the grey responsibility coefficient considering the ith factor can be shown as follows:

$$u_i^k = \frac{\sum_{j=1}^{n} b_{ij}^k}{\frac{1}{n}\sum_{i=1}^{n}\sum_{j=1}^{n} b_{ij}^k}; \; k = 1, 2, 3, \tag{5.40}$$

Also, we can indicate the grey influence coefficient of the jth factor as follows:

$$v_j^k = \frac{\sum_{i=1}^{n} b_{ij}^k}{\frac{1}{n}\sum_{i=1}^{n}\sum_{j=1}^{n} b_{ij}^k}; \; k = 1, 2,3 \;. \tag{5.41}$$

Step 10: Calculate the grey importance coefficients

Further, we can calculate the grey importance coefficients using Equation 5.33, where k = 1, 2, 3, is indicating the grey importance coefficients corresponding to critical, ideal, and the most typical values, respectively. Equation 5.42 is indicated as follows:

$$t_{ij}^k = u_i^k + v_j^k \; \forall i = j; \; k = 1, 2, 3. \tag{5.42}$$

Step 11: Observe the most influential factors and prioritize

Considering the calculated values of t_{ij}^k; k = 1, 2, 3, the most influential factors can be identified, which are corresponding to the critical, the ideal, and the most typical models, respectively. Further, the weighted mean (t_{ij}^k) of the values can be calculated using Equation 5.43, as follows:

$$t_{ij} = \frac{(t_{ij}^1 + (4 \times t_{ij}^2) + t_{ij}^3)}{l}, \tag{5.43}$$

here is indicating an arbitrary number (generally, 1, 2, …, 6). From the values , we can identify the most influential factors, usually following the Pareto principle, where the top 20 percentage of the factors can be selected and marked as highly important, considering their contributions to the entire system under consideration. Note that the Pareto principle suggests that in most of the cases 20 percent of factors can create or be responsible of 80 percent of the effects.

5.3.3 Sample Case Problem (Grey Influence Analysis)

We further consider the problem of improving the resilience capabilities of the frim XYZ, where analyzing the risk categories in supply chains are critically important for implementing approaches to risk mitigation. To this end, major risk categories in the supply chain was identified and these risk categories are mostly generic in nature, considering all manufacturing supply chains. We identify *seven* categories of risks particular to the study. These risks are *forecast risks* (FR), *procurement risks* (PR), *capacity risks* (CR), *inventory risks* (IR), *transportation risks* (TR), *delays* (DL), and *disruptions* (DS). As we can see that these categories of risks are particularly interlinked and a causal relation exist among themselves. Hence, identification and separation of the same appears to be important. The study is based on an expert response based study and relies on *eleven* experts. The causal relations amongst the *seven* category of risks are recorded in *five* point linguistic scales varying from *Very High* to *Very Low*. The step-wise implementation of the methodology is detailed below.

Step 1: The first step is the identification of the factors for the study. We have identified seven factors (categories of risk) to further analyze them for influence relations.

Step 2: The responses are recorded from *eleven* experts in a *five*-point linguistic scale, where the influence level of a factor over the other is recorded on a scale varying from *Very High* to *Very Low*. As we know that there are *seven* factors considered for analysis, we have 40 ((7 × 7) – 7) questions for getting the responses regarding the level of influences.

Step 3: The process of cleaning the responses is mandatory to avoid any biased responses and the responses were recorded initially by removing the biased responses. Hence, no responses were removed at this stage of the analysis.

Step 4: The initial responses were converted to grey scales using Equation 5.34. While aggregating the responses, equal weighting has been given to the ratings from different analysts, so as to avoid any potential biases in the analysis. The grey scale conversion is shown in Table 5.10.

Table 5.10 Grey scale conversion table

Rating	Linguistic Labels	Grey Scales
1	Very Low	(1, 3)
2	Low	(2, 5)
3	Medium	(4, 7)
4	High	(6, 9)
5	Very High	(8, 10)

Step 5: The collected *eleven* responses in grey values were aggregated based on the cumulative aggregation of responses using GINA, which is mentioned in Equations 5.35. The addition operation of grey numbers, as proposed by Deng (1989) is employed for this purpose. The responses are then whitenized.

Step 6: The grey number whitenization is processed by following the *three* models, the *critical*, the *ideal* and the most *typical* one. As there are *eleven* responses, all individual responses are not shown in the book, instead, the whitenized aggregated values are indicated as the initial matrices for analysis. The Excel formula and the initial matrices are shown in Tables 5.11 and 5.12, respectively.

Table 5.11 Excel formula: Whitenized values of aggregated responses

J7 | fx =SUM(C7:I7)

	A	B	C	D	E	F	G	H	I	J	K	L
1						Whitenized						
2		Critical	1	2	3	4	5	6	7			
3			FR	PR	CR	IR	TR	DL	DS	Sum		
4		1 FR	11	78	75	83	67	67	82	463	11*1	
5		2 PR	43	11	45	78	65	64	78	384	Sum of lower bounds	
6		3 CR	34	64	11	72	62	62	78	383	of the grey ratings	
7		4 IR	31	64	76	11	72	78	80	412		
8		5 TR	34	62	62	67	11	82	78	396		
9		6 DL	26	72	65	68	72	11	72	386		
10		7 DS	62	65	67	67	71	82	11	425	SUM(C10:I10)	
11		Sum	241	416	401	446	420	446	479	→	SUM(I4:I10)	
12												
13		Ideal	1	2	3	4	5	6	7			
14			FR	PR	CR	IR	TR	DL	DS	Sum		
15		1 FR	33	101	98	105	90	90	105	622	11*3	
16		2 PR	66	33	68	101	87	86	101	542	Sum of upper bounds	
17		3 CR	57	87	33	95	85	84	100	541	of the grey ratings	
18		4 IR	54	87	99	33	95	101	103	572		
19		5 TR	58	84	63	89	33	104	103	534		
20		6 DL	50	95	88	91	93	33	96	546		
21		7 DS	85	88	90	90	95	105	33	586	SUM(C21:I21)	
22		Sum	403	575	539	604	578	603	641	→	SUM(I15:I21)	
23												
24		Typical	1	2	3	4	5	6	7			
25			FR	PR	CR	IR	TR	DL	DS	Sum		
26		1 FR	22	90	87	94	79	79	94	545	11*2	
27		2 PR	55	22	57	90	76	75	90	465	Average of the bounds	
28		3 CR	46	76	22	84	74	73	89	464	of the grey ratings	
29		4 IR	43	76	88	22	84	90	92	495		
30		5 TR	46	73	63	78	22	93	91	466		
31		6 DL	38	84	77	80	83	22	84	468		
32		7 DS	74	77	79	79	83	94	22	508	SUM(C32:I32)	
33		Sum	324	498	473	527	501	526	562	→	SUM(I26:I32)	

Table 5.12 Whitenized values of aggregated responses

	A	B	C	D	E	F	G	H	I	J
1						Whitenized				
2		Critical	1	2	3	4	5	6	7	
3			FR	PR	CR	IR	TR	DL	DS	Sum
4		1 FR	11	78	75	83	67	67	82	463
5		2 PR	43	11	45	78	65	64	78	384
6		3 CR	34	64	11	72	62	62	78	383
7		4 IR	31	64	76	11	72	78	80	412
8		5 TR	34	62	62	67	11	82	78	396
9		6 DL	26	72	65	68	72	11	72	386
10		7 DS	62	65	67	67	71	82	11	425
11		Sum	241	416	401	446	420	446	479	
12										
13		Ideal	1	2	3	4	5	6	7	
14			FR	PR	CR	IR	TR	DL	DS	Sum
15		1 FR	33	101	98	105	90	90	105	622
16		2 PR	66	33	68	101	87	86	101	542
17		3 CR	57	87	33	95	85	84	100	541
18		4 IR	54	87	99	33	95	101	103	572
19		5 TR	58	84	63	89	33	104	103	534
20		6 DL	50	95	88	91	93	33	96	546
21		7 DS	85	88	90	90	95	105	33	586
22		Sum	403	575	539	604	578	603	641	
23										
24		Typical	1	2	3	4	5	6	7	
25			FR	PR	CR	IR	TR	DL	DS	Sum
26		1 FR	22	90	87	94	79	79	94	545
27		2 PR	55	22	57	90	76	75	90	465
28		3 CR	46	76	22	84	74	73	89	464
29		4 IR	43	76	88	22	84	90	92	495
30		5 TR	46	73	63	78	22	93	91	466
31		6 DL	38	84	77	80	83	22	84	468
32		7 DS	74	77	79	79	83	94	22	508
33		Sum	324	498	473	527	501	526	562	

Step 7: The Equations 5.36 and 5.37 are utilized for the construction of the direct influence coefficient matrix. The Excel formula for calculating the same and the final values are presented in Table 5.13.

Step 8: Further, the complete influence coefficient matrix is calculated following Equations 5.38 and 5.39. The Excel calculations for the same presented in Tables 5.14 and 5.15 and the and the final values are shown in Table 5.16.

Table 5.13 Direct influence coefficient matrices

U6 =ROUND(I6/I$11,3)

Whitenised

Critical	1 FR	2 PR	3 CR	4 IR	5 TR	6 DL	7 DS	Sum	
1 FR	11	78	75	83	67	67	82	463	11*1
2 PR	43	11	45	78	65	64	78	384	Sum of lower bounds
3 CR	34	64	11	72	62	62	78	383	of the grey ratings
4 IR	31	64	76	11	72	78	80	412	
5 TR	34	62	62	67	11	82	78	396	
6 DL	26	72	65	68	72	11	72	386	
7 DS	62	65	67	67	71	82	11	425	SUM(C10:I10)
Sum	241	416	401	446	420	446	479		SUM(I4:I10)

Ideal	1 FR	2 PR	3 CR	4 IR	5 TR	6 DL	7 DS	Sum	
1 FR	33	101	98	105	90	90	105	622	11*3
2 PR	66	33	68	101	87	86	101	542	Sum of upper bounds
3 CR	57	87	33	95	85	84	100	541	of the grey ratings
4 IR	54	87	99	33	95	101	103	572	
5 TR	58	84	63	89	33	104	103	534	
6 DL	50	95	88	91	93	33	96	546	
7 DS	85	88	90	90	95	105	33	586	SUM(C21:I21)
Sum	403	575	539	604	578	603	641		SUM(I15:I21)

Typical	1 FR	2 PR	3 CR	4 IR	5 TR	6 DL	7 DS	Sum	
1 FR	22	90	87	94	79	79	94	545	11*2
2 PR	55	22	57	90	76	75	90	465	Average of the bounds
3 CR	46	76	22	84	74	73	89	464	of the grey ratings
4 IR	43	76	88	22	84	90	92	495	
5 TR	46	73	63	78	22	93	91	466	
6 DL	38	84	77	80	83	22	84	468	
7 DS	74	77	79	79	83	94	22	508	SUM(C32:I32)
Sum	324	498	473	527	501	526	562		SUM(I26:I32)

Norm

Critical	1 FR	2 PR	3 CR	4 IR	5 TR	6 DL	7 DS	
1 FR	0.046	0.188	0.187	0.186	0.16	0.15	0.171	ROUND(C4/C$11,3)
2 PR	0.178	0.026	0.112	0.175	0.155	0.143	0.163	
3 CR	0.141	0.154	0.027	0.161	0.148	0.139	0.163	
4 IR	0.129	0.154	0.19	0.025	0.171	0.175	0.167	
5 TR	0.141	0.149	0.155	0.15	0.026	0.184	0.163	
6 DL	0.108	0.173	0.162	0.152	0.171	0.025	0.15	
7 DS	0.257	0.156	0.167	0.15	0.169	0.184	0.023	

Ideal	1 FR	2 PR	3 CR	4 IR	5 TR	6 DL	7 DS	
1 FR	0.082	0.176	0.182	0.174	0.156	0.149	0.164	ROUND(C15/C$22,3)
2 PR	0.164	0.057	0.126	0.167	0.151	0.143	0.158	
3 CR	0.141	0.151	0.061	0.157	0.147	0.139	0.156	
4 IR	0.134	0.151	0.184	0.055	0.164	0.167	0.161	
5 TR	0.144	0.146	0.117	0.147	0.057	0.172	0.161	
6 DL	0.124	0.165	0.163	0.151	0.161	0.055	0.15	
7 DS	0.211	0.153	0.167	0.149	0.164	0.174	0.051	

Typical	1 FR	2 PR	3 CR	4 IR	5 TR	6 DL	7 DS	
1 FR	0.068	0.181	0.184	0.178	0.158	0.15	0.167	ROUND(C26/C$33,3)
2 PR	0.17	0.044	0.121	0.171	0.152	0.143	0.16	
3 CR	0.142	0.153	0.047	0.159	0.148	0.139	0.158	
4 IR	0.133	0.153	0.186	0.042	0.168	0.171	0.164	
5 TR	0.142	0.147	0.133	0.148	0.044	0.177	0.162	
6 DL	0.117	0.169	0.163	0.152	0.166	0.042	0.149	
7 DS	0.228	0.155	0.167	0.15	0.166	0.179	0.039	

Table 5.14 Excel formula 1: Complete influence coefficient matrices

U44 {=ROUND(MINVERSE(C38:I44-O4:U10),3)}

	A	B	C	D	E	F	G	H	I
35				Identity					
36		Critical	1	2	3	4	5	6	7
37			FR	PR	CR	IR	TR	DL	DS
38		1 FR	1	0	0	0	0	0	0
39		2 PR	0	1	0	0	0	0	0
40		3 CR	0	0	1	0	0	0	0
41		4 IR	0	0	0	1	0	0	0
42		5 TR	0	0	0	0	1	0	0
43		6 DL	0	0	0	0	0	1	0
44		7 DS	0	0	0	0	0	0	1
45		Ideal	1	2	3	4	5	6	7
46			FR	PR	CR	IR	TR	DL	DS
47		1 FR	1	0	0	0	0	0	0
48		2 PR	0	1	0	0	0	0	0
49		3 CR	0	0	1	0	0	0	0
50		4 IR	0	0	0	1	0	0	0
51		5 TR	0	0	0	0	1	0	0
52		6 DL	0	0	0	0	0	1	0
53		7 DS	0	0	0	0	0	0	1
54		Typical	1	2	3	4	5	6	7
55			FR	PR	CR	IR	TR	DL	DS
56		1 FR	1	0	0	0	0	0	0
57		2 PR	0	1	0	0	0	0	0
58		3 CR	0	0	1	0	0	0	0
59		4 IR	0	0	0	1	0	0	0
60		5 TR	0	0	0	0	1	0	0
61		6 DL	0	0	0	0	0	1	0
62		7 DS	0	0	0	0	0	0	1

	N	O	P	Q	R	S	T	U	V
35			inv (I-A)						
36	Critical	1	2	3	4	5	6	7	
37		FR	PR	CR	IR	TR	DL	DS	
38	1 FR	1073.005	1072.107	1072.076	1071.157	1072.07	1072.059	1072.083	ROUND(MINVERSE(C38:I44-O4:U10),3)
39	2 PR	957.247	958.095	957.149	956.377	957.196	957.184	957.205	
40	3 CR	936.011	936.002	936.863	935.179	935.984	935.975	935.999	
41	4 IR	1000	1000	1000	1000	1000	1000	1000	
42	5 TR	964.539	964.527	964.504	963.673	965.404	964.538	964.527	
43	6 DL	937.289	937.321	937.285	936.475	937.308	938.177	937.294	
44	7 DS	1091.991	1091.892	1091.87	1090.92	1091.885	1091.892	1092.762	
45	Ideal	1	2	3	4	5	6	7	
46		FR	PR	CR	IR	TR	DL	DS	
47	1 FR	1231.13	1229.004	1230.176	1230.121	1230.126	1229.025	1231.242	ROUND(MINVERSE(C47:I53-O15:U21),3)
48	2 PR	1110.311	1110.121	1110.239	1110.229	1110.234	1109.239	1111.241	
49	3 CR	1092.585	1091.517	1093.471	1092.515	1092.525	1091.546	1093.518	
50	4 IR	1155.967	1154.843	1155.967	1156.806	1155.924	1154.898	1156.964	
51	5 TR	1085.28	1084.214	1085.219	1085.2	1086.136	1084.274	1086.209	
52	6 DL	1106.642	1105.587	1106.634	1106.581	1106.608	1106.527	1107.597	
53	7 DS	1216.953	1215.708	1216.873	1216.81	1216.842	1215.767	1218.838	
54	Typical	1	2	3	4	5	6	7	
55		FR	PR	CR	IR	TR	DL	DS	
56	1 FR	-229.3	-230.634	-230.404	-230.227	-230.652	-230.45	-230.029	ROUND(MINVERSE(C56:I62-O26:U32),3)
57	2 PR	-206.777	-206.281	-207.004	-206.801	-207.183	-207.002	-206.624	
58	3 CR	-203.171	-203.547	-202.442	-203.181	-203.55	-203.374	-203	
59	4 IR	-216.083	-216.475	-216.235	-215.191	-216.462	-216.264	-215.888	
60	5 TR	-204.457	-204.84	-204.649	-204.476	-203.932	-204.629	-204.281	
61	6 DL	-204.568	-204.913	-204.716	-204.562	-204.914	-203.838	-204.381	
62	7 DS	-230.209	-230.702	-230.465	-230.297	-230.693	-230.475	-229.191	

Table 5.15 Excel formula 2: Complete influence coefficient matrices

K75 f_x =ROUND(J75/$J$76,4)

	A	B	C	D	E	F	G	H	I	J	K	L
66					inv (I-A)-I							
67			1	2	3	4	5	6	7			
68		Critical	FR	PR	CR	IR	TR	DL	DS	Sum	Grey resp coeff	
69		1 FR	1072.005	1072.107	1072.076	1071.157	1072.07	1072.059	1072.083	7503.557	0.1541	O38-C38
70		2 PR	957.247	957.095	957.149	956.377	957.196	957.184	957.205	6699.453	0.1375	ROUND(SUM(C70:I70),3)
71		3 CR	936.011	936.002	935.863	935.179	935.984	935.975	935.999	6551.013	0.1345	ROUND(J71/$J$76,4)
72		4 IR	1000	1000	1000	999	1000	1000	1000	6999	0.1437	
73		5 TR	964.539	964.527	964.504	963.673	964.404	964.538	964.527	6750.712	0.1386	
74		6 DL	937.289	937.321	937.285	936.475	937.308	937.177	937.294	6560.149	0.1347	
75		7 DS	1091.991	1091.892	1091.87	1090.92	1091.885	1091.892	1091.762	7642.212	0.1569	
76			6959.082	6958.944	6958.747	6952.781	6958.847	6958.825	6958.87	48706.1		SUM(J69:J75)
77		Grey inf coeff	0.1429	0.1429	0.1429	0.1427	0.1429	0.1429	0.1429			ROUND(C76/$J$76,4)
78		Grey resp coeff	0.1541	0.1375	0.1345	0.1437	0.1386	0.1347	0.1569			K69
79		Sum (GIC, GRC)	0.297	0.2804	0.2774	0.2864	0.2815	0.2776	0.2998			ROUND(SUM(C77:C78),4)
80												
81		Ideal	FR	PR	CR	IR	TR	DL	DS	Sum	Grey resp coeff	
82		1 FR	1230.13	1229.004	1230.176	1230.121	1230.126	1229.025	1231.242	8609.824	0.1538	O47-C47
83		2 PR	1110.311	1109.121	1110.239	1110.229	1110.234	1109.239	1111.241	7770.614	0.1388	ROUND(SUM(C83:I83),3)
84		3 CR	1092.585	1091.517	1092.471	1092.515	1092.525	1091.546	1093.518	7646.677	0.1366	ROUND(J84/$J$89,4)
85		4 IR	1155.967	1154.843	1155.967	1155.806	1155.924	1154.898	1156.964	8090.369	0.1445	
86		5 TR	1085.28	1084.214	1085.219	1085.2	1085.136	1084.274	1086.209	7595.532	0.1357	
87		6 DL	1106.642	1105.587	1106.634	1106.581	1106.608	1105.527	1107.597	7745.176	0.1384	
88		7 DS	1216.953	1215.708	1216.873	1216.81	1216.842	1215.767	1217.838	8516.791	0.1522	
89			7997.868	7989.994	7997.579	7997.262	7997.395	7990.276	8004.609	55974.98		SUM(J82:J88)
90		Grey inf coeff	0.1429	0.1427	0.1429	0.1429	0.1429	0.1427	0.143			ROUND(C89/$J$89,4)
91		Grey resp coeff	0.1538	0.1388	0.1366	0.1445	0.1357	0.1384	0.1522			K82
92		Sum (GIC, GRC)	0.2967	0.2815	0.2795	0.2874	0.2786	0.2811	0.2952			ROUND(SUM(C90:C91),4)
93												
94		Typical	FR	PR	CR	IR	TR	DL	DS	Sum	Grey resp coeff	
95		1 FR	-230.3	-230.634	-230.404	-230.227	-230.652	-230.45	-230.029	-1612.7	0.1539	O56-C56
96		2 PR	-206.777	-207.281	-207.004	-206.801	-207.183	-207.002	-206.624	-1448.67	0.1383	ROUND(SUM(C96:I96),3)
97		3 CR	-203.171	-203.547	-203.442	-203.181	-203.55	-203.374	-203	-1423.27	0.1359	ROUND(J97/$J$102,4)
98		4 IR	-216.083	-216.475	-216.235	-216.191	-216.462	-216.264	-215.888	-1513.6	0.1445	
99		5 TR	-204.457	-204.84	-204.649	-204.476	-204.932	-204.629	-204.281	-1432.26	0.1367	
100		6 DL	-204.568	-204.913	-204.716	-204.562	-204.914	-204.838	-204.381	-1432.89	0.1368	
101		7 DS	-230.209	-230.702	-230.465	-230.297	-230.693	-230.475	-230.191	-1613.03	0.154	
102			-1495.57	-1498.39	-1496.915	-1495.74	-1498.39	-1497.03	-1494.39	-10476.4		SUM(J95:J101)
103		Grey inf coeff	0.1428	0.143	0.1429	0.1428	0.143	0.1429	0.1426			ROUND(C102/$J$102,4)
104		Grey resp coeff	0.1539	0.1383	0.1359	0.1445	0.1367	0.1368	0.154			K95
105		Sum (GIC, GRC)	0.2967	0.2813	0.2788	0.2873	0.2797	0.2797	0.2966			ROUND(SUM(C103:C104),4)

Table 5.16 Complete influence coefficient matrices

	A	B	C	D	E	F	G	H	I	J	K	L
66					inv (I-A)-I							
67			1	2	3	4	5	6	7			
68		Critical	FR	PR	CR	IR	TR	DL	DS	Sum	Grey resp coeff	
69		1 FR	1072.005	1072.107	1072.076	1071.157	1072.07	1072.059	1072.083	7503.557	0.1541	
70		2 PR	957.247	957.095	957.149	956.377	957.196	957.184	957.205	6699.453	0.1375	
71		3 CR	936.011	936.002	935.863	935.179	935.984	935.975	935.999	6551.013	0.1345	
72		4 IR	1000	1000	1000	999	1000	1000	1000	6999	0.1437	
73		5 TR	964.539	964.527	964.504	963.673	964.404	964.538	964.527	6750.712	0.1386	
74		6 DL	937.289	937.321	937.285	936.475	937.308	937.177	937.294	6560.149	0.1347	
75		7 DS	1091.991	1091.892	1091.87	1090.92	1091.885	1091.892	1091.762	7642.212	0.1569	
76			6959.082	6958.944	6958.747	6952.781	6958.847	6958.825	6958.87	48706.1		
77		Grey inf coeff	0.1429	0.1429	0.1429	0.1427	0.1429	0.1429	0.1429			
78		Grey resp coeff	0.1541	0.1375	0.1345	0.1437	0.1386	0.1347	0.1569			
79		Sum (GIC, GRC)	0.297	0.2804	0.2774	0.2864	0.2815	0.2776	0.2998			
80												
81		Ideal	FR	PR	CR	IR	TR	DL	DS	Sum	Grey resp coeff	
82		1 FR	1230.13	1229.004	1230.176	1230.121	1230.126	1229.025	1231.242	8609.824	0.1538	
83		2 PR	1110.311	1109.121	1110.239	1110.229	1110.234	1109.239	1111.241	7770.614	0.1388	
84		3 CR	1092.585	1091.517	1092.471	1092.515	1092.525	1091.546	1093.518	7646.677	0.1366	
85		4 IR	1155.967	1154.843	1155.967	1155.806	1155.924	1154.898	1156.964	8090.369	0.1445	
86		5 TR	1085.28	1084.214	1085.219	1085.2	1085.136	1084.274	1086.209	7595.532	0.1357	
87		6 DL	1106.642	1105.587	1106.634	1106.581	1106.608	1105.527	1107.597	7745.176	0.1384	
88		7 DS	1216.953	1215.708	1216.873	1216.81	1216.842	1215.767	1217.838	8516.791	0.1522	
89			7997.868	7989.994	7997.579	7997.262	7997.395	7990.276	8004.609	55974.00		
90		Grey inf coeff	0.1429	0.1427	0.1429	0.1429	0.1429	0.1427	0.143			
91		Grey resp coeff	0.1538	0.1388	0.1366	0.1445	0.1357	0.1384	0.1522			
92		Sum (GIC, GRC)	0.2967	0.2815	0.2795	0.2874	0.2786	0.2811	0.2952			
93												
94		Typical	FR	PR	CR	IR	TR	DL	DS	Sum	Grey resp coeff	
95		1 FR	-230.3	-230.634	-230.404	-230.227	-230.652	-230.45	-230.029	-1612.7	0.1539	
96		2 PR	-206.777	-207.281	-207.004	-206.801	-207.183	-207.002	-206.624	-1448.67	0.1383	
97		3 CR	-203.171	-203.547	-203.442	-203.181	-203.55	-203.374	-203	-1423.27	0.1359	
98		4 IR	-216.083	-216.475	-216.235	-216.191	-216.462	-216.264	-215.888	-1513.6	0.1445	
99		5 TR	-204.457	-204.84	-204.649	-204.476	-204.932	-204.629	-204.281	-1432.26	0.1367	
100		6 DL	-204.568	-204.913	-204.716	-204.562	-204.914	-204.838	-204.381	-1432.89	0.1368	
101		7 DS	-230.209	-230.702	-230.465	-230.297	-230.693	-230.475	-230.191	-1613.03	0.154	
102			-1495.57	-1498.39	-1496.915	-1495.74	-1498.39	-1497.03	-1494.39	-10476.4		
103		Grey inf coeff	0.1428	0.143	0.1429	0.1428	0.143	0.1429	0.1426			
104		Grey resp coeff	0.1539	0.1383	0.1359	0.1445	0.1367	0.1368	0.154			
105		Sum (GIC, GRC)	0.2967	0.2813	0.2788	0.2873	0.2797	0.2797	0.2966			

Step 9: The grey responsibility and influence coefficients are calculated following Equations 5.40 and 5.41. The Excel calculation and the values are presented in Table 5.16.

Step 10: Later, the grey importance coefficients are calculated following Equation 5.42. The Excel calculation for the same and the values are shown in Table 5.17. The same corresponds to all the three models of whitenization, the ideal, critical and the most typical models.

Table 5.17 Grey responsibility, influence and the importance coefficients

T69 | f_x =I77

	M	N	O	P	Q	R	S	T	U	V	W
67		1	2	3	4	5	6	7			
68		FR	PR	CR	IR	TR	DL	DS			
69	Critical: Grey inf coeff	0.1429	0.1429	0.1429	0.1427	0.1429	0.1429	0.1429			
70	Critical: Grey resp coeff	0.1541	0.1375	0.1345	0.1437	0.1386	0.1347	0.1569			
71	Critical: Sum (GIC, GRC)	0.297	0.2804	0.2774	0.2864	0.2815	0.2776	0.2998			
72	Ideal: Grey inf coeff	0.1429	0.1427	0.1429	0.1429	0.1429	0.1427	0.143			
73	Ideal: Grey resp coeff	0.1538	0.1388	0.1366	0.1445	0.1357	0.1384	0.1522			
74	Ideal: Sum (GIC, GRC)	0.2967	0.2815	0.2795	0.2874	0.2786	0.2811	0.2952			
75	Typical: Grey inf coeff	0.1428	0.143	0.1429	0.1428	0.143	0.1429	0.1426			
76	Typical: Grey resp coeff	0.1539	0.1383	0.1359	0.1445	0.1367	0.1368	0.154			
77	Typical: Sum (GIC, GRC)	0.2967	0.2813	0.2788	0.2873	0.2797	0.2797	0.2966			
78	Aggregate: Grey inf coeff	0.1428	0.1429	0.1429	0.1428	0.143	0.1429	0.1427			
79	Aggregate: Grey resp coeff	0.1539	0.1383	0.1358	0.1444	0.1369	0.1367	0.1542			
80	Total Influence	0.2968	0.2812	0.2787	0.2872	0.2798	0.2796	0.2969	ROUND((N71+N74+4*N77)/6, 4)		
81		FR	PR	CR	IR	TR	DL	DS			

Step 11: Thus, from the implementation of the GINA model and evaluation, we identify the risk factors are receiving the highest influence in the system as *procurement risks (PR), capacity risks (CR), delays (DL)*, considering the grey influence coefficients. Also, we understand that the factors *disruptions (DS), forecast risks (FR),* and *inventory risks (IR),* are the most influencing factors in the system, considering the grey responsibility coefficients. Considering the total importance coefficients, we can see that the factors *disruptions (DS)* and *forecast risks (FR)* appear to be of critical importance to the system.

5.4 CONCLUSION

The causal/ influence modelling techniques using grey theory are discussed in detail in this chapter. These are new additions to the basket of grey based methodologies. Two different methodologies are discussed—the grey causal modelling and the grey influence analysis. Grey causal modelling is mostly applicable to causal modelling situations with multiple objectives, and grey influence analysis can be better used when there are large number of evaluators as respondents for receiving the inputs. The detailed implementation steps along with the practical case implementations of the methodologies were also included in this chapter.

REFERENCES

Chouhan, M., Rajesh, R. and Sahu, R. (2025). Resilience enhancers and barriers analysis for Industry 4.0 in supply chains using grey influence analysis (GINA). *Journal of Industrial Information Integration*, 43, 100735.

Deng, J.L. (1989). Introduction to grey system theory. *The Journal of Grey System*, *1*(1), 1–24.

Kumar, P.S., Shriram, R.G., Rajesh, R. and Rammohan, A. (2024). Causal analysis of the challenges to electric vehicles' adoption using GINA: Implications to emerging economies. *Case Studies on Transport Policy*, 15, 101160.

Liu, S.F., Yang, Y.J. and Forrest, J. (2022). *Grey Systems Analysis*. Springer-Verlag, Berlin.

Luo, D. and Wang, X. (2012). The multi-attribute grey target decision method for attribute value within three-parameter interval grey number. *Applied Mathematical Modelling*, 36(5), 1957–1963.

Rajesh, R. (2023a). An introduction to grey causal modelling (GCM): applications to manufacturing, supply chains, resilience, and sustainability. *Artificial Intelligence Review*, 56(7), 6267–6293.

Rajesh, R. (2023b). Industry 5.0: analyzing the challenges in implementation using grey influence analysis. *Journal of Enterprise Information Management*, 36(5), 1349–1371.

Rajesh, R. (2023c). An introduction to grey influence analysis (GINA): Applications to causal modelling in marketing and supply chain research. *Expert Systems with Applications*, 212, 118816.

Rajesh, R. (2024a). Modelling the traits of consumer resilience: implications to emerging markets. *Marketing Intelligence and Planning*, 42(2), 234–261.

Sharma, R., Sundarakani, B. and Manikas, I. (2025). Integration of industry 4.0 technologies for agri-food supply chain resilience. *Computers in Industry*, 165, 104225.

Rajesh, R. (2024b). Managerial risk data analytics applications using grey influence analysis (GINA). *Data and Knowledge Engineering*, 151, 102312.

Singh, G., Rajesh, R., Daultani, Y. and Misra, S. C. (2023). Resilience and sustainability enhancements in food supply chains using Digital Twin technology: A grey causal modelling (GCM) approach. *Computers and Industrial Engineering*, 179, 109172.

Singh, G., Rajesh, R., Misra, S.C. and Singh, S. (2024). Analyzing the role of digital twins in developing a resilient sustainable manufacturing supply chain: A grey influence analysis (GINA) approach. *Technological Forecasting and Social Change*, 209, 123763.

Singh, S., Misra, S. and Singh, G. (2024). Evaluation of critical success determinants to the implementation of additive manufacturing technology in the spare parts supply chain: a grey causal modelling approach. *Business Process Management Journal*, 30(4), 1154–1184.

Yash, D. and Rajesh, R. (2024). Risk analysis of electrical power grids in India using best-worst method and grey causal modelling. *Benchmarking: An International Journal*, https://doi.org/10.1108/BIJ-03-2023-0149.

CHAPTER 6

Prediction Models

6.1 INTRODUCTION

Grey prediction models are often employed for forecasting with small datasets, where other prediction models may not be successfully applied. The prediction does not depend on the source of the data or how the values are obtained (Liu et al., 2022). Grey prediction models can be used to forecast the values particularly for the immediate future points, subject to a check for the prediction errors. The error measures have to be checked for ensuring a *level one* prediction (Liu and Lin, 2006; Tien, 2012).

6.2 BASIC GREY PREDICTION (GM (1, 1))

The basic grey prediction model, the GM (1, 1) is the most commonly used grey prediction model, where 1, 1 indicates the grey model of the first order and with one variable for prediction. The model is largely applied to predictions using small datasets. As the analysis is generally conducted for small datasets, there can be external disturbances in the data, making it to show too fast or slow developmental tendencies and the same can affect the system behavior. These disturbances are fixed using the data strengthening and weakening operations, which are applied as a part of the prediction model.

6.2.1 Step-wise Implementation

Grey prediction models can handle such data and the step-wise procedure of the implementation of the grey prediction model is elaborated as follows:

Step 1: Observe the sequence of data

The periodic sequence data for prediction are observed or extracted, shows the developmental tendencies of the data. Let the periodic indicators for the period $1 \le i \le n$ can be indicated as follows:

$$X^{(0)} = \left(x^{(0)}(i)\right)_{i=1}^{n} \tag{6.1}$$

For indicative example, we can say that $x^{(0)}(2)$ is indicating zero order periodical indicators for the second period. Further, we can indicate the time series as follows:

$$X = \left(x(1),\, x(2),\, x(3), \ldots,\, x(n)\right) \tag{6.2}$$

Step 2: Strengthening and weakening of data

Due to the effect of any uncontrollable shocks, the data may show fast or slow developmental tendencies, which is not the actual developmental tendency of the system. Hence, any conclusions based on predictions made from these sequences may not be reliable. For avoiding any such interference of shock waves, the data can be transformed using *strengthening* or *weakening* sequence operators. This process can enhance the prediction accuracy.

Suppose that D be a sequence operator applied on X, such that;

$$XD = \left(x(1)d,\, x(2)d,\, x(3)d, \ldots,\, x(n)d\right) \tag{6.3}$$

Considering for a monotonically increasing function, D can be shown as a *weakening* operator if,

$$x(k)d \geq x(k);\, k = 1, 2, 3\ldots, n\,, \tag{6.4}$$

and D can be regarded as a *strengthening* operator if,

$$x(k)d \leq x(k);\, k = 1, 2, 3\ldots, n \tag{6.5}$$

Similarly, we can say that for a monotonically decreasing function the contrary of Equations 6.4 and 6.5 hold true. Considering the case of a monotonically increasing sequence, the same expands while a weakening operator is applied and will shrink while a strengthening operator is applied. Suppose that we apply a second order weakening operator D^2, as shown;

$$X^{(0)}D = \left(x^{(0)}(1)d, x^{(0)}(2)d, x^{(0)}(3)d\ldots,\, x^{(0)}(n)d\right), \tag{6.6}$$

here,
$$x^{(0)}(k)d = \frac{1}{n-k+1}\left(x^{(0)}(k) + x^{(0)}(k+1) + x^{(0)}(k+2)\ldots, x^{(0)}(n)\right), \tag{6.7}$$

and
$$X^{(0)}D^2 = \left(x^{(0)}(1)d^2, x^{(0)}(2)d^2, x^{(0)}(3)d^2\ldots, x^{(0)}(n)d^2\right), \tag{6.8}$$

i.e.,
$$x^{(0)}(k)d^2 = \frac{1}{n-k+1}\left(x^{(0)}(k)d + x^{(0)}(k+1)d + x^{(0)}(k+2)d\ldots, x^{(0)}(n)d\right). \tag{6.9}$$

Suppose that $X^{(0)}D^2$ can be further indicated using a sequence $\tilde{X}$. This can be shown as follows:

$$X^{(0)}D^2 = \widetilde{X} = \left(\tilde{x}^{(0)}(1),\, \tilde{x}^{(0)}(2),\, \tilde{x}^{(0)}(3)\ldots,\, \tilde{x}^{(0)}(n)\right). \tag{6.10}$$

Step 3: Construct the first accumulating generating sequence (1st AGS)

Further, the first accumulating generating operator can be constructed as follows:

$$\widetilde{X}^{(1)} = \left(\tilde{x}^{(1)}(1),\, \tilde{x}^{(1)}(2),\, \tilde{x}^{(1)}(3)\ldots,\, \tilde{x}^{(1)}(n)\right), \tag{6.11}$$

here,
$$\tilde{x}^{(1)}(k) = \sum_{i=1}^{k} \tilde{x}^{(0)}(i);\; k = 1, 2, 3\ldots, n\,. \tag{6.12}$$

Step 4: Build the mean generating sequence (MGS)

Further, the mean generating sequence of adjacent neighboring elements of $\widetilde{X}^{(1)}$ can be calculated, which can be indicated using $\dot{X}^{(1)}$ and is shown as follows:

$$\dot{X}^{(1)} = \left(\dot{x}^{(1)}(1), \dot{x}^{(1)}(2), \dot{x}^{(1)}(3) \ldots, \dot{x}^{(1)}(n)\right), \tag{6.13}$$

here,

$$\dot{x}^{(1)}(1) = \left(\left(0.5 \times \tilde{x}^{(1)}(k)\right) + \left(0.5 \times \tilde{x}^{(1)}(k-1)\right)\right); k = 2,3,4\ldots,n. \tag{6.14}$$

Step 5: Simulate the indicator sequences

The data sequences can be simulated using the matrices Y and B, which is shown as follows:

$$Y = \begin{bmatrix} \tilde{x}^{(0)}(2) \\ \tilde{x}^{(0)}(3) \\ \tilde{x}^{(0)}(4) \\ \vdots \\ \tilde{x}^{(0)}(n) \end{bmatrix}; \; B = \begin{bmatrix} -\dot{x}^{(1)}(2) & 1 \\ -\dot{x}^{(1)}(3) & 1 \\ -\dot{x}^{(1)}(4) & 1 \\ \vdots & \vdots \\ -\dot{x}^{(1)}(n) & 1 \end{bmatrix}, \tag{6.15}$$

and

$$\frac{d\tilde{x}^{(1)}}{dt} + a\tilde{x}^{(1)} = b. \tag{6.16}$$

We can further estimate the values of a, b using the method of least squares as follows:

$$\hat{a} = [a, b]^T \tag{6.17}$$

here $\hat{a}$ is indicating the parameter sequence obtained as follows:

$$\hat{a} = \left(\left[B^T B\right]^{-1} B^T Y\right) \tag{6.18}$$

Further, expansion of the expression can be indicated below:

$$\hat{a} = \begin{bmatrix} \left(\dfrac{\left(\left(\frac{1}{n-1}\left(\sum_{k=2}^{n}\tilde{x}^{(0)}(k) \times \sum_{k=2}^{n}\dot{x}^{(1)}(k)\right)\right) - \left(\sum_{k=2}^{n}\left(\tilde{x}^{(0)}(k) \times \dot{x}^{(1)}(k)\right)\right)\right)}{\left(\sum_{k=2}^{n}\left[\dot{x}^{(1)}(k)\right]^2 - \frac{1}{n-1}\left[\sum_{k=2}^{n}\dot{x}^{(1)}(k)\right]^2\right)}\right) \\ \left(\frac{1}{n-1}\left(\sum_{k=2}^{n}\tilde{x}^{(0)}(k) + a\sum_{k=2}^{n}\dot{x}^{(1)}(k)\right)\right) \end{bmatrix} \tag{6.19}$$

The time response sequences can be constructed for the GM (1, 1) model after estimation of the parameters a, b, as follows:

$$\hat{x}^{(1)}(k+1) = \left(\left[\tilde{x}^{(0)}(1) - \left(\frac{b}{a}\right)\right]e^{-ak} + \left(\frac{b}{a}\right)\right); k = 0, 1, 2, 3\ldots, n-1 \tag{6.20}$$

$$\hat{x}^{(0)}(k+1) = \hat{x}^{(1)}(k+1) - \hat{x}^{(1)}(k) \tag{6.21}$$

The simulated sequences can be generated from Equations 6.20 and 6.21 as follows:

$$\hat{X} = \left(\hat{x}^{(0)}(k)\right)_{k=1}^{n} \tag{6.22}$$

Step 6: Observe the estimates of error

We can further calculate the error estimates to ensure the prediction accuracy. *Five* measures of errors are calculated and checked, so that a *level one* prediction accuracy can be ensured. Firstly, the differences in the forecast and actual values can be indicated as error sequences shown below:

$$\varepsilon^{(0)} = \left(\varepsilon^{(0)}(k)\right)_{k=1}^{n}, \tag{6.23}$$

here,
$$\varepsilon^{(0)}(k) = \left(\tilde{x}^{(0)}(k) - \hat{x}^{(0)}(k)\right). \tag{6.24}$$

The relative error sequences can be indicated as

$$\Delta = (\delta_k)_{k=1}^{n}, \tag{6.25}$$

here,
$$\delta_k = \frac{\left|\varepsilon^{(0)}(k)\right|}{\tilde{x}^{(0)}(k)} \tag{6.26}$$

and the mean relative error is shown as

$$\bar{\Delta} = \frac{1}{n}\left(\sum_{i=1}^{n}\delta_i\right), \tag{6.27}$$

Where the filtering error can be indicated as follows:

$$\varnothing = \delta_n \tag{6.28}$$

We can ensure for a *level one* prediction by checking for all these error measures to be in their permissible limits (<0.01). Further to this, the absolute degree of grey incidences (ε) of $\widetilde{X}$ and $\hat{X}$ can be calculated as follows:

$$\varepsilon = \frac{1+|s|+|\hat{s}|}{1+|s|+|\hat{s}|+|\hat{s}-s|}, \tag{6.29}$$

where
$$|s| = \left|\left(\sum_{k=2}^{n-1}\left[\tilde{x}(k)-\tilde{x}(1)\right]\right)+\left(\frac{1}{2}\left[\tilde{x}(n)-\tilde{x}(1)\right]\right)\right|, \tag{6.30}$$

and
$$|\hat{s}| = \left|\left(\sum_{k=2}^{n-1}\left[\hat{x}(k)-\hat{x}(1)\right]\right)+\left(\frac{1}{2}\left[\hat{x}(n)-\hat{x}(1)\right]\right)\right| \tag{6.31}$$

$$|\hat{s}-s| = \left|\begin{matrix}\left(\sum_{k=2}^{n-1}\left(\left[\hat{x}(k)-\hat{x}(1)\right]-\left[\tilde{x}(k)-\tilde{x}(1)\right]\right)\right)+\\ \left(\frac{1}{2}\left(\left[\hat{x}(n)-\hat{x}(1)\right]-\left[\tilde{x}(n)-\tilde{x}(1)\right]\right)\right)\end{matrix}\right| \tag{6.32}$$

i.e,
$$\varepsilon = \frac{1+|s|+|\hat{s}|}{1+|s|+|\hat{s}|+|\hat{s}-s|} \tag{6.33}$$

For ensuring a level one prediction. The level of incidence must be good (>0.9).

Further to this, we calculate the mean square deviation (C) as follows:

$$\overline{x} = \frac{1}{n}\sum_{k=1}^{n}\tilde{x}^{(0)}(k), \tag{6.34}$$

$$S_1^2 = \frac{1}{n}\sum_{k=1}^{n}\left[\tilde{x}^{(0)}(k) - \overline{x}\right]^2, \tag{6.35}$$

$$\overline{\varepsilon} = \frac{1}{n}\sum_{k=1}^{n}\varepsilon^{(0)}(k)), \tag{6.36}$$

$$S_2^2 = \frac{1}{n}\sum_{k=1}^{n}\left[\varepsilon^{(0)}(k) - \overline{\varepsilon}\right]^2, \tag{6.37}$$

and

$$C = \frac{S_2}{S_1}, \tag{6.38}$$

We ensure that the mean square deviation is in level one (<0.35).

Also, we compute the small error probability as follows:

$$\exists = 0.6745 \times S_1, \tag{6.39}$$

and we also ensure that $\left(P\left|\varepsilon^{(0)}(k) - \overline{\varepsilon}\right| < \exists\right)$ is in *level one* (>0.95).

Step 7: Forecast the sequences

After ensuring a *level one* prediction, we can use the GM (1, 1) model to forecast the periodic sequences, based on Equations 6.20 and 6.21. The grey prediction models are more useful in predicting the immediate future points, as small data is often employed. Hence, the predicted sequences for the next m periods can be indicated as follows.

$$\hat{X}^{(0)} = \left(\hat{x}^{(0)}(i)\right)_{i=n}^{n+m} \tag{6.40}$$

6.2.2 Sample Case Problem (Basic Grey Prediction)

As we see that basic grey prediction models are widely applied to business problems in literature (Rajesh, 2016; 2022). Here, we further consider the problem of improving the resilience performance indicators of the firm XYZ. The resilience performance indicators of the firm are evaluated using multiple indicators and are classified in *five* different categories, which are *flexibility, responsiveness, quality, productivity and accessibility*. From the data records of the firm, the overall periodic indicators of performances were measured under the *five* different categories considering a continuous period of *five* years. Later, the predictions for the resilience performances were made for the subsequent years, particularly for the very next year. The detailed step-wise implementation of the basic grey prediction model (GM (1,1)) for the case is indicated as follows:

Step 1: We employ a group constituting of *three* analysts to evaluate and extract the data considering the *five* indicators of resilience performances of firms. These indicators are named as the *resilience indicators* (RI) and the performance in *flexibility* (RI 1), *responsiveness* (RI 2), *quality* (RI 3), *productivity* (RI 4) *and accessibility* (RI 5) are measured, following Equations

6.1 to 6.5. The initial data indicating the values for the *five* performance indicators measured over a period from 2011 to 2015 are showed in Table 6.1.

Table 6.1 Periodic performances of indicators

	A	B	C	D	E	F
2	X sl no.	x(0)1	x(0)2	x(0)3	x(0)4	x(0)5
3	RI 1	2386	2399	3453	3645	4064
4	RI 2	1345	1876	2345	2784	3764
5	RI 3	674	567	453	363	278
6	RI 4	6784	5647	4563	3743	3345
7	RI 5	1763	2376	2763	2983	3216

Step 2: We apply the *first* order weakening operator on the sequences by employing Equations 6.6 – 6.9. Further to this, the *second* order weakening operator is applied following Equation 6.10 and the data for prediction are again smoothened. The Excel calculations for applying the *first* and *second* order weakening operators are shown in Table 6.2.

Table 6.2 Excel formula: First and second order weakening operators

F19 =ROUND(((1/(5-5+1))*(F13)),3)

	A	B	C	D	E	F	G
8	XD	x(0)1d	x(0)2d	x(0)3d	x(0)4d	x(0)5d	
9	RI 1	3189.4	3390.25	3720.667	3854.5	4064	ROUND(((1/(5-1+1))*(B3+C3+D3+E3+F3)),3)
10	RI 2	2422.8	2692.25	2964.333	3274	3764	ROUND(((1/(5-5+1))*(F4)),3)
11	RI 3	467	415.25	364.667	320.5	278	
12	RI 4	4816.4	4324.5	3883.667	3544	3345	
13	RI 5	2620.2	2834.5	2987.333	3099.5	3216	
14	XD2	x(0)1d^2	x(0)2d^2	x(0)3d^2	x(0)4d^2	x(0)5d^2	
15	RI 1	3643.763	3757.354	3879.722	3959.25	4064	ROUND(((1/(5-1+1))*(B9+C9+D9+E9+F9)),3)
16	RI 2	3023.477	3173.646	3334.111	3519	3764	ROUND(((1/(5-5+1))*(F10)),3)
17	RI 3	369.083	344.604	321.056	299.25	278	
18	RI 4	3982.713	3774.292	3590.889	3444.5	3345	
19	RI 5	2951.507	3034.333	3100.944	3157.75	3216	

Step 3: In order to smoothen the data sequences again, the first accumulating generator operators are employed utilizing Equations 6.12 and 6.13, the Excel calculations for the same are shown in Table 6.3.

Step 4: Further to this, the mean generating operators are employed on the sequences following Equations 6.25 and 6.26, the Excel calculations for the same are shown in the above table, Table 6.3 and the resulting values after all the transformation operations are presented in Table 6.4.

Step 5: The performance indicator sequences for the period 2010 to 2015 has been simulated using Equations 6.27–6.34. The time response sequences and the data sequences that are simulated are to be simulated now. For this, the B and Y matrices are to be constructed for all the *five* indicators. The values are taken from the proper matrices, which is indicated in Table 6.5. Later, for simulating the values, we construct the matrices of B^TB, B^TY, $(B^TB)^{-1}$, and finally $(B^TB)^{-1} \times B^TY$, to obtain the specific prediction parameters a and b, for all the *five* indicator sequences. The complete Excel calculations for the same are shown in Table 6.6 and the final values are shown in Table 6.7. Note that, here we employ the matrix operations in Excel, hence the 'MMULT', 'MINVERSE' functions are used. Please carry out this carefully,

Table 6.3 Excel formula and the results after weakening operators

F31 | f_x =ROUND((0.5*F25+0.5*E25),3)

	A	B	C	D	E	F	G	H	I
20	1 AGO	$\tilde{x}^{(0)}(1)$	$\tilde{x}^{(0)}(2)$	$\tilde{x}^{(0)}(3)$	$\tilde{x}^{(0)}(4)$	$\tilde{x}^{(0)}(5)$			
21	RI 1	3643.763	7401.117	11280.84	15240.089	19304.089	B15		
22	RI 2	3023.477	6197.123	9531.234	13050.234	16814.234	ROUND(B16+C16,3)		
23	RI 3	369.083	713.687	1034.743	1333.993	1611.993	ROUND(B17+C17+D17+E17+F17,3)		
24	RI 4	3982.713	7757.005	11347.89	14792.394	18137.394			
25	RI 5	2951.507	5985.84	9086.784	12244.534	15460.534			
26	Mean GS	$\dot{x}^{(1)}(1)$	$\dot{x}^{(1)}(2)$	$\dot{x}^{(1)}(3)$	$\dot{x}^{(1)}(4)$	$\dot{x}^{(1)}(5)$			
27	RI 1		5522.44	9340.978	13260.464	17272.089	ROUND((0.5*C21+0.5*B21),3)		
28	RI 2		4610.3	7864.179	11290.734	14932.234	ROUND((0.5*F22+0.5*E22),3)		
29	RI 3		541.385	874.215	1184.368	1472.993			
30	RI 4		5869.859	9552.45	13070.144	16464.894			
31	RI 5		4468.674	7536.312	10665.659	13852.534			

Table 6.4 The values obtained after the transformation operations

	A		B	C	D	E	F
2	X	sl no.	x(0)1	x(0)2	x(0)3	x(0)4	x(0)5
3		RI 1	2386	2399	3453	3645	4064
4		RI 2	1345	1876	2345	2784	3764
5		RI 3	674	567	453	363	278
6		RI 4	6784	5647	4563	3743	3345
7		RI 5	1763	2376	2763	2983	3216
8	XD		x(0)1d	x(0)2d	x(0)3d	x(0)4d	x(0)5d
9		RI 1	3189.4	3390.25	3720.667	3854.5	4064
10		RI 2	2422.8	2692.25	2961.333	3274	3764
11		RI 3	467	415.25	364.667	320.5	278
12		RI 4	4816.4	4324.5	3883.667	3544	3345
13		RI 5	2620.2	2834.5	2987.333	3099.5	3216
14	XD2		x(0)1d^2	x(0)2d^2	x(0)3d^2	x(0)4d^2	x(0)5d^2
15		RI 1	3643.763	3757.354	3879.722	3959.25	4064
16		RI 2	3023.477	3173.646	3334.111	3519	3764
17		RI 3	369.083	344.604	321.056	299.25	278
18		RI 4	3982.713	3774.292	3590.889	3444.5	3345
19		RI 5	2951.507	3034.333	3100.944	3157.75	3216
20	1 AGO		$\tilde{x}^{(0)}(1)$	$\tilde{x}^{(0)}(2)$	$\tilde{x}^{(0)}(3)$	$\tilde{x}^{(0)}(4)$	$\tilde{x}^{(0)}(5)$
21		RI 1	3643.763	7401.117	11280.84	15240.089	19304.089
22		RI 2	3023.477	6197.123	9531.234	13050.234	16814.234
23		RI 3	369.083	713.687	1034.743	1333.993	1611.993
24		RI 4	3982.713	7757.005	11347.89	14792.394	18137.394
25		RI 5	2951.507	5985.84	9086.784	12244.534	15460.534
26	Mean GS		$\dot{x}^{(1)}(1)$	$\dot{x}^{(1)}(2)$	$\dot{x}^{(1)}(3)$	$\dot{x}^{(1)}(4)$	$\dot{x}^{(1)}(5)$
27		RI 1		5522.44	9340.978	13260.464	17272.089
28		RI 2		4610.3	7864.179	11290.734	14932.234
29		RI 3		541.385	874.215	1184.368	1472.993
30		RI 4		5869.859	9552.45	13070.144	16464.894
31		RI 5		4468.674	7536.312	10665.659	13852.534

as these are array operations and it is done by selecting the dimensions of the resulting cells (row and column), type the formula in the topmost cell in the left corner, press the F2 key, and then press the 'Control + Shift + Enter' tabs to populate the entire matrix. Further, the sequences are simulated, where the Excel calculations are shown in Tables 6.8 and 6.9. The final values are shown in Table 6.10.

Table 6.5 Construction of the *B* and *Y* matrices

O37 =F31*-1

	A	B	C	D	E	F	G	H	I	J	K	L	M	N	O	P	Q
33	Y1	Y2	Y3	Y4	Y5		B1		B2		B3		B4		B5		
34	3757.354	3173.646	344.604	3774.292	3034.333	C15	-5522.44	1	-4610.3	1	-541.385	1	-5869.86	1	-4468.67	1	C27*-1
35	3879.722	3334.111	321.056	3590.889	3100.944	D16	-9340.978	1	-7864.179	1	-874.215	1	-9552.45	1	-7536.31	1	D31*-1
36	3959.25	3519	299.25	3444.5	3157.75		-13260.464	1	-11290.734	1	-1184.37	1	-13070.1	1	-10665.7	1	
37	4064	3764	278	3345	3216		-17272.089	1	-14932.234	1	-1472.99	1	-16464.9	1	-13852.5	1	

Table 6.6 Excel formula: Calculation of the prediction parameters

G50 {=MMULT(G43:H44,G46:G47)}

	A	B	C	D	E	F	G	H	I	J	K
39	B1 T B1		B2 T B2		B3 T B3		B4 T B4		B5 T B5		
40	591916177.5	-45395.97	433552463.9	-38697.4	4629785.522	-4072.961	567625944.3	-44957.3	382414026	-36523.18	MMULT(TRANSPOSE(G34:H37),G34:H37)
41	-45395.971	4	-38697.447	4	-4072.961	4	-44957.347	4	-36523.179	4	MMULT(TRANSPOSE(O34:P37),O34:P37)
42	inv (B1 T B1)		inv (B2 T B2)		inv (B3 T B3)		inv (B4 T B4)		inv (B5 T B5)		
43	1.30348E-08	0.0001479	1.68978E-08	0.000163	2.0724E-06	0.002110199	1.60423E-08	0.00018	2.0438E-08	0.000187	MINVERSE(A40:B41)
44	0.000147932	1.9288792	0.000163475	1.831519	0.002110199	2.398690063	0.000180305	2.276507	0.00018662	1.953948	MINVERSE(I40:J41)
45	B1 T Y		B2 T Y		B3 T Y		B4 T Y		B5 T Y		
46	-179685421.7		-136788528		-1231149.586		-156551531		-115158361		MMULT(TRANSPOSE(G34:H37),A34:A37)
47	15660.326		13790.757		1242.91		14154.681		12509.027		MMULT(TRANSPOSE(O34:P37),E34:E37)
48	inv (B1 T B1)*(B1 T Y)		inv (B1 T B1)*(B1 T Y)		inv (B1 T B1)*(B1 T Y)		inv (B1 T B1)*(B1 T Y)		inv (B1 T B1)*(B1 T Y)		
49	-0.025502552		-0.05697519		0.071355587		0.040710484		-0.0192322		MMULT(A43:B44,A46:A47)
50	3625.653218		2896.490632		383.3846304		3996.229087		2951.65108		MMULT(I43:J44,I46:I47)
51	a1	b1	a2	b2	a3	b3	a4	b4	a5	b5	
52	-0.025502552	3625.6532	-0.05697519	2896.491	0.071355587	383.3846304	0.040710484	3996.229	-0.0192322	2951.651	
53	A49	A50									

Table 6.7 Results showing the prediction parameters for *five* indicators

	A	B	C	D	E	F	G	H	I	J
39	B1 T B1		B2 T B2		B3 T B3		B4 T B4		B5 T B5	
40	591916177.5	-45395.97	433552463.9	-38697.4	4629785.522	-4072.961	567625944.3	-44957.3	382414026	-36523.18
41	-45395.971	4	-38697.447	4	-4072.961	4	-44957.347	4	-36523.179	4
42	inv (B1 T B1)		inv (B2 T B2)		inv (B3 T B3)		inv (B4 T B4)		inv (B5 T B5)	
43	1.30343E-08	0.0001479	1.68978E-08	0.000163	2.0724E-06	0.002110199	1.60423E-08	0.00018	2.0438E-08	0.000187
44	0.000147932	1.9288792	0.000163475	1.831519	0.002110199	2.398690063	0.000180305	2.276507	0.00018662	1.953948
45	B1 T Y		B2 T Y		B3 T Y		B4 T Y		B5 T Y	
46	-179685421.7		-136788528		-1231149.586		-156551531		-115158361	
47	15660.326		13790.757		1242.91		14154.681		12509.027	
48	inv (B1 T B1)*(B1 T Y)		inv (B1 T B1)*(B1 T Y)		inv (B1 T B1)*(B1 T Y)		inv (B1 T B1)*(B1 T Y)		inv (B1 T B1)*(B1 T Y)	
49	-0.025502552		-0.05697519		0.071355587		0.040710484		-0.0192322	
50	3625.653218		2896.490632		383.3846304		3996.229087		2951.65108	
51	a1	b1	a2	b2	a3	b3	a4	b4	a5	b5
52	-0.025502552	3625.6532	-0.05697519	2896.491	0.071355587	383.3846304	0.040710484	3996.229	-0.0192322	2951.651

Table 6.8 Excel formula: The simulated 1-AGO sequences

K64 =ROUND(K63-J63,3)

	A	B	C	D	E	F	G	H	I	J	K	L
54	**Simulated (AGO)**	2011	2012	2013	2014	2015	2016	2017	2018	2019	2020	
55	RI 1. x(1)(k+1)	3643.763	7410.164	11273.85	15237.343	19303.212	23474.104	27752.73	32141.881	36644.4	41263.23	ROUND((((B15-(B52/A52))*EXP(-A52*0))+(B52/A52)),3)
56	RI 1. x(0)(k+1)	3643.763	3766.401	3863.689	3963.49	4065.869	4170.892	4278.629	4389.148	4502.522	4618.825	B55
57	RI 2. x(1)(k+1)	3023.477	6181.336	9524.34	13063.342	16809.834	20775.981	24974.66	29419.51	34124.96	39106.28	
58	RI 2. x(0)(k+1)	3023.477	3157.859	3343.004	3539.002	3746.492	3966.147	4198.681	4444.848	4705.446	4981.326	ROUND(C57-B57,3)
59	RI 3. x(1)(k+1)	369.083	713.69	1034.565	1333.341	1611.541	1870.581	2111.782	2336.371	2545.493	2740.212	
60	RI 3. x(0)(k+1)	369.083	344.607	320.875	298.776	278.2	259.04	241.201	224.589	209.122	194.719	ROUND(K59-J59,3)
61	RI 4. x(1)(k+1)	3982.713	7739.808	11347.02	14810.334	18135.484	21327.983	24393.13	27335.989	30161.45	32874.2	ROUND((((B18-(H52/G52))*EXP(-G52*9))+(H52/G52)),3)
62	RI 4. x(0)(k+1)	3982.713	3757.095	3607.214	3463.312	3325.15	3192.499	3065.142	2942.864	2825.464	2712.749	
63	RI 5. x(1)(k+1)	2951.507	5989.038	9085.553	12242.197	15460.137	18740.566	22084.69	25493.76	28969.03	32511.77	
64	RI 5. x(0)(k+1)	2951.507	3037.531	3096.515	3156.644	3217.94	3280.429	3344.128	3409.066	3475.265	3542.749	

Table 6.9 Excel formula: The simulated actual sequences

K76 =K64

	A	B	C	D	E	F	G	H	I	J	K	L	M
66	**Simulated (Actual)**	2011	2012	2013	2014	2015	2016	2017	2018	2019	2020		
67	RI 1. x(1)(k+1)	3643.763	7410.164	11273.85	15237.343	19303.212	23474.104	27752.73	32141.881	36644.4	41263.23	B55	
68	RI 2. x(1)(k+1)	3023.477	6181.336	9524.34	13063.342	16809.834	20775.981	24974.66	29419.51	34124.96	39106.28	B57	
69	RI 3. x(1)(k+1)	369.083	713.69	1034.565	1333.341	1611.541	1870.581	2111.782	2336.371	2545.493	2740.212	B59	
70	RI 4. x(1)(k+1)	3982.713	7739.808	11347.02	14810.334	18135.484	21327.983	24393.13	27335.989	30161.45	32874.2		
71	RI 5. x(1)(k+1)	2951.507	5989.038	9085.553	12242.197	15460.137	18740.566	22084.69	25493.76	28969.03	32511.77	Trends	
72	RI 1. x(0)(k+1)	3643.763	3766.401	3863.689	3963.49	4065.869	4170.892	4278.629	4389.148	4502.522	4618.825	2.5830394	((G72-F72)/F72)*100
73	RI 2. x(0)(k+1)	3023.477	3157.859	3343.004	3539.002	3746.492	3966.147	4198.681	4444.848	4705.446	4981.326	5.8629513	
74	RI 3. x(0)(k+1)	369.083	344.607	320.875	298.776	278.2	259.04	241.201	224.589	209.122	194.719	-6.8871316	
75	RI 4. x(0)(k+1)	3982.713	3757.095	3607.214	3463.312	3325.15	3192.499	3065.142	2942.864	2825.464	2712.749	-3.9893238	
76	RI 5. x(0)(k+1)	2951.507	3037.531	3096.515	3156.644	3217.94	3280.429	3344.128	3409.066	3475.265	3542.749	1.9418945	((G76-F76)/F76)*100

Table 6.10 The simulated 1-AGO and the simulated actual sequences

	A	B	C	D	E	F	G	H	I	J	K	L
54	**Simulated (AGO)**	2011	2012	2013	2014	2015	2016	2017	2018	2019	2020	
55	RI 1. x(1)(k+1)	3643.763	7410.164	11273.85	15237.343	19303.212	23474.104	27752.73	32141.881	36644.4	41263.23	
56	RI 1. x(0)(k+1)	3643.763	3766.401	3863.689	3963.49	4065.369	4170.892	4278.629	4389.148	4502.522	4618.825	
57	RI 2. x(1)(k+1)	3023.477	6181.336	9524.34	13063.342	16809.834	20775.981	24974.66	29419.51	34124.96	39106.28	
58	RI 2. x(0)(k+1)	3023.477	3157.859	3343.004	3539.002	3746.492	3966.147	4198.681	4444.848	4705.446	4981.326	
59	RI 3. x(1)(k+1)	369.083	713.69	1034.565	1333.341	1611.541	1870.581	2111.782	2336.371	2545.493	2740.212	
60	RI 3. x(0)(k+1)	369.083	344.607	320.875	298.776	278.2	259.04	241.201	224.589	209.122	194.719	
61	RI 4. x(1)(k+1)	3982.713	7739.808	11347.02	14810.334	18135.484	21327.983	24393.13	27335.989	30161.45	32874.2	
62	RI 4. x(0)(k+1)	3982.713	3757.095	3607.214	3463.312	3325.15	3192.499	3065.142	2942.864	2825.464	2712.749	
63	RI 5. x(1)(k+1)	2951.507	5989.038	9085.553	12242.197	15460.137	18740.566	22084.69	25493.76	28969.03	32511.77	
64	RI 5. x(0)(k+1)	2951.507	3037.531	3096.515	3156.644	3217.94	3280.429	3344.128	3409.066	3475.265	3542.749	
65												
66	**Simulated (Actual)**	2011	2012	2013	2014	2015	2016	2017	2018	2019	2020	
67	RI 1. x(1)(k+1)	3643.763	7410.164	11273.85	15237.343	19303.212	23474.104	27752.73	32141.881	36644.4	41263.23	
68	RI 2. x(1)(k+1)	3023.477	6181.336	9524.34	13063.342	16809.834	20775.981	24974.66	29419.51	34124.96	39106.28	
69	RI 3. x(1)(k+1)	369.083	713.69	1034.565	1333.341	1611.541	1870.581	2111.782	2336.371	2545.493	2740.212	
70	RI 4. x(1)(k+1)	3982.713	7739.808	11347.02	14810.334	18135.484	21327.983	24393.13	27335.989	30161.45	32874.2	
71	RI 5. x(1)(k+1)	2951.507	5989.038	9085.553	12242.197	15460.137	18740.566	22084.69	25493.76	28969.03	32511.77	Trends
72	RI 1. x(0)(k+1)	3643.763	3766.401	3863.689	3963.49	4065.869	4170.892	4278.629	4389.148	4502.522	4618.825	2.5830394
73	RI 2. x(0)(k+1)	3023.477	3157.859	3343.004	3539.002	3746.492	3966.147	4198.681	4444.848	4705.446	4981.326	5.8629513
74	RI 3. x(0)(k+1)	369.083	344.607	320.875	298.776	278.2	259.04	241.201	224.589	209.122	194.719	-6.8871316
75	RI 4. x(0)(k+1)	3982.713	3757.095	3607.214	3463.312	3325.15	3192.499	3065.142	2942.864	2825.464	2712.749	-3.9893238
76	RI 5. x(0)(k+1)	2951.507	3037.531	3096.515	3156.644	3217.94	3280.429	3344.128	3409.066	3475.265	3542.749	1.9418945

Step 6: Later, we check for the measures of residuals to ensure for a Level 1 prediction. We observe the absolute and relative measures of errors for this. The sequence of error measures (residuals) are calculated following Equations 6.35–6.51. The mean relative errors are calculated and the same is checked for an acceptable threshold of *less than* 0.01. The measures of the absolute degree of grey incidences (ADGI) are calculated and checked for the acceptance limits, which needs to be *greater than* 0.9. The absolute degrees of grey incidences were calculated and are checked for the acceptable limits of *greater than* 0.90. Further, we calculate the ratio of mean square deviations and ensure it to be in the acceptable threshold value of *less than* 0.35. We also ensure that the values for small error probabilities are *greater than* 0.95. The Excel calculations for the measures of residuals are indicated in Tables 6.11 and 6.12., and the final values of the residuals are presented in Table 6.13. If the error measures are within the permissible limits, we ensure that the prediction is at Level 1.

Table 6.11 Excel formula: Residuals (error, relative error, and the mean relative error)

F87 | fx =ROUND((ABS(F80)/F16),3)

	A		B	C	D	E	F	G	H	I	J
78	Error		2011	2012	2013	2014	2015				
79		RI 1	0	-9.047	16.033	-4.24	-1.869	ROUND(B15-B56,3)			
80		RI 2	0	15.787	-8.893	-20.002	17.508				
81		RI 3	0	-0.003	0.181	0.474	-0.2				
82		RI 4	0	17.197	-16.325	-18.812	19.85				
83		RI 5	0	-3.198	4.429	1.106	-1.94	ROUND(F19-F64,3)			
84											
85	Rel. error		2011	2012	2013	2014	2015				
86		RI 1	0	0.002	0.004	0.001	0	ROUND((ABS(B79)/B15),3)			
87		RI 2	0	0.005	0.003	0.006	0.005				
88		RI 3	0	0	0.001	0.002	0.001				
89		RI 4	0	0.005	0.005	0.005	0.006				
90		RI 5	0	0.001	0.001	0	0.001	ROUND((ABS(F83)/F19),3)			
91											
92	Mean rel. err.				Filt. Error						
93		RI 1	0.001		0	<	0.01	<.01	ROUND(AVERAGE(B86:F86),3)		
94		RI 2	0.004		0.005	<	0.01	level 1			
95		RI 3	0.001		0.001	<	0.01		F88		
96		RI 4	0.004		0.006	<	0.01				
97		RI 5	0.001		0.001	<	0.01				

Table 6.12 Excel formula: Residuals (ADGI, ratio of MSD, B and Y small error probabilities)

G119 | f_x =ROUND(0.6745*SQRT(C112),3)

	A	B	C	D	E	F	G	H	I	J	K	L
99	**Abs. Deg. GI**	$\lvert s\rvert$	s	$\lvert\hat{s}\rvert$	$\hat{s}$	$\lvert\hat{s}-s\rvert$	ϵ					
100	RI 1	875.156	875.156	873.344	873.344	1.812	0.999	>	0.9	>0.90	ROUND((ABS(((C15-B15)+(D15-B15)+(E15-B15))+(0.5*(F15-B15)))),3)	
101	RI 2	1326.588	1326.588	1330.942	1330.942	4.354	0.998	>	0.9	level 1	ROUND(((C16-B16)+(D16-B16)+(E16-B16))+(0.5*(F16-B16)),3)	
102	RI 3	187.881	-187.881	188.433	-188.433	0.552	0.999	>	0.9		ROUND((ABS(((C60-B60)+(D60-B60)+(E60-B60))+(0.5*(F60-B60)))),3)	
103	RI 4	1457.315	-1457.315	1449.3	-1449.3	8.015	0.997	>	0.9		ROUND(((C62-B62)+(D62-B62)+(E62-B62))+(0.5*(F62-B62)),3)	
104	RI 5	570.753	570.753	569.385	569.385	1.368	0.999	>	0.9		ABS(E104-C104)	
105							ROUND(((1+B104+D104)/(1+B104+D104+F104)),3)					
106												
107	**Ratio of MSD**	$\bar{x}$	S_1^2	$\bar{\varepsilon}$	S_2^2	C						
108	RI 1	3860.818	21829.363	0.175	72.044	0.057	<	0.35	<0.35	ROUND(AVERAGE(B15:F15),3)		
109	RI 2	3362.847	67420.452	0.88	206.211	0.055	<	0.35	level 1	ROUND((((B16-B109)^2+(C16-B109)^2+(D16-B109)^2+(E16-B109)^2+(F16-B109)^2)/5),3)		
110	RI 3	322.399	1036.282	0.09	0.051	0.007	<	0.35		ROUND(AVERAGE(B81:F81),3)		
111	RI 4	3627.479	52471.956	0.382	261.885	0.071	<	0.35		ROUND((((B82-D111)^2+(C82-D111)^2+(D82-D111)^2+(E82-D111)^2+(F82-D111)^2)/5),3)		
112	RI 5	3092.107	8568.553	0.079	6.96	0.029	<	0.35		ROUND((SQRT(E112)/SQRT(C112)),3)		
113												
114	**Small er. Prb.**	2011	2012	2013	2014	2015	measure	p value				
115	$\varepsilon^{(0)}(k)-\bar{\varepsilon}$ RI 1	0.175	9.222	15.858	4.415	2.044	99.656	1	>	0.95	>0.95	ROUND(ABS(B79-D108),3)
116	RI 2	0.88	14.907	9.773	20.882	16.628	175.137	1	>	0.95	level 1	ROUND(ABS(F80-D109),3)
117	RI 3	0.09	0.093	0.091	0.384	0.29	21.713	1	>	0.95		ROUND(0.6745*SQRT(C110),3)
118	RI 4	0.382	16.815	16.707	19.194	19.468	154.506	1	>	0.95		ROUND((IF(B118<G118,1,0)+IF(C118<G118,1,0)+IF(D118<G118,1,0)+IF(E118<G118,1,0)+IF(F118<G118,1,0))/5,3)
119	RI 5	0.079	3.277	4.35	1.027	2.019	62.436	1	>	0.95		

Table 6.13 Final obtained value of residuals

	A	B	C	D	E	F	G	H	I	J	K
78	Error	2011	2012	2013	2014	2015					
79	RI 1	0	-9.047	16.033	-4.24	-1.869					
80	RI 2	0	15.787	-8.893	-20.002	17.508					
81	RI 3	0	-0.003	0.181	0.474	-0.2					
82	RI 4	0	17.197	-16.325	-18.812	19.85					
83	RI 5	0	-3.198	4.429	1.106	-1.94					
84											
85	Rel. error	2011	2012	2013	2014	2015					
86	RI 1	0	0.002	0.004	0.001	0					
87	RI 2	0	0.005	0.003	0.006	0.005					
88	RI 3	0	0	0.001	0.002	0.001					
89	RI 4	0	0.005	0.005	0.005	0.006					
90	RI 5	0	0.001	0.001	0	0.001					
91											
92	Mean rel. err.			Filt. Error							
93	RI 1	0.001		0	<	0.01	<.01				
94	RI 2	0.004		0.005	<	0.01	level 1				
95	RI 3	0.001		0.001	<	0.01					
96	RI 4	0.004		0.006	<	0.01					
97	RI 5	0.001		0.001	<	0.01					
98											
99	Abs. Deg. GI	$\lvert s \rvert$	s	$\lvert \hat{s} \rvert$	$\hat{s}$	$\lvert \hat{s} - s \rvert$	ϵ				
100	RI 1	875.156	875.156	873.344	873.344	1.812	0.999	>	0.9	>0.90	
101	RI 2	1326.588	1326.588	1330.94	1330.942	4.354	0.998	>	0.9	level 1	
102	RI 3	187.881	-187.881	188.433	-188.433	0.552	0.999	>	0.9		
103	RI 4	1457.315	-1457.315	1449.3	-1449.3	8.015	0.997	>	0.9		
104	RI 5	570.753	570.753	569.385	569.385	1.368	0.999	>	0.9		
105											
106											
107	Ratio of MSD	$\bar{x}$	S_1^2	$\bar{\varepsilon}$	S_2^2	C					
108	RI 1	3860.818	21829.363	0.175	72.044	0.057	<	0.35	<0.35		
109	RI 2	3362.847	67420.452	0.88	206.211	0.055	<	0.35	level 1		
110	RI 3	322.399	1036.282	0.09	0.051	0.007	<	0.35			
111	RI 4	3627.479	52471.956	0.382	261.885	0.071	<	0.35			
112	RI 5	3092.107	8568.553	0.079	6.96	0.029	<	0.35			
113											
114	Small er. Prb.	2011	2012	2013	2014	2015	measure	p value			
115	$\varepsilon^{(0)}(k) - \bar{\varepsilon}$ RI 1	0.175	9.222	15.858	4.415	2.044	99.656	1	>	0.95	>0.95
116	RI 2	0.88	14.907	9.773	20.882	16.628	175.137	1	>	0.95	level 1
117	RI 3	0.09	0.093	0.091	0.384	0.29	21.713	1	>	0.95	
118	RI 4	0.382	16.815	16.707	19.194	19.468	154.506	1	>	0.95	
119	RI 5	0.079	3.277	4.35	1.027	2.019	62.436	1	>	0.95	

Step 7: Following Equation 6.52, we generate the time response sequences and then construct the predicted sequences based on the simulated values of resilience indicators (RI). The Excel formula for the time response sequences (1-AGO) and the simulated sequences of RI are shown in Table 6.14. The final values of the simulated predicted sequences are shown in Table 6.15.

Table 6.14 Excel formula: 1-AGO and the predicted sequences

F133 | f_x | =K64

	A	B	C	D	E	F	
120	i = 6 to 10						
121	**Predicted (AGO)**	2016	2017	2018	2019	2020	
122	RI 1. x(1)(k+1)	23474.104	27752.733	32141.88	36644.403	41263.228	G55
123	RI 2. x(1)(k+1)	20775.981	24974.662	29419.51	34124.956	39106.282	K57
124	RI 3. x(1)(k+1)	1870.581	2111.782	2336.371	2545.493	2740.212	
125	RI 4. x(1)(k+1)	21327.983	24393.125	27335.99	30161.453	32874.202	
126	RI 5. x(1)(k+1)	18740.566	22084.694	25493.76	28969.025	32511.774	
127							
128	**Predicted (Actual)**	2016	2017	2018	2019	2020	
129	RI 1. x(0)(k+1)	4170.892	4278.629	4389.148	4502.522	4618.825	G56
130	RI 2. x(0)(k+1)	3966.147	4198.681	4444.848	4705.446	4981.326	K58
131	RI 3. x(0)(k+1)	259.04	241.201	224.589	209.122	194.719	
132	RI 4. x(0)(k+1)	3192.499	3065.142	2942.864	2825.464	2712.749	
133	RI 5. x(0)(k+1)	3280.429	3344.128	3409.066	3475.265	3542.749	

Table 6.15 1-AGO and the predicted sequences of the *five* indicators

	A	B	C	D	E	F
120	i = 6 to 10					
121	**Predicted (AGO)**	2016	2017	2018	2019	2020
122	RI 1. x(1)(k+1)	23474.104	27752.733	32141.88	36644.403	41263.228
123	RI 2. x(1)(k+1)	20775.981	24974.662	29419.51	34124.956	39106.282
124	RI 3. x(1)(k+1)	1870.581	2111.782	2336.371	2545.493	2740.212
125	RI 4. x(1)(k+1)	21327.983	24393.125	27335.99	30161.453	32874.202
126	RI 5. x(1)(k+1)	18740.566	22084.694	25493.76	28969.025	32511.774
127						
128	**Predicted (Actual)**	2016	2017	2018	2019	2020
129	RI 1. x(0)(k+1)	4170.892	4278.629	4389.148	4502.522	4618.825
130	RI 2. x(0)(k+1)	3966.147	4198.681	4444.848	4705.446	4981.326
131	RI 3. x(0)(k+1)	259.04	241.201	224.589	209.122	194.719
132	RI 4. x(0)(k+1)	3192.499	3065.142	2942.864	2825.464	2712.749
133	RI 5. x(0)(k+1)	3280.429	3344.128	3409.066	3475.265	3542.749

6.3 GREY DISASTER PREDICTION

The disaster prediction models using grey theory are the extension of the basic grey prediction models, the GM (1, 1) models (Liu and Lin, 2006). Here, we observe the sequences of any abnormalities or catastrophes for making the prediction. Grey disaster prediction models are also helpful for the prediction of any catastrophe or contingency, when the period considered for prediction is small.

Suppose that the raw data sequence with values be indicated as follows:

$$Y = \left(y(1), y(2), \ldots, y(n)\right). \tag{6.41}$$

Suppose that the sub-sequences of Y indicating an upper abnormal (as fixed by the user) or a catastrophe value ξ, having m values is indicated as follows:

$$Y_{\xi} = \left(y[p(1)], y[p(2)], \ldots, y[p(m)]\right), \tag{6.42}$$

i.e.,

$$Y_{\xi} = \left\{\frac{y[p(i)]}{y[p(i)]} \geq \xi,\ i = 1, 2, \ldots, m\right\}. \tag{6.43}$$

Similarly, suppose that the sub-sequences of Y indicating an lower abnormal (as fixed by the user) or a catastrophe value ζ, having l values is indicated as follows:

$$Y_{\zeta} = \left(y[q(1)], y[q(2)], \ldots, y[q(l)]\right), \tag{6.44}$$

i.e.,

$$Y_{\zeta} = \left\{\frac{y[q(i)]}{y[q(i)]} \leq \zeta,\ i = 1, 2, \ldots, l\right\}. \tag{6.45}$$

These sub-sequences can be referred to as catastrophe sequences, which are indicating the upper and lower abnormal sequences.

Assume that

$$Y_{\xi} = \left(y[p(1)], y[p(2)], \ldots, y[p(m)]\right) \subset Y, \tag{6.46}$$

is indicating the catastrophic sequence of Y, then

$$P^{(0)} = \left(p(1), p(2), \ldots, p(m)\right), \tag{6.47}$$

can represent a catastrophe date sequence, which can be used for predicting the future date of occurrence of any abnormal events. The disaster prediction models using GM (1, 1) can be hence constructed for the catastrophe date sequences.

6.3.1 Implementation of Grey Disaster Prediction

The disaster prediction model using grey theory can be constructed for the catastrophic date sequences. Initially, we calculate the first accumulative generating operator (1-AGO) of the sequences of $P_{(0)}$ can be built as follows:

$$P^{(1)} = \left(p^{(1)}(1), p^{(1)}(2), \ldots, p^{(1)}(m)\right), \tag{6.48}$$

here

$$p^{(1)}(i) = \sum_{j=1}^{i} p(j),\ i = 1, 2, \ldots, m. \tag{6.49}$$

Further, the mean generating operator sequence (MGO) considering the adjacent neighbors of $P^{(1)}$ can be indicated as follows:

$$Z^{(1)} = \left(z^{(1)}(1), z^{(1)}(2), \ldots, z^{(1)}(m)\right), \tag{6.50}$$

here
$$z^{(1)}(1) = p^{(1)}(1) \tag{6.51}$$

and
$$z^{(1)}(i) = \frac{1}{2}\left[p^{(1)}(i) + p^{(1)}(i-1)\right], i = 2,3,\ldots,m. \tag{6.52}$$

Further, the catastrophe prediction sequences can be built as follows:

$$b = p^{(0)}(k) + az^{(1)}(k). \tag{6.53}$$

Further, we assess the least square estimates of the GM (1, 1) model as follows:

$$\hat{a} = [a \quad b]^T,$$

where the ordinality responses considering the catastrophic date sequences are indicated as follows:

$$\begin{cases} \hat{p}^{(1)}(k+1) = \left[p(1) - \dfrac{b}{a}\right] \times e^{-ak} + \dfrac{b}{a} \\ \hat{p}(k+1) = \hat{p}^{(1)}(k+1) - \hat{p}^{(1)}(k) \end{cases} \tag{6.54}$$

i.e.,
$$\hat{p}(k+1) = \left[p(1) - \frac{b}{a}\right] \times e^{-ak} - \left[p(1) - \frac{b}{a}\right] \times e^{-a(k-1)}, \tag{6.55}$$

and
$$\hat{p}(k+1) = \left(1 - e^{a}\right) \times \left[p(1) - \frac{b}{a}\right] \times e^{-ak} \tag{6.56}$$

The prediction parameters ($\hat{a} = [a \quad b]^I$) can be calculated from the matrices, B, B^T, and Y, as follows:

$$\hat{a} = [a \quad b]^T = [B^T \quad B]^{-1} \times (B^T Y), \tag{6.57}$$

here
$$B = \begin{bmatrix} -z^{(1)}(2) & 1 \\ -z^{(1)}(3) & 1 \\ \vdots & \vdots \\ -z^{(1)}(m) & 1 \end{bmatrix}, \tag{6.58}$$

and
$$Y = \begin{bmatrix} p(2) \\ p(3) \\ \vdots \\ p(m) \end{bmatrix}. \tag{6.59}$$

Further to this, the error estimates need to be calculated and the prediction accuracy can be determined. The standard error sequence can be constructed as follows:

$$\varepsilon(k) = p(k) - \hat{p}(k); k = 1,2,\ldots,m \tag{6.60}$$

Further to this, the relative error sequences can be constructed as follows:

$$\left\{ \Delta_k = \frac{\varepsilon(k)}{p(k)}; \; k = 1, 2, \ldots, m, \text{ where } \Delta = \{\Delta_1, \Delta_2, \ldots, \Delta_m\} \right. \tag{6.61}$$

The average relative error $(\bar{\Delta})$ can also be obtained as below:

$$\bar{\Delta} = \frac{1}{m-1} \sum_{k=2}^{m} \Delta_k . \tag{6.62}$$

Also, we can calculate the accuracy of predictions using the measures of average relative accuracy (ϑ) and the filtering accuracy (φ), as follows:

$$\begin{cases} \vartheta = 1 - \bar{\Delta}, \text{ and} \\ \varphi = 1 - \Delta_m \end{cases} \tag{6.63}$$

Suppose that the last date of occurrence of any abnormal event or a catastrophe being $p(m)(\leq n)$, then $\hat{p}(m+1)$ indicate the forecasted date of occurrence of the next abnormal event. Also, the predicted value $\hat{p}(m+k)$ can indicate the date of occurrence of the kth abnormal event in the future.

6.3.2 Seasonal Disaster Prediction

Let us consider the disaster prediction model for seasonal disaster prediction (Liu et al., 2022). Suppose that the overall period for the study is $\Omega = [a\ b]$, and assume that there are s seasons. Further, consider a season in the time period $\omega_i = [a_i\ b_i] \subset \Omega = [a\ \text{b}]$, $i = 1, 2, \ldots, s$. Suppose that ω_i can satisfy the following conditions:

$$\Omega = \bigcup_{i=1}^{s} \omega_i , \tag{6.64}$$

and

$$\omega_i \cap \omega_j = \varnothing, \text{ for any } j \neq i . \tag{6.65}$$

Then, ω_i; $i = 1, 2, \ldots, s$, can be regarded as a season or time zone within Ω,

and

$$P'^{(0)} = \left(p'(1), p'(2), \ldots, p'(m)\right), \tag{6.66}$$

can be regarded as a seasonal catastrophe date sequence.

Let us further assume that

$$\omega_i = [a_i \quad b_i]\Omega, a_i > 0. \tag{6.67}$$

Let

$$Y' = \left(y'(1), y'(2), \ldots, y'(n)\right)\omega_i = [a_i \quad b_i], \tag{6.68}$$

be considered as a positive sequence of raw data, where

$$x(k) = y'(k) - a_i \, , \tag{6.69}$$

here a_i be assumed as the lower bound of a particular season.

Here, the distinguishing rates of the sequences can be calculated as follows:

$$X = \left(x(1), x(2), \ldots, x(n)\right). \tag{6.70}$$

We can see that the distinguishing rates for these sequences are better than the original sequences, Y'.

Let us calculate the distinguishing rates for the X sequence as follows:

$$\frac{x(k+1)-x(k)}{x(k)} = \frac{y'(k+1)-a_i-y'(k)+a_i}{y'(k)-a_i} = \frac{y'(k+1)-y'(k)}{y'(k)-a_i}. \tag{6.71}$$

Applying the initial assumption of $a_i > 0$, we can assume that $y'(k)-a_i < y'(k)$, hence,

$$\frac{x(k+1)-x(k)}{x(k)} = \frac{y'(k+1)-y'(k)}{y'(k)-a_i} > \frac{y'(k+1)-y'(k)}{y'(k)}, \tag{6.72}$$

indicates an improved distinguishing rates for the sequences.

6.3.3 Sample Case Problem (Seasonal Disaster Prediction)

The seasonal disaster prediction model has been applied for the flood prediction in India, where the time sequences of the flood related disasters are extracted to predict the future occurrences of any such events. The monsoons in India represents the rainy seasons and is regarded as the major source of flood related events. This represents period of early monsoons (June-August) and the late monsoons (September-November), where almost 90 percentage of the rains are received in India. The raw data for the flood occurrences in India are collected for a period of 2007 to 2017 (Rajesh and Rajendran, 2019). This is shown in Table 6.16. The date sequences of the occurrences of floods, period of disaster, the fatalities count are shown. This is a general prediction, as the limited data is employed and we observe to understand whether there is a major flood occurrence during the early or late monsoons? And whether there is any possibility of flood occurrence with a large number of fatalities?

Table 6.16 Major flood events in India (2007–2017)

No.	Year	Flood name	Affected states	Period affected	Fatalities
1	2007	Bihar floods	Bihar	August	41
2	2008	Kosi floods	Bihar	August–September	527
3	2009	Krishna floods	Andhra Pradesh and Karnataka	October	300
4	2010	Jammu floods	Jammu & Kashmir	August	257
5	2011	Odisha floods	Odisha	September	45
6	2012	Uttarakhand floods	Uttarakhand	August–September	52
7	2013	Himalayan floods	Uttarakhand and Himachal Pradesh	June–July	5748
8	2013	Andhra floods	Andhra Pradesh	October–November	53
9	2013	Odisha floods	Odisha	October	145
10	2014	J&K floods	Jammu & Kashmir	September–October	300
11	2015	Amreli floods	Gujarat	June–July	70
12	2015	Chennai floods	Tamil Nadu	November–December	421
13	2016	Assam floods	Assam	July–August	28
14	2017	Gujarat floods	Gujarat	July–August	200

As we consider two different periods, the early monsoons and the late monsoons, two separate catastrophe date sequences (CDS) are generated. Further, the fatality sequences are also generated based on the date sequences. The flood is considered to be critical assuming if the fatalities are higher than 100. Thus, the data corresponds to a period of 11 years, with 14 data points considered for the study. Suppose that the initial sequences are indicated by Y_1, Y_2, and Y_3. Further, the two CDS for early and late monsoons ($P_{(1)}^{(0)}$, $P_{(2)}^{(0)}$) and one CDS for fatalities ($P_{(3)}^{(0)}$) are generated, which are shown below:

$$Y_1 = \left(y_1(1), y_1(2), \ldots, y_1(l)\right), \tag{6.73}$$

$$Y_2 = \left(y_2(1), y_2(2), \ldots, y_2(m)\right), \tag{6.74}$$

$$Y_3 = \left(y_3(1), y_3(2), \ldots, y_3(n)\right), \tag{6.75}$$

and the CDS consistent to Y_1, Y_2, and Y_3 are shown as follows.

$$P_{(1)}^{(0)} = \left(p_1(1), p_1(2), \ldots, p_1(l)\right), \tag{6.76}$$

$$P_{(2)}^{(0)} = \left(p_2(1), p_2(2), \ldots, p_2(m)\right), \tag{6.77}$$

and

$$P_{(3)}^{(0)} = \left(p_3(1), p_3(2), \ldots, p_3(n)\right), \tag{6.78}$$

where l, m, n is indicating the limits of the three sequences, respectively.

The step-wise implementation of the prediction model is shown as follows:

Step 1: Built the seasonal catastrophe sequences

Considering the date sequences as shown in Table 6.16, we convert the considered date as a number (Say for instance, March 3 can be assigned as 62) and the same is considered to be a subset of [1–365]. The date of initiation of the event is regarded as the raw data considered for analysis (we have two seasonal catastrophe sequences and one fatality sequence). The seasonal catastrophe sequences (SCS) indicated by Y_1, Y_2, and Y_3 are constructed, which is shown in Table 6.17.

Table 6.17 Seasonal catastrophe sequences of the raw data

Series of year	Date of occurrence	Date in [1–365]	Raw data sequences	Fatalities	SCS June 1st/ Aug 31st (152–243)	SCS Sept 1st/ Nov 30th (244–334)	SCS of fatalities
1	3/8/2007	215	63	41	63	0	0
2	18/08/2008	231	79	527	79	0	527
3	5/10/2009	278	126	300	0	126	300
4	6/8/2010	218	66	257	66	0	257
5	11/9/2011	254	102	45	0	102	0
6	3/8/2012	216	64	52	64	0	0

Series of year	Date of occurrence	Date in [1–365]	Raw data sequences	Fatalities	SCS June 1st/ Aug 31st (152–243)	SCS Sept 1st/ Nov 30th (244–334)	SCS of fatalities
7	16/06/2013	167	15	5748	15	0	5748
7	28/10/2013	301	149	53	0	149	0
7	4/10/2013	277	125	145	0	125	145
8	2/9/2014	245	93	300	0	93	300
9	22/06/2015	173	21	70	21	0	0
9	9/11/2015	313	161	421	0	161	421
10	17/07/2016	199	47	28	47	0	0
11	21/07/2017	202	50	200	50	0	200

Step 2: Built the catastrophe date sequences

From the SCS, the CDS are generated for the considered three sequences. Further, the 1-AGO and MGO series were also constructed for the considered three sequences, following Equations 6.48–6.52. The generated sequences are indicted in Table 6.18. The Excel calculations for the same are shown in Table 6.19 and the results are shown in Table 6.20. Also, the Excel formula for generation of CDS is shown in Table 6.21. As we see that, there are leap years in the calculations, appropriate adjustments in the formula are made to generate the sequences. The 1st AGO sequences and the MGS sequences and the Excel calculations are shown in Table 6.22, also the final sequences are shown in Table 6.23.

Table 6.18 CDS, 1-AGO, and MGS series

CDS			1st AGO			MGS		
June–Aug	Sept–Nov	Fatalities	June-Aug	Sept–Nov	Fatalities	June–Aug	Sept-Nov	Fatalities
1	3	2	1	3	2	1	3	2
2	5	3	3	8	5	2	5.5	3.5
4	7	4	7	15	9	5	11.5	7
6	8	7	13	23	16	10	19	12.5
7	9	8	20	32	24	16.5	27.5	20
9		9	29		33	24.5		28.5
10		11	39		44	34		38.5
11			50			44.5		

Table 6.19 Excel formula: Seasonal catastrophe sequences (SCS)

J16 =IF(K16>=100,K16,0)

	A	B	C	D	E	F	G	H	I	J	K	L	M
1								Period: 152- 243	Period: 244- 334				
2	Sl. No.	Year No.	Dates	Date 1-365		Months	Dates	Period (June- Aug)	Period (Sept- Nov)	Catastrophe fatality	Fatalities		
3	1	1	3/8/2007	215	212	31	63	63	0	0	41	E3+3	
4	2	2	18/08/2008	231	212	28	79	79	0	527	527	SUM($F$3:$F$9)	
5	3	3	5/10/2009	278	273	31	126	0	126	300	300	D5-152	
6	4	4	6/8/2010	218	212	30	66	66	0	257	257	IF(G6<91,G6,0)	
7	5	5	11/9/2011	254	243	31	102	0	102	0	45	IF(G7>=91,G7,0)	
8	6	6	3/8/2012	216	212	30	64	64	0	0	52	IF(K8>=100,K8,0)	
9	7	7	16/06/2013	167	151	31	15	15	0	5748	5748		
10	8	7	28/10/2013	301	273	31	149	0	149	0	53		
11	9	7	4/10/2013	277	273	30	125	0	125	145	145		
12	10	8	2/9/2014	245	243	31	93	0	93	300	300		
13	11	9	22/06/2015	173	151	30	21	21	0	0	70		
14	12	9	9/11/2015	313	304	31	161	0	161	421	421		
15	13	10	17/07/2016	199	181		47	47	0	0	28	E15+18	
16	14	11	21/07/2017	202	181		50	50	0	200	200		
17							Y	Y1	Y2	Y3			
18								Upperlimit= 91	Lowerlimit= 91	>100 (limit)			

Table 6.20 Seasonal catastrophe sequences (SCS)

	A	B	C	D	E	F	G	H	I	J	K
1								Period: 152- 243	Period: 244- 334		
2	Sl. No.	Year No.	Dates	Date 1-365		Months	Dates	Period (June- Aug)	Period (Sept- Nov)	Catastrophe fatality	Fatalities
3	1	1	3/8/2007	215	212	31	63	63	0	0	41
4	2	2	18/08/2008	231	212	28	79	79	0	527	527
5	3	3	5/10/2009	278	273	31	126	0	126	300	300
6	4	4	6/8/2010	218	212	30	66	66	0	257	257
7	5	5	11/9/2011	254	243	31	102	0	102	0	45
8	6	6	3/8/2012	216	212	30	64	64	0	0	52
9	7	7	16/06/2013	167	151	31	15	15	0	5748	5748
10	8	7	28/10/2013	301	273	31	149	0	149	0	53
11	9	7	4/10/2013	277	273	30	125	0	125	145	145
12	10	8	2/9/2014	245	243	31	93	0	93	300	300
13	11	9	22/06/2015	173	151	30	21	21	0	0	70
14	12	9	9/11/2015	313	304	31	161	0	161	421	421
15	13	10	17/07/2016	199	181		47	47	0	0	28
16	14	11	21/07/2017	202	181		50	50	0	200	200
17							Y	Y1	Y2	Y3	
18								Upperlimit= 91	Lowerlimit= 91	>100 (limit)	

Table 6.21 Catastrophe date sequences (CDS)

C35 | f_x =IF(J16=0,0,B16)

	A	B	C	D	E
20	Catastrophe date sequence				
21	June- Aug	Sept-Nov	Fatality		
22	1	0	0	IF(H3=0,0,B3)	
23	2	0	2	IF(I4=0,0,B4)	
24	0	3	3	IF(J5=0,0,B5)	
25	4	0	4		
26	0	5	0		
27	6	0	0		
28	7	0	7		
29	0	7	0		
30	0	7	7		
31	0	8	8		
32	9	0	0		
33	0	9	9		
34	10	0	0		
35	11	0	11		

Step 3: Construct the decision matrices

We further construct the *first*, *second*, and the *third* decision matrices considering the data from Tables 6.17 and 6.18 and by following Equations 6.53–6.55. The Excel calculations for the same are shown in Tables 6.24 and 6.25 and the obtained prediction parameters are indicated in Table 6.26.

Table 6.22 Excel formula: 1st AGO and MGS sequences

C35 =IF(J16=0,0,B16)

	A	B	C	D	E	F	G	H	I	J	K	L
37	Catastrophe date seqnce					1 AGO				MGS		
38	June- Aug	Sept-Nov	Fatality		June- Aug	Sept-Nov	Fatality		June- Aug	Sept-Nov	Fataliy	
39	1	3	2		1	3	2		1	3	2	A39
40	2	5	3		3	8	5		2	5.5	3.5	B40+F39
41	4	7	4		7	15	9		5	11.5	7	C41+G40
42	6	8	7		13	23	16		10	19	12.5	(E41+E42)/2
43	7	9	8		20	32	24		16.5	27.5	20	(F42+F43)/2
44	9		9		29		33		24.5		28.5	(G43+G44)/2
45	10		11		39		44		34		38.5	
46	11				50				44.5			

Table 6.23 1st AGO and MGS sequences

	A	B	C	D	E	F	G	H	I	J	K
37	Catastrophe date sequence					1 AGO				MGS	
38	June- Aug	Sept-Nov	Fatality		June- Aug	Sept-Nov	Fatality		June- Aug	Sept-Nov	Fatality
39	1	3	2		1	3	2		1	3	2
40	2	5	3		3	8	5		2	5.5	3.5
41	4	7	4		7	15	9		5	11.5	7
42	6	8	7		13	23	16		10	19	12.5
43	7	9	8		20	32	24		16.5	27.5	20
44	9		9		29		33		24.5		28.5
45	10		11		39		44		34		38.5
46	11				50				44.5		
47											
48		B1		B2		B3			Y1	Y2	Y3
49		June- Aug		Sept-Nov		Fatality			June- Aug		Sept-Nov
50									1		3
51		-2	1	-5.5	1	-3.5	1		2		5
52		-5	1	-11.5	1	-7	1		4		7
53		-10	1	-19	1	-12.5	1		6		8
54		-16.5	1	-27.5	1	-20	1		7		9
55		-24.5	1			-28.5	1		9		
56		-34	1			-38.5	1		10		
57		-44.5	1						11		

Table 6.24 *B* and *Y* matrices

I56 | =A46

	A	B	C	D	E	F	G	H	I	J	K	L
48		B1		B2		B3			Y1	Y2	Y3	
49		June- Aug		Sept-Nov		Fatality			June- Aug	Sept-Nov	Fatality	
50		-2	1	-5.5	1	-3.5	1		2	5	3	-(I40)
51		-5	1	-11.5	1	-7	1		4	7	4	-(J41)
52		-10	1	-19	1	-12.5	1		6	8	7	-(K42)
53		-16.5	1	-27.5	1	-20	1		7	9	8	
54		-24.5	1			-28.5	1		9		9	
55		-34	1			-38.5	1		10		11	
56		-44.5	1						11			

Table 6.25 Excel formula: First, second, and the third decision matrices

H76 | {=MMULT(A75:B76,E75:E76)}

	A	B	C	D	E	F	G	H	I	J	K	L	M	N
58		June- Aug	Transpose B1						June- Aug	B1 trans* B1				
59	-2	-5	-10	-16.5	-24.5	-34	-44.5		4137.75	-136.5		TRANSPOSE(B50:C56)		
60	1	1	1	1	1	1	1		-136.5	7		MMULT(A59:G60,B50:C56)		
61		Sept-Nov	Transpose B2						Sept-Nov	B2 trans* B2				
62	-5.5	-11.5	-19	-27.5					1279.75	-63.5		TRANSPOSE(D50:E53)		
63	1	1	1	1					-63.5	4		MMULT(A62:D63,D50:E53)		
64		Fatality	Transpose B3						Fatality	B3 trans* B3				
65	-3.5	-7	-12.5	-20	-28.5	-38.5			2912	-110		TRANSPOSE(F50:G55)		
66	1	1	1	1	1	1			-110	6		MMULT(A65:F66,F50:G55)		
67														
68	Inv(B1 trans*B1)				B1 trans*Y1			(inv (B1 trans*B1))*(B1 trans*Y1)						
69	0.000678	0.013211	June- Aug		-1249.5		June- Aug	-0.199186992	a1	MINVERSE(I59:J60)				
70	0.013211	0.400479			49			3.115853659	b1	MMULT(A59:G60,I50:I56)				
71	Inv(B2 trans*B2)		Sept-Nov		B2 trans*Y2		Sept-Nov	(inv (B2 trans*B2))*(B2 trans*Y2)						
72	0.003681	0.058431			-507.5			-0.173452956	a2	MINVERSE(I62:J63)				
73	0.058431	1.177594			29			4.496434323	b2	MMULT(A72:B73,E72:E73)				
74	Inv(B3 trans*B3)		Fatality		B3 trans*Y3		Fatality	(inv (B3 trans*B3))*(B3 trans*Y3)						
75	0.001117	0.020477			-966			-0.218912882	a3					
76	0.020477	0.54207			42			2.986597171	b3					

Table 6.26 First, second, and the third decision matrices

	A	B	C	D	E	F	G	H	I	J	K
59		June- Aug	Transpose B1						June- Aug	B1 trans* B1	
60	-2	-5	-10	-16.5	-24.5	-34	-44.5		4137.75	-136.5	
61	1	1	1	1	1	1	1		-136.5	7	
62		Sept-Nov	Transpose B2						Sept-Nov	B2 trans* B2	
63	-5.5	-11.5	-19	-27.5					1279.75	-63.5	
64	1	1	1	1					-63.5	4	
65		Fatality	Transpose B3						Fatality	B3 trans* B3	
66	-3.5	-7	-12.5	-20	-28.5	-38.5			2912	-110	
67	1	1	1	1	1	1			-110	6	
68											
69	Inv(B1 trans*B1)				B1 trans*Y1			(inv (B1 trans*B1))*(B1 trans*Y1)			
70	0.000678	0.013211	June- Aug		-1249.5		June- Aug	-0.199186992	a1		
71	0.013211	0.400479			49			3.115853659	b1		
72	Inv(B2 trans*B2)		Sept-Nov		B2 trans*Y2		Sept-Nov	(inv (B2 trans*B2))*(B2 trans*Y2)			
73	0.003681	0.058431			-507.5			-0.173452956	a2		
74	0.058431	1.177594			29			4.496434323	b2		
75	Inv(B3 trans*B3)		Fatality		B3 trans*Y3		Fatality	(inv (B3 trans*B3))*(B3 trans*Y3)			
76	0.001117	0.020477			-966			-0.218912882	a3		
77	0.020477	0.54207			42			2.986597171	b3		

Step 4: Built the simulated sequence of data

The sequences are simulated using the prediction parameters obtained in the previous step and thus, the 1-AGO sequences are constructed. The actual sequences generated on simulation are constructed using Equations 6.56–6.59. The Excel calculations for the same are included in Table 6.27 and the final values obtained are shown in Table 6.28.

Step 5: Evaluate the residuals

The residuals (error estimates) of the simulated sequences are calculated using Equations 6.60 – 6.63, where the accuracy of prediction is ensured at Level 1 (>95%) and at Level 2 (>80). The predictions below that accuracy levels are mostly not used in practice and further grey higher order prediction models can be used for such data. The Excel calculations for the estimation of residuals are shown in Table 6.29 and the values are presented in Table 6.30.

Step 6: Forecast the data for future periods

As we see that the accuracy of prediction is at Level 2, the model can be used with caution for prediction of the immediate sequences. From the results of prediction, we can see that there is chance of a flood occurrence in the year 2018 during the early monsoon period that can be critical and the fatalities may rise above 100. We see that there was a critical flood occurrence in the early monsoon period (in August) in Kerala and the same resulted in a death toll of above 400 people, which agrees to the results of prediction.

6.4 GREY PREDICTION OF HIGHER ORDER (GREY–VERHULST MODELS)

The GM (1,1) model is widely used in the prediction of linear patterns, by applying suitable transformation operators. Grey higher order prediction models are also used when the data is showing non-monotonic wavelike progress sequences or saturated sigmoidal sequences (Liu and Lin, 2006; Liu et al., 2022). A Grey-Verhulst model is a widely used higher order prediction model, which is a GM (2,1) model, or a grey model of the second order and with one variable for prediction. These prediction models are used often for saturated a sigmoidal sequence, which is often seen while measuring an indicator with a slow initial growth phase, a fast middle period growth phase, and a slow or saturated phase of end growth. These sigmoidal sequences are often seen commonly, while measuring any indicators of performances, and Grey-Verhulst models can represent the same with minimal errors.

6.4.1 GM (2, 1) Prediction Model

As said prior, Verhulst model is using a GM (2,1) model for prediction, where the model is employed, when the data sequences show saturated sigmoidal tendencies. For implementation, a general understanding of the GM (2,1) model and the related functions are required, which are elaborated as follows:

Table 6.27 Excel formula: The predicted 1st AGO and the simulated sequences

G87 =ROUND(((($C$39-($H$76/$H$75))*EXP(-$H$75*B87))+($H$76/$H$75)),3)

	A	B	C	D	E	F	G	H	I	J	K	L
78			AGO	Actual	AGO	Actual	AGO	Actual				
79		k	June- Aug		Sept-Nov		Fatality		June- Aug	Sept-Nov	Fatality	
80		0	1		3		2		3.668	5.478	3.828	ROUND(((($A$39-($H$70/$H$69))*EXP(-$H$69*B80))+($H$70/$H$69)),3)
81		1	4.668	3.668	10.857	7.857	5.828	3.828	4.477	6.516	4.765	ROUND(((($A$39-($H$70/$H$69))*EXP(-$H$69*B81))+($H$70/$H$69)),3)
82		2	9.145	4.477	20.653	9.796	10.593	4.765	5.464	7.75	5.931	ROUND(C82-C81,3)
83		3	14.609	5.464	31.157	10.504	16.524	5.931	6.667	9.218	7.383	ROUND((((B42-($H$73/$H$72))*EXP(-$H$72*B83))+($H$73/$H$72)),3)
84		4	21.276	6.667	43.97	12.813	23.907	7.383	8.138		9.189	ROUND(E84-E83,3)
85		5	29.414	8.138	35.784		33.096	9.189	9.93		11.438	ROUND(((($C$39-($H$76/$H$75))*EXP(-$H$75*B85))+($H$76/$H$75)),3)
86		6	39.344	9.93	47.472		44.534	11.438	12.12			ROUND(G86-G85,3)
87		7	51.464	12.12			58.771					
88		8	66.255									

Table 6.28 The predicted 1st AGO and the simulated sequences

	A	B	C	D	E	F	G	H	I	J	K
79			AGO	Actual	AGO	Actual	AGO	Actual			
80		k	June- Aug		Sept-Nov		Fatality		June- Aug	Sept-Nov	Fatality
81		0	1		3		2		3.668	5.478	3.828
82		1	4.668	3.668	8.478	5.478	5.828	3.828	4.477	6.516	4.765
83		2	9.145	4.477	14.994	6.516	10.593	4.765	5.464	7.75	5.931
84		3	14.609	5.464	22.744	7.75	16.524	5.931	6.667	9.218	7.383
85		4	21.276	6.667	31.962	9.218	23.907	7.383	8.138		9.189
86		5	29.414	8.138	42.925		33.096	9.189	9.93		11.438
87		6	39.344	9.93	55.965		44.534	11.438	12.12		
88		7	51.464	12.12			58.771				
89		8	66.255								

Table 6.29 Excel formula: Estimation of residuals

G97 | f_x =ABS(ROUND(C97/C45,4))

	A	B	C	D	E	F	G	H	I	J	K
90	Errors					Rel. error			Prediction period		
91	June- Aug	Sept-Nov	Fatality		June- Aug	Sept-Nov	Fatality		June- Aug	Sept-Nov	Fatality
92	-1.668	-2.857	-0.828		0.834	0.5714	0.276		14.791	-8.186	14.237
93	-0.477	-2.796	-0.765		0.1193	0.3994	0.1913			11.688	
94	0.536	-2.504	1.069		0.0893	0.313	0.1527				
95	0.333	-3.813	0.617		0.0476	0.4237	0.0771		14	13	14
96	0.862		-0.189		0.0958		0.021		C88-C87	E86-E85	G87-G86
97	0.07		-0.438		0.007		0.0398				
98	-1.12				0.1018						
99											
100				June- Aug	Sept-Nov	Fatality		>0.95	level 1		
101			Ave. rel. errors	0.185	0.4269	0.1263		>0.80	level 2		
102			Relative accuracy	0.815	0.5731	0.8737		>0.70	level 3		
103			Perc. accuracy	81.5	57.31	87.37		<=0.70	level 4		
104			Filtering accuracy	89.82	57.63	96.02					

Table 6.30 Estimation of residuals

	A	B	C	D	E	F	G	H	I	J	K
91	Errors					Rel. error			Prediction period		
92	June- Aug	Sept-Nov	Fatality		June- Aug	Sept-Nov	Fatality		June- Aug	Sept-Nov	Fatality
93	-1.668	-0.478	-0.828		0.834	0.0956	0.276		14.791	10.963	14.237
94	-0.477	0.484	-0.765		0.1193	0.0691	0.1913			13.04	
95	0.536	0.25	1.069		0.0893	0.0313	0.1527				
96	0.333	-0.218	0.617		0.0476	0.0242	0.0771		14	13	14
97	0.862		-0.189		0.0958		0.021				
98	0.07		-0.438		0.007		0.0398				
99	-1.12				0.1018						
100											
101				June- Aug	Sept-Nov	Fatality		>0.95	level 1		
102			Ave. rel. errors	0.185	0.0551	0.1263		>0.80	level 2		
103			Relative accuracy	0.815	0.9449	0.8737		>0.70	level 3		
104			Perc. accuracy	81.5	94.49	87.37		<=0.70	level 4		
105			Filtering accuracy	89.82	97.58	96.02					

Suppose that

$$X^{(0)} = \left(x^{(0)}(1),\, x^{(0)}(2),\, x^{(0)}(3), \ldots,\, x^{(0)}(n)\right), \tag{6.79}$$

is indicating a raw data sequence as follows:

$$X^{(0)} = \left(x^{(0)}(i)\right)_{i=1}^{n}. \tag{6.80}$$

Further, the sequence of first aggregate generating operator (1st AGO), $X^{(1)}$ can be shown as follows:

$$X^{(1)} = \left(x^{(1)}(1), x^{(1)}(2), x^{(1)}(3), \ldots, x^{(1)}(n)\right), \tag{6.81}$$

here

$$x^{(1)}(k) = \sum_{i=1}^{k} x^{(0)}(i); k = 1,2,\ldots,n. \tag{6.82}$$

The inverse aggregating generator operator (1st IAGO) can be employed on the sequence $X^{(1)}$ as below:

$$\alpha^{(1)}X^{(0)} = \left(\alpha^{(1)}x^{(0)}(1),\, \alpha^{(1)}x^{(0)}(2),\, \alpha^{(1)}x^{(0)}(3), \ldots,\, \alpha^{(1)}x^{(0)}(n)\right), \tag{6.83}$$

where

$$\alpha^{(1)}x^{(0)}(k) = x^{(0)}(k) - x^{(0)}(k-1);\ k = 1,\, 2,\, \ldots,\, n. \tag{6.84}$$

We can further calculate the mean generating operator sequence considering adjacent neighbors as follows:

$$Z^{(1)} = \left(z^{(1)}(1), z^{(1)}(2), z^{(1)}(3), \ldots, z^{(1)}(n)\right), \tag{6.85}$$

here

$$z^{(1)}(k) = \frac{1}{2}\left[x^{(1)}(k) + x^{(1)}(k-1)\right]; k = 1,2,\ldots,n. \tag{6.86}$$

Hence,

$$\alpha^{(1)}X^{(0)} + a_1X^{(0)} + a_2Z^{(1)} = b, \tag{6.87}$$

is representing the GM (2, 1) differential equation of the grey model and we can represent the whitenization equation as below:

$$\frac{d^2x^{(1)}}{dt} + a_1\frac{dx^{(1)}}{dt} + a_2x^{(1)} = b. \tag{6.88}$$

In most cases, for constructing the Verhulst model, we may encounter difficulties while dealing with the saturated sigmoidal sequences. For handling this, the original sequence can be indicated using $X^{(1)}$ and the 1st IAGO sequences can be represented using $X^{(0)}$ for constructing the Verhulst model, so as to directly simulate the sequence $X^{(1)}$.

6.4.2 Methodology Using Grey–Verhulst Model

The step-wise procedure for implementation of the Grey-Verhulst model is elaborated below:

Step 1: Data collection and representation

The original primary or secondary data can be collected, which can indicate the time sequence of performance of any attribute or criteria over a considered period of study. Observe the trend in the data and confirm a raw trend of saturated sigmoidal sequence. Suppose that $X^{(1)}$ is indicating the raw data collected through primary or secondary sources. The initial raw data sequence can be indicated as follows:

$$X^{(1)} = \left(x^{(1)}(1), x^{(1)}(2), x^{(1)}(3), \ldots, x^{(1)}(m)\right). \tag{6.89}$$

Further, the first IAGO sequence of $X^{(1)}$ can be built and can be indicated as $X^{(0)}$, as shown below:

$$X^{(0)} = \left(x^{(0)}(1), x^{(0)}(2), x^{(0)}(3), \ldots, x^{(0)}(m)\right). \tag{6.90}$$

Further, the mean generating sequences considering consecutive neighbors are calculated and represented as follows:

$$Z^{(1)} = \left(z^{(1)}(1), z^{(1)}(2), z^{(1)}(3), \ldots, z^{(1)}(m)\right). \tag{6.91}$$

Step 2: Construct the Verhulst matrices

Let us consider the period of study be k, where $k = (1, 2, \ldots, m)$ for the evaluation of n factors where $i = (1, 2, \ldots, n)$. Thus, the Verhulst matrices, B_{ki} corresponding to the evaluation can be indicated as follows:

$$B_{ki} = \left[\left(-z^{(1)}_{(k=(2-m);i=(1-n))}\right) \left(z^{(1)}_{(k=(2-m);i=(1-n))}\right)^2\right]. \tag{6.92}$$

Considering the case for example, $k = (2 - m)$; $i = 1$, we can represent the matrix as follows:

$$B_{11} = \begin{bmatrix} -z^{(1)}(2) & \left(z^{(1)}(2)\right)^2 \\ -z^{(1)}(3) & \left(z^{(1)}(3)\right)^2 \\ \vdots & \vdots \\ -z^{(1)}(m) & \left(z^{(1)}(m)\right)^2 \end{bmatrix}. \tag{6.93}$$

Further to this, we can represent the transpose of the matrix y_{ki} as follows:

$$T(y_{ki}) = \left[x^{(0)}_{(k=(2-m);\, i=(1-n))}\right]. \tag{6.94}$$

Consider for example, while $k = (2 - m)$; $i = 1$, we can represent the matrix as:

$$T(y_{11}) = \left(x^{(0)}(2), x^{(0)}(3), \ldots, x^{(0)}(m)\right)^T \tag{6.95}$$

Step 3: Construct the decision matrices

We can construct the *first*, *second*, and *third* decision matrices using the equations below, where the first decision matrices correspond to the following:

$$A_{ki} = \left[\left(B_{ki}\right)^T \times \left(B_{ki}\right) \right]. \tag{6.96}$$

Further, the second and third decision matrices are constructed respectively as follows:

$$C_{ki} = \left(A_{ki}\right)^{-1}. \tag{6.97}$$

$$D_{ki} = \left[\left(B_{ki}\right)^T \times \left(Y_{ki}\right) \right]. \tag{6.98}$$

Step 4: Model the Verhulst sequences

The Verhulst sequences for various factors i for the period k can be constructed as follows:

$$\hat{a}_i = \left(C_{ki} \times D_{ki}\right) \forall k = (2 - m) = \begin{bmatrix} a_i \\ b_i \end{bmatrix}, \tag{6.99}$$

and

$$\hat{x}^{(1)}_{((k+1),i)} = \left[\frac{\left(a_i \times x^{1}_{(0,i)}\right)}{\left(\left(b_i \times x^{1}_{(0,\,i)}\right) + \left(\left(a_i - \left(b_i \times x^{1}_{(0,i)}\right)\right) \times e^{k \times a_i}\right)\right)} \right]. \tag{6.100}$$

i.e., for; $i = 1$, we can reduce the equation to,

$$\hat{x}^{(1)}_{(k+1)} = \left[\frac{\left(a \times x^{(1)}_{(0)}\right)}{b x^{(1)}_{(0)} + \left(\left(a - \left(b \times x^{(1)}_{(0)}\right)\right) e^{ak}\right)} \right], \tag{6.101}$$

here a and b is indicating a_{11} and b_{11}, respectively.

Step 5: Error checks

The constructed Verhulst model need to be checked for errors to endorse the results. We estimate the errors, in a similar way to that of the GM (1, 1) model. The sequence of error estimates for the factor i considering the period k can be shown as follows:

$$\in_i (k) = x^{(1)}_{(k,\,i)} - \hat{x}^{(1)}_{(k,i)} \forall i, k. \tag{6.102}$$

Further, the relative errors are computed as follows:

$$\Delta_i(k) = \left| \frac{\in_i (k)}{x^{(1)}_{(k,i)}} \right| \forall i, k. \tag{6.103}$$

The prediction accuracy can be determined using the following equation as:

$$\theta_i(k) = \left(1 - \Delta_i(k)\right) \times 100 \forall i, k. \tag{6.104}$$

We can ensure for an acceptable level of the accuracy of prediction (~ >85%). After satisfying the condition for accuracy, the Verhulst model can be used to predict the data sequences for the future.

6.4.3 Sample Case Problem (Grey–Verhulst Model)

Grey higher order models are also applied in literature to different social science and management problems (Rajesh, 2019). The problem of improving the resilience performance indicators of the firm XYZ is again considered as the case problem. As we see that the resilience performance indicators of the firm are estimated using multiple indicators and are classified in *five* different categories, which are *flexibility, responsiveness, quality, productivity and accessibility*. Combining the secondary and primary data records of the firm regarding the overall periodic indicators of performances, we can see that these performance records fall into *five* different categories and the evaluation has been done for a continuous period of *six* years from 2011 to 2016. Here, the primary data on performances over the considered years were obtained from the ratings on evaluation of *three* analysts and the secondary data is from multiple sources considering the indicators of performances for *five* different categories, including *flexibility, responsiveness, quality, productivity and accessibility*. Further, the predictions for the resilience performances were made for the succeeding years, chiefly applicable for the very next year. Here, we can see that the data indicators show sigmoidal developmental tendencies, which is showing nonlinear pattern. Hence, the basic grey prediction model (GM (1,1)) may not be suitable for the case. Here, we can use a GM (2, 1) model, which is showed as a Grey–Verhulst model. Here, we consider the observed sequences as the 1st AGO sequences and the Inverse Accumulative Generator Operator (IAGO) is performed to convert them to the original sequences. The step-wise procedure for the implementation of the Grey–Verhulst model for the case is detailed as follows:

Step 1: Considering the primary and secondary data regarding the resilience performances of the firm, the evaluation has been made considering the *five* indicators of resilience performances of firms. The indicators, named here as the *resilience indicators* (RI) are evaluated based on performance in *flexibility* (RI 1), *responsiveness* (RI 2), *quality* (RI 3), *productivity* (RI 4) *and accessibility* (RI 5). Following Equations 6.79 – 6.91, the initial sequences are regarded as the 1st AGO sequences and the Inverse Accumulative Generator Operator (IAGO) is performed to construct the original sequences. Further, the mean generating operators (MGO) are employed on the sequences. The initial data indicating the scores for the *five* performance indicators captured during the period from 2011 to 2016, the Excel calculations for the IAGO sequences, and the mean generating sequences are displayed in Table 6.31.

***Step 2*:** Further, the Verhulst matrices are constructed following Equations 6.92 – 6.95, as we see that a GM (2, 1) model may fit the purpose, as the data sequences appear to have a saturated sigmoidal developmental tendency. The Excel formula for the construction of the Verhulst matrices are indicated in Table 6.32, and the final obtained values are shown in Table 6.33. Also, the transpose of the matrix constructed after applying the IAGO on sequences is shown.

***Step 3*:** The first, second and the third set of decision matrices were constructed based on Equations 6.96–6.98. The Excel calculations for the same are shown in Table 6.34 and the results showing the prediction parameters and are shown in Table 6.35.

Table 6.31 Excel formula: Initial, IAGO, and the MGO sequences

H21 | f_x =AVERAGE(G7:H7)

	A	B	C	D	E	F	G	H	I
1	X(1)				Period				
2	Sl. No.	RI's	2011	2012	2013	2014	2015	2016	
3		1 RI 1	230	234	325	355	359	362	
4		2 RI 2	94	98	192	218	268	272	
5		3 RI 3	265	271	330	342	351	355	
6		4 RI 4	221	226	252	312	323	327	
7		5 RI 5	117	121	159	226	248	252	
8									
9	1st IAGO (X(0))		2011	2012	2013	2014	2015	2016	
10		1 RI 1	230	4	91	30	4	3	C3
11		2 RI 2	94	4	94	26	50	4	D4-C4
12		3 RI 3	265	6	59	12	9	4	E5-D5
13		4 RI 4	221	5	26	60	11	4	
14		5 RI 5	117	4	38	67	22	4	
15									
16	MGS		2011	2012	2013	2014	2015	2016	
17		1 RI 1	230	232	279.5	340	357	360.5	C3
18		2 RI 2	94	96	145	205	243	270	AVERAGE(C4:D4)
19		3 RI 3	265	268	300.5	336	346.5	353	
20		4 RI 4	221	223.5	239	282	317.5	325	
21		5 RI 5	117	119	140	192.5	237	250	

Table 6.32 Excel formula: Verhulst matrices

K29 | =H21*-1

	A	B	C	D	E	F	G	H	I	J	K	L	M
23			RI 1		RI 2		FI 3		RI 4		RI 5		
24	Verhulst matrices		-Z1	Z1^2	-Z2	Z2^2	-Z3	Z3^2	-Z4	Z4^2	-Z5	Z5^2	
25	1	RI 1	-232	53824	-96	9216	-268	71824	-223.5	49952.25	-119	14161	D17*-1
26	2	RI 2	-279.5	78120.25	-145	21025	-300.5	90300.25	-239	57121	-140	19600	C26^2
27	3	RI 3	-340	115600	-205	42025	-336	112896	-282	79524	-192.5	37056.25	
28	4	RI 4	-357	127449	-243	59049	-346.5	120062.25	-317.5	100806.25	-237	56169	G21*-1
29	5	RI 5	-360.5	129960.25	-270	72900	-353	124609	-325	105625	-250	62500	K29^2
30													
31	Transpose (X(0))		RI 1	RI 2	RI 3	RI 4	RI 5						
32		2012	4	4	6	5	4	D10					
33		2013	91	94	59	26	38	E10					
34		2014	30	26	12	60	67	F10					
35		2015	4	50	9	11	22	G10					
36		2016	3	4	4	4	4	H10					

Table 6.33 Constructing the Verhulst matrices from the initial sequences

	A	B	C	D	E	F	G	H	I	J	K	L
1	X(1)				Period							
2	Sl. No.	RI's	2011	2012	2013	2014	2015	2016				
3	1	RI 1	230	234	325	355	359	362				
4	2	RI 2	94	98	192	218	268	272				
5	3	RI 3	265	271	330	342	351	355				
6	4	RI 4	221	226	252	312	323	327				
7	5	RI 5	117	121	159	226	248	252				
8												
9	1st IAGO (X(0)		2011	2012	2013	2014	2015	2016				
10	1	RI 1	230	4	91	30	4	3				
11	2	RI 2	94	4	94	26	50	4				
12	3	RI 3	265	6	59	12	9	4				
13	4	RI 4	221	5	26	60	11	4				
14	5	RI 5	117	4	38	67	22	4				
15												
16	MGS		2011	2012	2013	2014	2015	2016				
17	1	RI 1	230	232	279.5	340	357	360.5				
18	2	RI 2	94	96	145	205	243	270				
19	3	RI 3	265	268	300.5	336	346.5	353				
20	4	RI 4	221	223.5	239	282	317.5	325				
21	5	RI 5	117	119	140	192.5	237	250				
22												
23			RI 1		RI 2		RI 3		RI 4		RI 5	
24	Verhulst matrices		-Z1	Z1^2	-Z2	Z2^2	-Z3	Z3^2	-Z4	Z4^2	-Z5	Z5^2
25	1	RI 1	-232	53824	-96	9216	-268	71824	-223.5	49952.25	-119	14161
26	2	RI 2	-279.5	78120.25	-145	21025	-300.5	90300.25	-239	57121	-140	19600
27	3	RI 3	-340	115600	-205	42025	-336	112896	-282	79524	-192.5	37056.25
28	4	RI 4	-357	127449	-243	59049	-346.5	120062.25	-317.5	100806.25	-237	56169
29	5	RI 5	-360.5	129960.25	-270	72900	-353	124609	-325	105625	-250	62500
30												
31	Transpose (X(0))		RI 1	RI 2	RI 3	RI 4	RI 5					
32		2012	4	4	6	5	4					
33		2013	91	94	59	26	38					
34		2014	30	26	12	60	67					
35		2015	4	50	9	11	22					
36		2016	3	4	4	4	4					

Table 6.34 Excel formula: First, second, and the third decision matrices

E52 | {=MMULT(F43:G44,D47:D48)}

	A	B	C	D	E	F	G	H	I	J	K	L	M	N	O
38	BTB	RI 1		RI 2		RI 3		RI 4		RI 5					
39		504953.5	-165975741	204215	-46580393	519691.5	-169905659.8	393028.5	-113576124.3	189486.25	-40499540.1	MMULT(TRANSPOSE(C25:D29),C25:D29)			
40		-1.66E+08	55496070617	-46580393	11094280307	-169905660	56000675698	-113576124.3	33400643161	-40499540.13	9019066146	MMULT(TRANSPOSE(K25:L29),K25:L29)			
41															
42	Inv (BTB)	RI 1		RI 2		RI 3		RI 4		RI 5					
43		0.0001168	3.49431E-07	0.000115703	4.85792E-07	0.000238157	7.22566E-07	0.000146578	4.98428E-07	0.000131136	5.88859E-07	MINVERSE(B39:C40)			
44		3.494E-07	1.06309E-09	4.85792E-07	2.12978E-09	7.22566E-07	2.21012E-09	4.98428E-07	1.7248E-09	5.88859E-07	2.75511E-09	MINVERSE(J39:K40)			
45															
46	BTY	RI 1	RI 2	RI 3	RI 4	RI 5									
47		-39072	-32574	-27900	-29044	-24907.5	MMULT(TRANSPOSE(C25:D29),C32:C36)								
48		11691916	6349914	8692407	8037716	4769930.75	MMULT(TRANSPOSE(I25:J29),F32:F36)								
49															
50	(Inv (BTB)		RI 1	RI 2	RI 3	RI 4	RI 5								
51	* BTY)	a	-0.479523473	-0.68418726	-0.3637365	-0.25100268	-0.457459924	MMULT(B43:C44,B47:B48)							
52		b	-0.001223462	-0.002300266	-0.00094835	-0.00061287	-0.001525323	MMULT(H43:I44,E47:E48)							

Table 6.35 Decision matrices and the prediction parameters

	A	B	C	D	E	F	G	H	I	J	K
38	BTB	RI 1		RI 2		RI 3		RI 4		RI 5	
39		504953.5	-165975741	204215	-46580393	519691.5	-169905659.8	393028.5	-113576124.3	189486.25	-40499540.1
40		-1.66E+08	55496070617	-46580393	11094280307	-169905660	56000675698	-113576124.3	33400643161	-40499540.13	9019066146
41											
42	Inv (BTB)	RI 1		RI 2		RI 3		RI 4		RI 5	
43		0.0001168	3.49431E-07	0.000115703	4.85792E-07	0.000238157	7.22566E-07	0.000146578	4.98428E-07	0.000131136	5.88859E-07
44		3.494E-07	1.06309E-09	4.85792E-07	2.12978E-09	7.22556E-07	2.21012E-09	4.98428E-07	1.7248E-09	5.88859E-07	2.75511E-09
45											
46	BTY	RI 1	RI 2	RI 3	RI 4	RI 5					
47		-39072	-32574	-27900	-29044	-24907.5					
48		11691916	6349914	8692407	8037716	4769930.75					
49											
50	(Inv (BTB)		RI 1	RI 2	RI 3	RI 4	RI 5				
51	* BTY)	a	-0.479523473	-0.68418726	-0.3637365	-0.25100268	-0.457459924				
52		b	-0.001223462	-0.002300266	-0.00094835	-0.00061287	-0.001525323				

Step 4: Based on the prediction parameters, the simulated IAGO sequences and the original sequences are constructed following Equations 6.99–6.101. The Excel calculations for the same are shown in Table 6.36 and the resulting simulated sequences are shown in Table 6.37.

Step 5: The Verhulst sequences are constructed and there is a need for checking the same for residuals to ensure the accuracy of prediction. For this, we calculate the estimated errors, relative errors and accuracy of prediction following Equations 6.102–6.104. Further, we calculate the overall accuracy of prediction using the measures of the grand mean accuracy (GMA), which are obtained as 93.95%, which does not ensure a Level 1 prediction. The Excel calculations for the same are shown in Table 6.38 and the resulting values are shown in Table 6.39. Hence, we can make only make immediate predictions (say for the next *two* years), applying the Grey-Verhulst model. The Excel formula for the same are shown in Table 6.40 and the prediction results are shown in Table 6.41. We can see from the results of prediction that all of the resilience indicators of performance showed slight, but consistent increase during the predicted periods of 2017 and 2018.

6.5 GREY–MARKOV MODELS

The basic grey prediction model, GM (1, 1) can be used for prediction of small data sequences, subject to a check for the measures of accuracy of prediction. Still, the prediction results can be further improved using various measures; where, one way is to predict the error measures and adjust the prediction models (Liu et al., 2022). Researchers have often used the same prediction model (GM $(1,1)$) for predicting the error (residual) sequences and further adjust the prediction results based on that. This model is called as a residual prediction model of GM $(1,1)$. Further, researchers have incorporated Markov models for error prediction, which can appropriately predict the future state that the residual can fall into, and thereby adjust the prediction results (Zhan-Li and Jin-Hua, 2011; Elgharbi et al., 2020). This incorporated model can be considered as a grey Markov model, which can improve the exactitude of the prediction results, even when limited information or data are available for prediction. The detailed step-wise procedure for implementation is elaborated as follows:

6.5.1 The (GM (1, 1)) Model

The GM $(1,1)$ model is elaborated in the starting of the chapter. The initial prediction of the sequences is done using the GM $(1,1)$ model. Let us assume that the sequence indicating the performance of an attribute or factor for period $1 \le i \le n$, be represented as follows:

$$Z^{(0)} = \left(z^{(0)}(i)\right)_{i=1}^{n}, \tag{6.105}$$

This can be further indicated as the sequence of data as;

$$Z = \left(z(1), z(2), z(3), \ldots, z(n)\right). \tag{6.106}$$

Table 6.36 Excel formula: Construction of simulated sequences

C55 =($C$51*$C3)/(($C$52*$C3)+(($C$51-($C$52*$C3))*EXP($C$51*C$60)))

	A	B	C	D	E	F	G	H	I
54	X(1) (Simulated)		2011	2012	2013	2014	2015	2016	
55		RI 1	230	272.9605334	308.6512688	335.8362347	355.2042199	368.355551	($C$51*$C3)/(($C$52*$C3)+(($C$51-($C$52*$C3))*EXP($C$51*D$60)))
56		RI 2	94	142.1885796	191.7914429	232.7555307	260.8648895	277.7898869	
57		RI 3	265	292.5737694	315.3835184	333.4532331	347.2834051	357.5922985	
58		RI 4	221	246.1564343	270.0748177	292.1617231	312.0142665	329.4302174	
59		RI 5	117	150.7527503	184.4248713	214.7877071	239.7708392	258.8241256	($G$51*$C7)/(($G$52*$C7)+(($G$51-($G$52*$C7))*EXP($G$51*G$60)))
60		k	0	1	2	3	4	5	

Table 6.37 Construction of simulated sequences

	A	B	C	D	E	F	G	H
54	X(1) (Simulated)		2011	2012	2013	2014	2015	2016
55		RI 1	230	272.9605334	308.6512688	335.8362347	355.2042199	368.355551
56		RI 2	94	142.1885796	191.7914429	232.7555307	260.8648895	277.7898869
57		RI 3	265	292.5737694	315.3835184	333.4532331	347.2834051	357.5922985
58		RI 4	221	246.1564343	270.0748177	292.1617231	312.0142665	329.4302174
59		RI 5	117	150.7527503	184.4248713	214.7877071	239.7708392	258.8241256
60		k	0	1	2	3	4	5

Table 6.38 Excel formula: Estimation of residuals

I72 | =AVERAGE(C70:H74)

	A	B	C	D	E	F	G	H	I	J
62	Error		2011	2012	2013	2014	2015	2016		
63		RI 1	0	-38.96053338	16.34873118	19.16376528	3.795780089	-6.355551042	D3-D55	
64		RI 2	0	-44.1885796	0.208557128	-14.7555307	7.135110468	-5.789886912		
65		RI 3	0	-21.57376944	14.6164816	8.546766851	3.716594903	-2.59229851		
66		RI 4	0	-20.15643426	-18.0748177	19.83827691	10.98573351	-2.430217417		
67		RI 5	0	-29.75275031	-25.4248713	11.21229293	8.229160846	-6.824125623	G7-G59	
68										
69	Prediction accuracy		2011	2012	2013	2014	2015	2016	GMA	
70		RI 1	100	83.35019941	94.96962118	94.60175626	98.94267964	98.24432292	(1-(ABS(D63/D3)))*100	
71		RI 2	100	54.90961265	99.8913765	93.23140796	97.33764535	97.87136511		
72		RI 3	100	92.03919947	95.57076315	97.50094537	98.94114105	99.26977507	93.95036005	
73		RI 4	100	91.08122378	92.8274533	93.64157791	96.59884411	99.25681425		
74		RI 5	100	75.41095016	84.0095149	95.03880844	96.68178998	97.29201364	(1-(ABS(G67/G7)))*100	

Table 6.39 The residuals of prediction

	A	B	C	D	E	F	G	H	I
62	Error		2011	2012	2013	2014	2015	2016	
63		RI 1	0	-38.96053338	16.34873118	19.16376528	3.795780089	-6.355551042	
64		RI 2	0	-44.1885796	0.208557128	-14.7555307	7.135110468	-5.789886912	
65		RI 3	0	-21.57376944	14.6164816	8.546766851	3.716594903	-2.59229851	
66		RI 4	0	-20.15643426	-18.0748177	19.83827691	10.98573351	-2.430217417	
67		RI 5	0	-29.75275031	-25.4248713	11.21229293	8.229160846	-6.824125623	
68									
69	Prediction accuracy		2011	2012	2013	2014	2015	2016	GMA
70		RI 1	100	83.35019941	94.96962118	94.60175626	98.94267964	98.24432292	
71		RI 2	100	54.90961265	99.8913765	93.23140796	97.33764535	97.87136511	
72		RI 3	100	92.03919947	95.57076315	97.50094537	98.94114105	99.26977507	93.95036005
73		RI 4	100	91.08122378	92.8274533	93.64157791	96.59884411	99.25681425	
74		RI 5	100	75.41095016	84.0095149	95.03880844	96.68178998	97.29201364	

Table 6.40 Excel formula: Predicted sequences

D81 | =($G$51*$C7)/(($G$52*$C7)+(($G$51-($G$52*$C7))*EXP($G$51*D$82)))

	A	B	C	D	E	F	G	H	I
76	X(1) (Predicted)		2017	2018					
77		RI 1	376.9967663	382.5525367	($C$51*$C3)/(($C$52*$C3)+(($C$51-($C$52*$C3))*EXP($C$51*C$82)))				
78		RI 2	287.1902341	292.1783525	($D$51*$C4)/(($D$52*$C4)+(($D$51-($D$52*$C4))*EXP($D$51*D$82)))				
79		RI 3	365.1258869	370.5520672					
80		RI 4	344.3860003	356.995546					
81		RI 5	272.5302919	281.9808742					
82		k	6	7					

Table 6.41 Predicted sequences for next five years

	A	B	C	D
76	X(1) (Predicted)		2017	2018
77		RI 1	376.9967663	382.5525367
78		RI 2	287.1902341	292.1783525
79		RI 3	365.1258869	370.5520672
80		RI 4	344.3860003	356.995546
81		RI 5	272.5302919	281.9808742
82		k	6	7

Step 1: Transforming data (data weakening)

As mentioned earlier, due to the effect of shock waves, the sequences indicating data can exhibit too fast or too slow developmental tendencies, which may not represent the true developmental patterns of the system. Due to these interferences, the data as such cannot be used in any statistical evaluations for drawing conclusions. Hence, we apply strengthening or weakening sequence operators to moderate the effect of such shock waves.

Suppose that τ is a sequence operator, which is applied on the sequence of data Z as;

$$Z\tau = \left(z(1)\tau,\ z(2)\tau,\ z(3)\tau, \ldots,\ z(n)\tau\right). \tag{6.107}$$

Suppose that Z is a monotonically increasing sequence, then τ can be categorized as a weakening operator if,

$$z(k)\tau \geq z(k);\ k = 1,\ 2,\ 3, \ldots,\ n. \tag{6.108}$$

On the reverse, τ can be considered as a strengthening operator on the monotonically increasing sequence of data Z, if this satisfies the condition:

$$z(k)\tau \leq z(k);\ k = 1,\ 2,\ 3, \ldots,\ n. \tag{6.109}$$

As we mentioned prior, the reverse of Equations 6.108 and 6.109 holds true. As we can see for a monotonically increasing sequence of data, the data can expand by the application of a weakening operator and the same will shrink on the application of a strengthening operator. The reverse holds true for a monotonically decreasing sequence of data. We can further apply the operator τ^2 as follows:

$$Z^{(0)}\tau = \left(z^{(0)}(1)\tau,\ z^{(0)}(2)\tau,\ z^{(0)}(3)\tau, \ldots,\ z^{(0)}(n)\tau\right), \tag{6.110}$$

here
$$z^{(0)}(k)\tau = \frac{1}{n-k+1}\left(z^{(0)}(k) + z^{(0)}(k+1) + z^{(0)}(k+2), \ldots,\ z^{(0)}(n)\right), \tag{6.111}$$

and
$$Z^{(0)}\tau^2 = \left(z^{(0)}(1)\tau^2,\ z^{(0)}(2)\tau^2,\ z^{(0)}(3)\tau^2, \ldots,\ z^{(0)}(n)\tau^2\right), \tag{6.112}$$

here
$$z^{(0)}(k)\tau^2 = \frac{1}{n-k+1}\left(z^{(0)}(k)\tau + z^{(0)}(k+1)\tau + z^{(0)}(k+2)\tau, \ldots,\ z^{(0)}(n)\tau\right). \tag{6.113}$$

We can represent the sequence $\tilde{Z}$ to indicate the sequence after applying the weakening operator of the second order ($Z^{(0)}\tau^2$), as follows:

$$Z^{(0)}\tau^2 = \tilde{Z} = \left(\tilde{z}^{(0)}(1),\ \tilde{z}^{(0)}(2),\ \tilde{z}^{(0)}(3), \ldots,\ \tilde{z}^{(0)}(n)\right). \tag{6.114}$$

Step 2: Transforming the data (Accumulating generator)

The first accumulating generator operator (1-AGO) can be applied on the sequence $\tilde{Z}$ as follows:

$$\tilde{Z}^{(1)} = \left(\tilde{z}^{(1)}(1),\ \tilde{z}^{(1)}(2),\ \tilde{z}^{(1)}(3), \ldots,\ \tilde{z}^{(1)}(n)\right), \tag{6.115}$$

here
$$\tilde{z}^{(1)}(k) = \sum_{i=1}^{k} \tilde{z}^{(0)}(i);\ k = 1,\ 2,\ 3, \ldots,\ n, \tag{6.116}$$

The cumulative sum till k^{th} value can be indicated by $\tilde{z}^{(1)}(k)$.

Step 3: Transforming the data (Mean generator operator)

Further to this, we construct the mean generator sequences $\dot{Z}^{(1)}$, which uses the adjacent neighborhood values of $\tilde{Z}^{(1)}$ and this can be indicated as follows:

$$\dot{Z}^{(1)} = \left(\dot{z}^{(1)}(1), \dot{z}^{(1)}(2), z^{(1)}(3), \ldots, \dot{z}^{(1)}(n)\right), \tag{6.117}$$

here $$\dot{z}^{(1)}(1) = \left(\left(0.5 \times \tilde{z}^{(1)}(k)\right) + \left(0.5 \times \tilde{z}^{(1)}(k-1)\right)\right); k = 2, 3, 4, \ldots, n. \tag{6.118}$$

Step 4: Simulate the sequence of indicators

We can employ the basic grey prediction model (GM (1, 1)) for simulating the sequences the corresponding matrices of Υ and B can be constructed as follows:

$$\Upsilon = \begin{bmatrix} \tilde{z}^{(0)}(2) \\ \tilde{z}^{(0)}(3) \\ z^{(0)}(4) \\ \vdots \\ \tilde{z}^{(0)}(n) \end{bmatrix}; \; B = \begin{bmatrix} -\dot{z}^{(1)}(2) & 1 \\ -\dot{z}^{(1)}(3) & 1 \\ -z^{(1)}(4) & 1 \\ \vdots & \vdots \\ -\dot{z}^{(1)}(n) & 1 \end{bmatrix}. \tag{6.119}$$

For prediction, we can employ the equation,

$$\frac{d\tilde{z}^{(1)}}{dt} + a\tilde{z}^{(1)} = b. \tag{6.120}$$

Here, a, b indicate the prediction parameters and can be further represented as follows:

$$\hat{a} = [a, b]^T, \tag{6.121}$$

where $\hat{a}$ represents the column vector of prediction parameters obtained as follows:

$$\hat{a} = ([B^T B]^{-1} B^T \Upsilon). \tag{6.122}$$

Further, expansion of Equation 6.122 can be shown as follows:

$$\hat{a} = \begin{bmatrix} \left(\dfrac{\left(\left(\dfrac{1}{n-1}\left(\sum_{k=2}^{n} \tilde{z}^{(0)}(k) \times \sum_{k=2}^{n} \dot{z}^{(1)}(k)\right)\right) - \left(\sum_{k=2}^{n}\left(\tilde{z}^{(0)}(k) \times \dot{z}^{(1)}(k)\right)\right)\right)}{\left(\sum_{k=2}^{n}\left[\dot{z}^{(1)}(k)\right]^2 - \dfrac{1}{n-1}\left[\sum_{k=2}^{n} \dot{z}^{(1)}(k)\right]^2\right)} \right) \\ \left(\dfrac{1}{n-1}\left(\sum_{k=2}^{n} \tilde{z}^{(0)}(k) + a\sum_{k=2}^{n} \dot{z}^{(1)}(k)\right)\right) \end{bmatrix}. \tag{6.123}$$

The time response sequences can be further constructed for the grey prediction (GM (1, 1)) model using the obtained parameters a, b as follows:

$$\hat{z}^{(1)}(k+1) = \left(\left[\tilde{z}^{(0)}(1) - \left(\frac{b}{a}\right)\right] e^{-ak} + \left(\frac{b}{a}\right)\right); k = 0, 1, 2, 3\ldots, n-1, \tag{6.124}$$

and $$\hat{z}^{(0)}(k+1)=\hat{z}^{(1)}(k+1)-\hat{z}^{(1)}(k). \tag{6.125}$$

Considering Equations 6.124 and 6.125, the sequence of indicators can be simulated and can be indicated as follows:

$$\hat{Z}=\left(\hat{z}^{(0)}(k)\right)_{k=1}^{n}. \tag{6.126}$$

Step 5: Error estimates

The residuals (errors) are estimated to observe the accuracy of predictions. As mentioned prior, we propose to ensure for a level one prediction, where the sequence of errors being:

$$\varepsilon^{(0)}=\left(\varepsilon^{(0)}(k)\right)_{k=1}^{n}, \tag{6.127}$$

here $$\varepsilon^{(0)}(k)=\left(\tilde{z}^{(0)}(k)-\hat{z}^{(0)}(k)\right), \tag{6.128}$$

and the relative errors can be calculated as;

$$\Delta=\left(\delta_k\right)_{k=1}^{n}, \tag{6.129}$$

here $$\delta_k=\frac{\left|\varepsilon^{(0)}(k)\right|}{\tilde{z}^{(0)}(k)}, \tag{6.130}$$

where the mean relative errors being;

$$\bar{\Delta}-\frac{1}{n}\left(\sum_{i=1}^{n}\delta_i\right), \tag{6.131}$$

and we can further calculate the filtering errors as follows:

$$\varnothing=\delta_n. \tag{6.132}$$

Though the estimates of error, we ensure for a level one prediction, as mentioned prior.

6.5.2 Grey-based Markov Model

Suppose that $\{Y_n : n \in T\}$ is indicating a stochastic process; here, considering any integer $n \in T$ and the states, $s_0, s_1,\ldots, s_n \in$ I, then $\{Y_n : n \in T\}$ can be regarded as a Markov chain, if the following is satisfied.

$$P\left(Y_{n+1}=s_{n+1}\middle|Y_j=s_i;i,j=0,1,\ldots,n\right)=P\left(Y_{n+1}=s_{n+1}\middle|Y_n=s_n\right). \tag{6.133}$$

Considering Equation 6.133, the future state at a point of time $t = n + 1$ is independent of the past states and is dependent only on the current state, $t = n$; Hence, the future state is independent of the states $t \leq n - 1$. Consider the following equation:

$$P_{ij}(n)=P(Y_{n+1}=j|Y_n=i), \tag{6.134}$$

If it is true for any random state $\in T$ and $i, j \in I$, then, we can represent the moving probability of the Markov chain as $P_{ij}(n)$. Suppose that the moving probability $P_{ij}(n)$ has no relation to n, then we can refer $\{Y_n : n \in T\}$ as a homogenous Markov chain. Considering the case of a homogenous Markov chain, we can represent the moving probability matrix as follows:

$$P=\left[p_{ij}\right]=\begin{bmatrix} p_{11} & p_{12} & \cdots & p_{1n} & \cdots \\ p_{21} & p_{22} & \cdots & p_{2n} & \cdots \\ \cdots & \cdots & \cdots & \cdots & \cdots \end{bmatrix}. \tag{6.135}$$

Suppose that the elements considering a moving probability matrix may fulfill the following conditions;

$$p_{ij}\geq 0,\ i,j\in I;\ \text{and}\ \sum_{j\in I}p_{ij}=1,\ \text{for all i} \in I,$$

which indicates that the row sum of the elements of P is always 1. Further, we can calculate the nth step moving probability considering the Markov chain as follows:

$$P_{ij}^{(n)}=P\left(Y_{m+n}=j\middle|Y_m=i\right),i,j\in I,n\geq 1 \tag{6.136}$$

Hence, the nth step moving probability matrix can be represented as, $P^{(n)}=\left[p_{ij}^{(n)}\right]$, which satisfies the conditions; $p_{ij}^{(n)}\geq 0,i,j\in I$; $\sum_{j\in I}p_{ij}^{(n)}=1$, for all $i \in I$; and $P^{(n)} = P_n$. Suppose that we further assume that the moving probability matrix of Markov chain is consisting of grey values; then, the Markov chain is referred to as a Grey–Markov chain. Consider an initial state distribution for a finite Grey–Markov chain as follows:

$$P^T(0)=\left(p_1,p_2,\ldots,p_n\right), \tag{6.137}$$

Further, the moving probability matrix for the same can be indicated as follows:

$$P(\otimes)=\left[P_{ij}(\otimes)\right]. \tag{6.138}$$

The next state distribution of the system can be further indicated as follows:

$$P^T(1)=P^T(0)\times P(\otimes), \tag{6.139}$$

Hence, the second state distribution can be indicated as below:

$$P^T(2)=P^T(0)\times P^2(\otimes). \tag{6.140}$$

Continuing the same for the nth state, the system distribution can be characterized as follows:

$$P^T(n)=P^T(0)\times P^n(\otimes). \tag{6.141}$$

Thus, we can predict the next and the future state distributions of the system by knowing the initial distribution and the moving probability matrix.

6.5.3 Grey State Markov Model

Suppose that the raw data sequences are indicated as $Z=(z(1), z(2), \ldots, z(n))$ and the simulated data sequences using the GM (1, 1) model be indicated as $\hat{Z}=(\hat{z}(1), \hat{z}(2), \ldots, \hat{z}(n))$. Further to this, we assume that $\hat{Z}$ is showing the same trend as that of the original sequence Z. We assume that Z is an instable stochastic sequence and the same satisfies the requirements of a Markov chain, where we can construct n states for consideration, which can be represented as follows:

$$\otimes_i = \left[\widetilde{\otimes}_{1i}, \widetilde{\otimes}_{2i}\right], \widetilde{\otimes}_i \in_i ,$$

and
$$\widetilde{\otimes}_{1i} = \hat{z}(k) + A_i; \widetilde{\otimes}_{2i} = \hat{z}(k) + B_i, i = 1, 2, \ldots, n. \quad (6.142)$$

The state moving probability of the data sample having size $M_{ij}(m)$, which is representing the development of a system state from $\otimes_i$ to $\otimes_j$ over m steps. The size of the data sample remaining at state $\otimes_i$ can be considered as M_i, where the state moving probability can be further indicated as follows:

$$P_{ij}(m) = \frac{M_{ij}(m)}{M_i}, i = 1, 2, \ldots, n \quad (6.143)$$

This is the indication of the one-step moving probability matrix represented by P and we can assume that the forecasted value be lying in the state $\otimes_k$. Then, we can verify whether the kth row of P can satisfy the condition as follows:

$$\max_j p_{kj} = p_{kl}. \quad (6.144)$$

If this condition is fulfilled, then the system can develop from state $\otimes_k$ to $\otimes_l$. Further, if the probability measures in the kth row of the matrix P are equal, we can calculate the nth step moving probability matrices, which are indicated as, $P^{(2)}$, $P^{(3)}$, and $P^{(n)}$.

6.5.4 Sample Case Problem (Grey–Markov Model)

Grey–Markov model are also applied to many problems in literature considering business and social sciences area (Rajesh et al., 2021; Rajesh, 2023a). We have used a case problem of the resilience prediction of a retail town center, YYZ. The level of resilience are measured using *five* indicators, over a period of ten years from 2010 to 2019. These indicators are *vacancy rates, retail turnover, tenant structure, slow burns,* and *economic crises*. The details of the indicators are not elaborated here, rather we use the combined score for retail resilience of the case town center, which are measured based on the performance of the town center on the five indicative measures as mentioned above. The combined score for resilience over a period of 10 years is shown in Table 6.42. As the data series corresponds to a period of ten years only, a prediction model for small data can be suitably used. Here, we use the basic grey prediction model (GM (1, 1) model) followed by a moving probability Markov-based error correction model (Abhinav and Rajesh, 2025).

Step 1: Firstly, we apply the data weakening operators of the first order and of the second order for transforming the data sequences and thereafter we apply the first accumulating generator operator and the mean generator operator on the transformed data sequences. This makes so as to enable the data for a prediction. The Excel calculations for the same are also shown in Table 6.42. The resulting values are indicated in Table 6.43.

Step 2: Further, using the method of least squares, prediction parameters a, b are obtained and the sequences are simulated. Also, prediction for the very next year is made. The Excel calculations for the same are shown in Table 6.44 and the values are shown in Table 6.45.

Table 6.42 Excel formula: The transformational sequences of retail resilience

J6 =ROUND((I5+J5)/2,3)

	A	B	C	D	E	F	G	H	I	J	K	L
1	Year	2010	2011	2012	2013	2014	2015	2016	2017	2018	2019	
2	Resilience	7.5	51.25	58.75	88	168.75	156.75	169	182.25	222	244	
3	XD	134.825	148.972	161.188	175.821	190.458	194.8	204.313	216.083	233	244	ROUND(((1/(10-1+1))*(SUM(B2:$K$2))),3)
4	XD2	190.346	196.515	202.458	208.354	213.776	218.439	224.349	231.028	238.5	244	ROUND(((1/(10-1+1))*(SUM(B3:$K$3))),3)
5	1 AGO	190.346	386.861	589.319	797.673	1011.449	1229.888	1454.237	1685.265	1923.765	2167.765	ROUND(SUM($B$4:C4),3)
6	Mean GS		288.604	488.09	693.496	904.561	1120.669	1342.063	1569.751	1804.515	2045.765	ROUND((B5+C5)/2,3)

Table 6.43 The transformational sequences of retail resilience

	A	B	C	D	E	F	G	H	I	J	K
1	Year	2010	2011	2012	2013	2014	2015	2016	2017	2018	2019
2	Resilience	7.5	51.25	58.75	88	168.75	156.75	169	182.25	222	244
3	XD	134.825	148.972	161.188	175.821	190.458	194.8	204.313	216.083	233	244
4	XD2	190.346	196.515	202.458	208.354	213.776	218.439	224.349	231.028	238.5	244
5	1 AGO	190.346	386.861	589.319	797.673	1011.449	1229.888	1454.237	1685.265	1923.765	2167.765
6	Mean GS		288.604	488.09	693.496	904.561	1120.669	1342.063	1569.751	1804.515	2045.765

Table 6.44 Excel formula: Prediction parameter estimates

I20 | {=ROUND((($A$9-($F$23/$F$22))*EXP(-$F$22*B19))+($F$23/$F$22),3)}

	A	B	C	D	E	F	G	H	I	J	K	L	M
8	Y	k											
9	190.346	0	Mean GS	B		BTB		Year	Pred. AGO	Pred. Act.	Error	Er. State	
10	196.515	1	288.604	-288.604	1	14583270.55	-10257.514	2010	190.346	190.346	0	2	MMULT(TRANSPOSE(D10:E18),D10:E18)
11	202.458	2	488.09	-488.09	1	-10257.514	9	2011	387.166	196.82	-0.305	2	ROUND((($A$9-($F$23/$F$22))*EXP(-$F$22*B10))+($F$23/$F$22),
12	208.354	3	693.496	-693.496	1			2012	589.35	202.184	0.274	3	I12-I11
13	213.776	4	904.561	-904.561	1	BTB inv		2013	797.045	207.695	0.659	4	ROUND(A12-J13,3)
14	218.439	5	1120.669	-1120.67	1	3.45717E-07	0.000394022	2014	1010.399	213.354	0.422	3	MINVERSE(F10:G11)
15	224.349	6	1342.063	-1342.06	1	0.000394022	0.56018743	2015	1229.569	219.17	-0.731	1	
16	231.028	7	1569.751	-1569.75	1			2016	1454.711	225.142	-0.793	1	
17	238.5	8	1804.515	-1804.52	1	BTY		2017	1685.989	231.278	-0.25	2	
18	244	9	2045.765	-2045.77	1	-2331487.07		2018	1923.57	237.581	0.919	4	MMULT(TRANSPOSE(D10:E18),A10:A18)
19		10				1977.419		2019	2167.626	244.056	-0.056	2	
20	B4		C6	-C10				2020	2418.334	250.708			
21						Inv BTB * BTY			Er. State	Er. Interval	Er. Correction		
22						-0.02688836			1	> -.99 to -.5	-0.75		MMULT(F14:G15,F18:F19)
23						189.0679139			2	> -.5 to 0	-0.25		
24									3	> 0 to .5	0.25		
25									4	> .5 to .99	0.75		

Table 6.45 Prediction parameter estimates

	A	B	C	D	E	F	G	H	I	J	K	L
8	**Y**	**k**										
9	190.346	0	**Mean GS**	**B**		**BTB**		**Year**	**Pred. AGO**	**Pred. Act.**	**Error**	**Er. State**
10	196.515	1	288.604	-288.604	1	14583270.55	-10257.514	2010	190.346	190.346	0	2
11	202.458	2	488.09	-488.09	1	-10257.514	9	2011	387.166	196.82	-0.305	2
12	208.354	3	693.496	-693.496	1			2012	589.35	202.184	0.274	3
13	213.776	4	904.561	-904.561	1	**BTB inv**		2013	797.045	207.695	0.659	4
14	218.439	5	1120.669	-1120.67	1	3.45717E-07	0.000394022	2014	1010.399	213.354	0.422	3
15	224.349	6	1342.063	-1342.06	1	0.000394022	0.56018743	2015	1229.569	219.17	-0.731	1
16	231.028	7	1569.751	-1569.75	1			2016	1454.711	225.142	-0.793	1
17	238.5	8	1804.515	-1804.52	1	**BTY**		2017	1685.989	231.278	-0.25	2
18	244	9	2045.765	-2045.77	1	-2331487.07		2018	1923.57	237.581	0.919	4
19		10				1977.419		2019	2167.626	244.056	-0.056	2
20								2020	2418.334	250.708		
21						**Inv BTB * BTY**			**Er. State**	**Er. Interval**	**Er. Correction**	
22						-0.02688836			1	> -.99 to -.5	-0.75	
23						189.0679139			2	> -.5 to 0	-0.25	
24									3	>0 to .5	0.25	
25									4	> .5 to .99	0.75	

Step 3: The error sequences are calculated based on the differences of the predicted values from the actual. The measures of relative error, mean relative error, and filtering error are observed to be in the permissible limits, considering a Level 1 prediction. The calculations are similar to that in Section 6.2. The basic error sequences are used further and the same are shown in Table 6.44 and 6.45.

Step 4: The prediction accuracy can be improved by predicting the error state and thereby adjusting the prediction results. Here, we use a moving probability-based Markov model for error prediction. From the calculation of the residual sequences, we observe that the error sequences vary from –0.99 to –0.99. This error interval is made to *four* nearly even intervals, which constitute the error states (1–4). These error states vary from State 1 (–0.99, –0.5), State 2 (–0.5, 0.0), State 3 (0.0, 0.5), and State 4 (0.5. 0.99). The error states are also indicated in Tables 6.44 and 6.45. Further, we calculate the state moving probabilities, P_1, P_2, P_3, and P_4, which are constructed from the Table 6.45. Here P_1 indicates the one-step moving probability matrix, P_2 represents the two-step moving probability matrix, and so on. The one-step probability indicates the probability of moving from one state to other in one-step interval.

Considering an example for the error states considered during the period, 2016, 2017, 2018, 2019 are State 1, State 2, State 4, and State 2. This can be inferred from Table 6.45. Here, we find the one-step moving probability for moving from 2016 to 2017 and from 2017 to 2018, as the probabilities for moving from State 1 to State 2 and from State 2 to State 4, respectively. Two-step moving probability is the probability of moving from one state to another in two step intervals. Consider the calculations assuming the loop to be circular. The transition probabilities can be manually calculated and the same are indicated in Tables 6.46 and 6.47. We only consider a recent four-year period (2016–2019) for the prediction of errors for the period 2020. The present state of error is assumed to be in either of the four states (State1 – State 4). The probabilities are also indicated in Tables 6.46 and 6.47.

We can calculate the future state of the error by multiplying the transpose of each state moving probability matrices with the present state probabilities. The Excel calculations for the same are shown in Table 6.46 and the values are shown in Table 6.47. The values for one-step, two-step, three-step, and four-step moving probabilities are separately calculated and the Markov probabilities for remaining in each states are calculated and are shown in Table 6.46, where the values are shown in Table 6.47. The cumulative sum of probabilities is also calculated and the same are also shown in Tables 6.46 and 6.47. Form the calculations, we can see that the future state of error can be assumed to be in State 2, where the error interval assumed is 0.5 and 0, and the mean error can be taken as –0.25. Thus, the final prediction results can be adjusted with the estimated error. For clarity of understanding, the calculation of moving probabilities are shown in Figures 6.1–6.4. Thus, for 2020, the retail resilience measure is 250.708 – 0.25 = 250.458.

Table 6.46 Excel formula: Grey moving probability Markov based error prediction

H37 | {=MMULT(TRANSPOSE(B34:E37),G34:G37)}

	A	B	C	D	E	F	G	H	I	J	K	L	M	N	O	P
27	P1	1	2	3	4	States	Probability	Cum. Prob.	Er. states	Sum of prob.	Error for prediction					
28	1	0.5	0.5	0	0	1	0.25	0.125	State 1	0.5			H28+H34+H40+H46			
29	2	0	0.5	0.25	0.25	2	0.5	0.5	State2	1.875	State 2 (>0.5 to 0)		H29+H35+H41+H47			
30	3	0.5	0	0	0.5	4	0	0.25	State3	0.875			H30+H36+H42+H48			
31	4	0	0.5	0.5	0	2	0.25	0.125	State4	0.75			H31+H37+H43+H49			
32																
33	P2	1	2	3	4	States	Probability	Cum. Prob.	Er. states							
34	1	0	0.5	0	0.5	1	0.25	0.125	State 1				MMULT(TRANSPOSE(B34:E37),G34:G37)			
35	2	0	0.5	0.25	0.25	2	0.5	0.5	State2							
36	3	0.5	0	0.5	0	4	0	0.125	State3							
37	4	0.5	0.5	0	0	2	0.25	0.25	State4							
38																
39	P3	1	2	3	4	States	Probability	Cum. Prob.	Er. states							
40	1	0	0.5	0	0.5	1	0.25	0.125	State 1				MMULT(TRANSPOSE(B40:E43),G40:G43)			
41	2	0	0.25	0.5	0.25	2	0.5	0.375	State2							
42	3	0.5	0.5	0	0	4	0	0.25	State3							
43	4	0.5	0.5	0	0	2	0.25	0.25	State4							
44																
45	P4	1	2	3	4	States	Probability	Cum. Prob.	Er. states							
46	1	0	1	0	0	1	0.25	0.125	State 1				MMULT(TRANSPOSE(B46:E49),G46:G49)			
47	2	0.25	0.25	0.25	0.25	2	0.5	0.5	State2							
48	3	0.5	0	0	0.5	4	0	0.25	State3							
49	4	0	0.5	0.5	0	2	0.25	0.125	State4							

Table 6.47 Grey moving probability Markov based error prediction

	A	B	C	D	E	F	G	H	I	J	K	L
27	**P1**	1	2	3	4	**States**	**Probability**	**Cum. Prob**	**Er. states**	**Sum of prob.**	**Error for prediction**	
28	1	0.5	0.5	0	0	1	0.25	0.125	**State 1**	0.5		
29	2	0	0.5	0.25	0.25	2	0.5	0.5	**State2**	1.875	**State 2 (>0.5 to 0)**	
30	3	0.5	0	0	0.5	4	0	0.25	**State3**	0.875		
31	4	0	0.5	0.5	0	2	0.25	0.125	**State4**	0.75		
32												
33	**P2**	1	2	3	4	**States**	**Probability**	**Cum. Prob**	**Er. states**			
34	1	0	0.5	0	0.5	1	0.25	0.125	**State 1**			
35	2	0	0.5	0.25	0.25	2	0.5	0.5	**State2**			
36	3	0.5	0	0.5	0	4	0	0.125	**State3**			
37	4	0.5	0.5	0	0	2	0.25	0.25	**State4**			
38												
39	**P3**	1	2	3	4	**States**	**Probability**	**Cum. Prob**	**Er. states**			
40	1	0	0.5	0	0.5	1	0.25	0.125	**State 1**			
41	2	0	0.25	0.5	0.25	2	0.5	0.375	**State2**			
42	3	0.5	0.5	0	0	4	0	0.25	**State3**			
43	4	0.5	0.5	0	0	2	0.25	0.25	**State4**			
44												
45	**P4**	1	2	3	4	**States**	**Probability**	**Cum. Prob**	**Er. states**			
46	1	0	1	0	0	1	0.25	0.125	**State 1**			
47	2	0.25	0.25	0.25	0.25	2	0.5	0.5	**State2**			
48	3	0.5	0	0	0.5	4	0	0.25	**State3**			
49	4	0	0.5	0.5	0	2	0.25	0.125	**State4**			

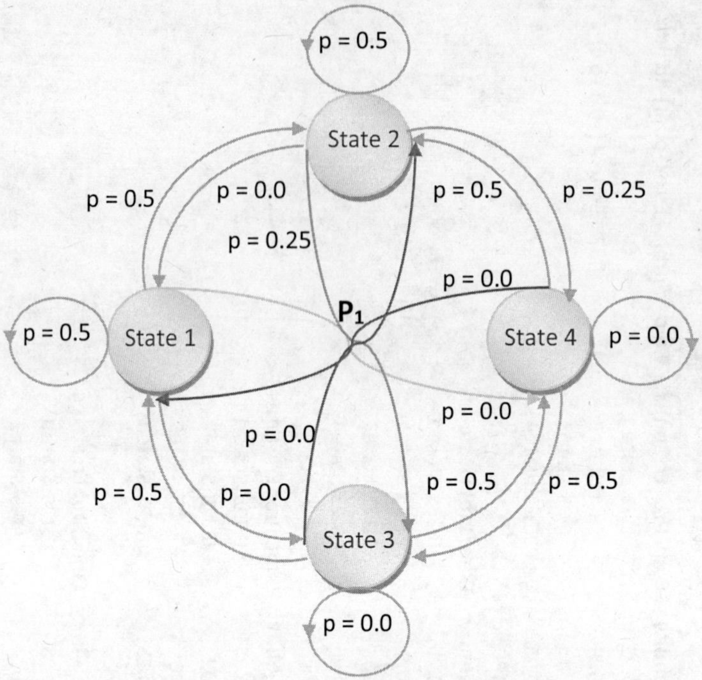

Figure 6.1 One-step moving probabilities for error prediction.

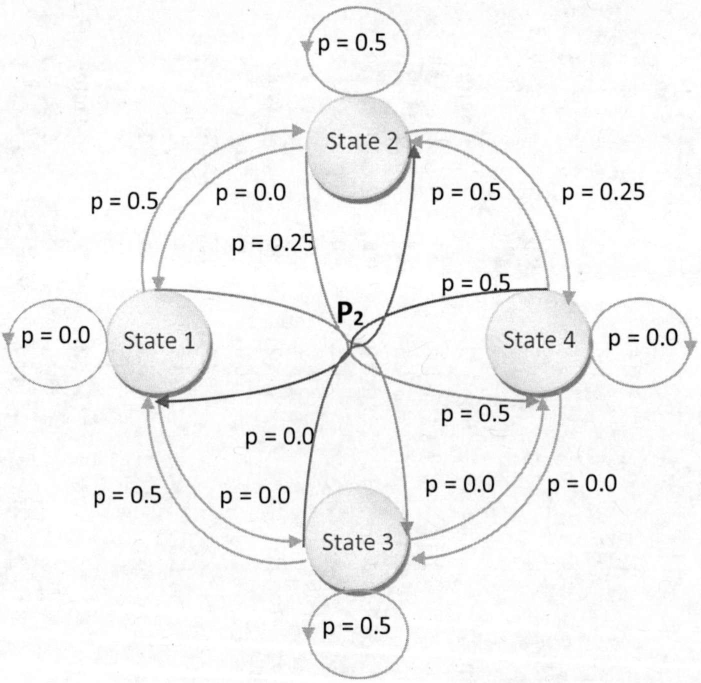

Figure 6.2 Two-step moving probabilities for error prediction.

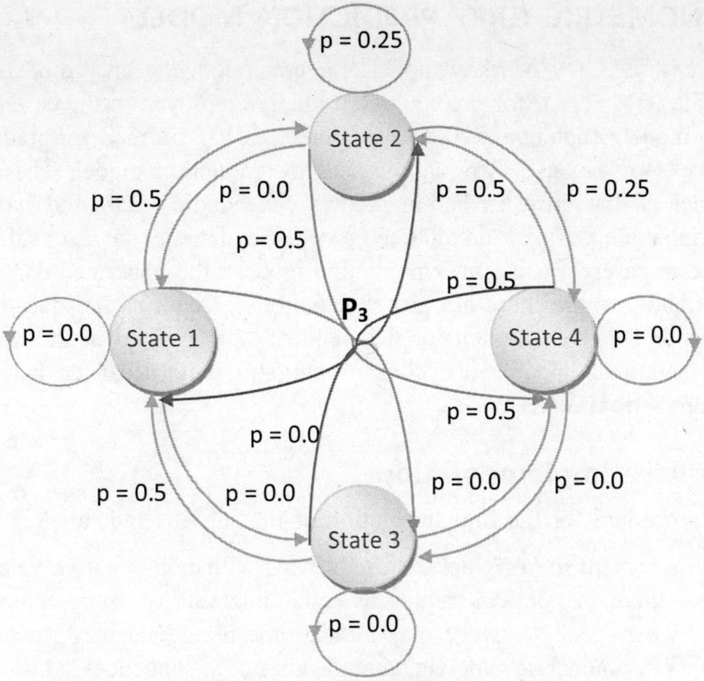

Figure 6.3 Three step moving probabilities for error prediction.

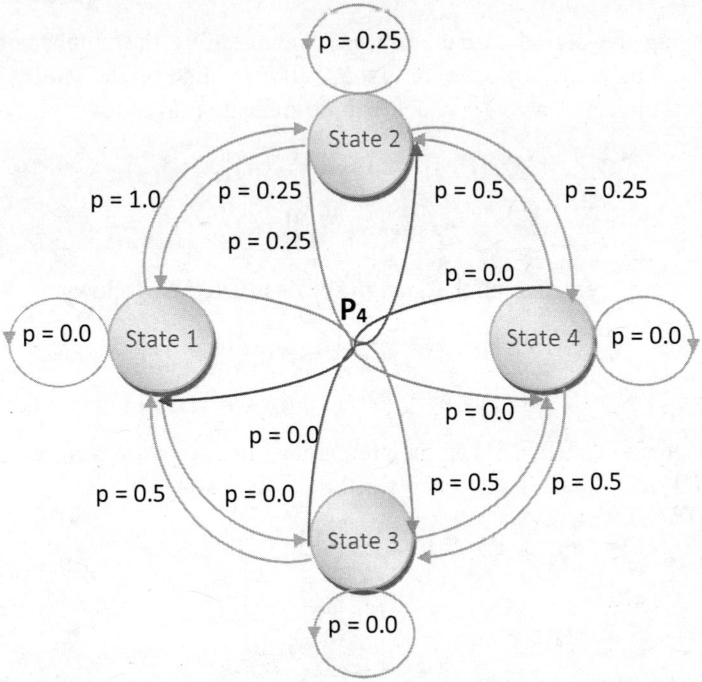

Figure 6.4 Four-step moving probabilities for error prediction.

6.6. TRIGONOMETRIC GREY PREDICTION MODEL

Similar to the case of Grey–Markov models for prediction, the grey model of the first order with one variable (GM (1, 1)) for prediction is initially employed in the case of a trigonometric grey prediction model (Zhou et al., 2006; Wang et al., 2019). Further, for predicting the residual (error) sequences, we can use a trigonometric grey prediction model. The advantage of this prediction model is that grey prediction models can handle small and incomplete datasets, whereas the trigonometric grey prediction models can handle the cyclical variations in the data. As we see in cases of using grey prediction models, the generated data shows increasing or decreasing trends, where there are also fluctuations in data as the data is often measured for a small period. This can account for the frequent sign reversal of the residuals, making it follow a combination of linear and cyclical trend. This pattern can be better captured using trigonometric prediction models.

6.6.1 Step-wise Implementation

The step-wise procedure for the implementation of the same is indicated as follows:

Step 1: We can represent the original data sequences with non-negative values and measured over n periods, where the periods represent equal intervals of time. Suppose, there are m such sequences, where each sequence may indicate the periodical performance of a particular attribute or simply periodical developmental tendencies of m sequences. This can be represented as below:

$$X_i^{(0)} = \left\{x_i^{(0)}(1), x_i^{(0)}(2), \ldots, x_i^{(0)}(n)\right\},\ i = 1, 2, \ldots, m; \tag{6.145}$$

here n is indicating the period of data and m is representing the number of such sequences. The first accumulating generator operator (1st AGO) is applied on the sequences, the sequences obtained after are indicated as $X_i^{(1)}$, which can be indicated as follows:

$$X_i^{(1)} = \left\{x_i^{(1)}(1), x_i^{(1)}(2), \ldots, x_i^{(1)}(n)\right\}, i = 1, 2, \ldots, m, \tag{6.146}$$

here

$$x_i^{(1)}(k) = \sum_{i=1}^{k} x_i^{(1)}(k) \tag{6.147}$$

Step 2: Further, the grey differential equation is constructed as follows:

$$x_i^{(0)}(k) + a_i z_i^{(1)}(k) = u_i;\ i = 1, 2, \ldots, m;\ k = 2, 3\ldots, n, \tag{6.148}$$

here

$$z_i^{(1)}(k) = 0.5 \times x_i^{(1)}(k) + 0.5 \times x_i^{(1)}(k-1) \tag{6.149}$$

Step 3: The developing coefficient and the grey input value a_i and u_i, respectively are calculated using the method of ordinary least-squares (OLS) as follows:

$$[a_i, u_i]^T = \left(U_i^T U_i\right)^{-1} \times U_i^T X_i^n, \tag{6.150}$$

here

$$U_i = \begin{bmatrix} -z_i^{(1)}(2) & 1 \\ -z_i^{(1)}(3) & 1 \\ \vdots & \vdots \\ -z_i^{(1)}(n) & 1 \end{bmatrix}, \tag{6.151}$$

and $$X_i^n = \left[x_i^{(0)}(2), x_i^{(0)}(3), \ldots, x_i^{(0)}(n)\right]^T. \tag{6.152}$$

Step 4: The whitenized differential equation of the first order for prediction can be obtained as follows:

$$\frac{dx_i^{(1)}}{dt} + a_i x_i^{(1)} = u_i, \tag{6.153}$$

and $$x_i^{(1)}(1) = x_i^{(0)}(1) \forall i = 1, 2, \ldots, m. \tag{6.154}$$

Step 5: The differential equation as in Equation 6.153 can be solved and the predicted sequence of first accumulating generator operator (1-AGO) sequences can be constructed, which is indicated below:

$$\hat{x}_i^{(1)}(k) = \left[x_i^{(0)}(1) - \frac{u_i}{a_i}\right] e^{-a_i(k-1)} + \frac{u_i}{a_i};\ k = 0, 1, 2, \ldots, n, n+1..;\ i = 1, 2, \ldots, m. \tag{6.155}$$

Further, the inverse accumulating generator operator (IAGO) can be applied on sequences shown in Equation 6.155 and the simulated data sequence can be constructed. Also, the future state predictions can be made based on the following equations;

$$\hat{x}_i^{(0)}(1) = x_i^{(0)}(1), \tag{6.156}$$

and $$\hat{x}_i^{(0)}(k) = \left(1 - e^{a_i}\right)\left[x_i^{(0)}(1) - \frac{u_i}{a_i}\right] e^{-a_i(k-1)};\ k = 0, 1, 2, \ldots, n, n+1..;\ i = 1, 2, \ldots, m. \tag{6.157}$$

Step 6: Following this, the residual sequences are constructed for the GM (1,1) model as follows:

$$r_i^{(0)} = \left\{r_i^{(0)}(2), r_i^{(0)}(3), \ldots, r_i^{(0)}(n)\right\},\ i = 1, 2, \ldots, m, \tag{6.158}$$

here $$r_i^{(0)}(k) = x_i^{(0)}k - \hat{x}_i^{(0)}(k);\ k = 2, \ldots, n;\ i = 1, 2, \ldots, m. \tag{6.159}$$

Step 7: We can use a generalized trigonometric model for representing the residual series as indicated below:

$$r_i^{(0)}(k+1) = b_{0i} + b_{1i}k + b_{2i}\sin\frac{2\pi k}{L} + b_{3i}\cos\frac{2\pi k}{L} + \varepsilon_{ki};\ k = 0, 1, 2\ldots;\ i = 1, 2, \ldots, m. \tag{6.160}$$

The parameter L is user defined, which can change based on the cyclical variations and ε_{ki} is indicating the random error component. Consider for a particular study, the period (k) is 10 years and L is fixed as 8.

Step 8: We use the method of ordinary least squares (OLS) for obtaining the trigonometric residual prediction coefficients, which is indicated as follows:

$$[b_{0i}, b_{1i}, b_{2i}, b_{3i}]^T = \left(B_i^T B_i\right)^{-1} \times B_i^T R_i^n \ \forall i, \tag{6.161}$$

here
$$B_i = \begin{bmatrix} 1 & 1 & \sin\frac{2\pi}{L} & \cos\frac{2\pi}{L} \\ 1 & 2 & \sin\frac{4\pi}{L} & \cos\frac{4\pi}{L} \\ \vdots & \vdots & \vdots & \vdots \\ 1 & n-1 & \sin\frac{2(n-1)\pi}{L} & \cos\frac{2(n-1)\pi}{L} \end{bmatrix} \forall i , \quad (6.162)$$

and
$$R_i^n = \left[r_i^{(0)}(2), r_i^{(0)}(3), \ldots, r_i^{(0)}(n)\right]^T ;\ i = 1, 2, \ldots, m . \quad (6.163)$$

Step 9: The residual sequences can be constructed based on the trigonometric grey prediction model as follows:

$$\hat{r}_i^{(0)}(k+1) = b_{0i} + b_{1i}k + b_{2i}\sin\frac{2\pi k}{L} + b_{3i}\cos\frac{2\pi k}{L};\ k = 0, 1, 2\ldots;\ i = 1, 2, \ldots, m . \quad (6.164)$$

The trigonometric terms and the constant terms as in Equation 6.160 can be considered similar to that of a Fourier residual model, where $L = n - 1$ and the term $b_{1i}k$ is considered as a linear trend for other terms in the Fourier residual model, which can reduce the occupied degree of freedom.

Step 10: Equation 6.164 can be used to construct the trigonometric residual prediction model and further the future state predictions can be made. The predicted sequences can be represented as follows:

$$\hat{x}_{i(tr)}^{(0)}(1) = x_i^{(0)}(1) , \quad (6.165)$$

and
$$\hat{x}_{i(tr)}^{(0)}(k) = \hat{x}_i^{(0)}(k) + \hat{r}_i^{(0)}(k);\ k = 0, 1, 2\ldots;\ i = 1, 2, \ldots, m , \quad (6.166)$$

here $\hat{x}_{i(tr)}^{(0)}(k)$ is indicating the predicted value using the trigonometric grey prediction model, whereas $\hat{x}_i^{(0)}(k)$ is representing the output from the GM (1, 1) model. Considering the degree of freedom, the GM (1, 1) model has two parameters and the residual prediction model has *four* parameters, making an overall degree of freedom as equal to *six*.

6.6.2 Sample Case Problem (Trigonometric Grey Prediction Model)

Let us consider the problem of considering the resilience performances of *three* Indian manufacturing firms, measured for a period of *nine* years (2010–2018), considering the reported information form the secondary data (Rajesh, 2023b). Several performance indicators were considered to generate a composite evaluation score for resilience. These scores reflect their performances considering the indicators *flexibility, responsiveness, quality, productivity*, and *accessibility*. We aim to predict the resilience performances of these firms for the successive periods and generate some insights. Knowing and predicting the level of resilience can enhance firms to adjust their strategies to suitably enhance the resilience capabilities. The firm names are not provided due to privacy concerns and are indicated as *Firm 1, Firm 2,* and *Firm 3*. The initial sequences indicating the composite resilience scores are shown in Table 6.48. The step-wise procedure for the implementation of the trigonometric grey prediction model is elaborated as follows:

Step 1: Firstly, the 1st AGO sequences of the data are constructed following Equations 6.146 and 6.147 and the Excel calculations for the generating sequences are also shown in Table 6.48. The final values are shown in Table 6.49.

Step 2: Further, the grey differential equation is developed and the mean generating sequences are built based on Equations 6.148 and 6.149. The Excel calculations for the mean generating sequences are also shown in Table 6.48 and the final values are indicated in Table 6.49. The construction of the matrix *U* is also indicated in Tables 6.48 and 6.49.

Table 6.48 Excel formula: Periodical resilience scores and the conversion sequences

E30 =0.5*D29+0.5*D30

	A	B	C	D	E	F	G	H	I
1		Year	Resilience score	x(1)k	z(1)k	k	U		
2	Firm 1	2010	48	48		1			
3		2011	47	95	71.5	2	-71.5	1	SUM($C$2:C3)
4		2012	52	147	121	3	-121	1	0.5*D3+0.5*D4
5		2013	55	202	174.5	4	-174.5	1	-E5
6		2014	58	260	231	5	-231	1	
7		2015	54	314	287	6	-287	1	
8		2016	57	371	342.5	7	-342.5	1	
9		2017	59	430	400.5	8	-400.5	1	
10		2018	61	491	460.5	9	-460.5	1	
11						10			
12	Firm 2	2010	28	28		1			
13		2011	26	54	41	2	-41	1	SUM($C$12:C13)
14		2012	18	72	63	3	-63	1	0.5*D13+0.5*D14
15		2013	19	91	81.5	4	-81.5	1	-E15
16		2014	21	112	101.5	5	-101.5	1	
17		2015	28	140	126	6	-126	1	
18		2016	24	164	152	7	-152	1	
19		2017	32	196	180	8	-180	1	
20		2018	35	231	213.5	9	-213.5	1	
21						10			
22	Firm 3	2010	55	55		1			
23		2011	58	113	84	2	-84	1	
24		2012	49	162	137.5	3	-137.5	1	
25		2013	43	205	183.5	4	-183.5	1	
26		2014	50	255	230	5	-230	1	
27		2015	52	307	281	6	-281	1	
28		2016	59	366	336.5	7	-336.5	1	
29		2017	68	434	400	8	-400	1	
30		2018	65	499	466.5	9	-466.5	1	
31						10			

Table 6.49 Periodical resilience scores and the transformation sequences

	A	B	C	D	E	F	G	H
1		Year	Resilience score	x(1)k	z(1)k	k	U	
2	Firm 1	2010	48	48		1		
3		2011	47	95	71.5	2	-71.5	1
4		2012	52	147	121	3	-121	1
5		2013	55	202	174.5	4	-174.5	1
6		2014	58	260	231	5	-231	1
7		2015	54	314	287	6	-287	1
8		2016	57	371	342.5	7	-342.5	1
9		2017	59	430	400.5	8	-400.5	1
10		2018	61	491	460.5	9	-460.5	1
11						10		
12	Firm 2	2010	28	28		1		
13		2011	26	54	41	2	-41	1
14		2012	18	72	63	3	-63	1
15		2013	19	91	81.5	4	-81.5	1
16		2014	21	112	101.5	5	-101.5	1
17		2015	28	140	126	6	-126	1
18		2016	24	164	152	7	-152	1
19		2017	32	196	180	8	-180	1
20		2018	35	231	213.5	9	-213.5	1
21						10		
22	Firm 3	2010	55	55		1		
23		2011	58	113	84	2	-84	1
24		2012	49	162	137.5	3	-137.5	1
25		2013	43	205	183.5	4	-183.5	1
26		2014	50	255	230	5	-230	1
27		2015	52	307	281	6	-281	1
28		2016	59	366	336.5	7	-336.5	1
29		2017	68	434	400	8	-400	1
30		2018	65	499	466.5	9	-466.5	1

Step 3: The developmental coefficients a_i and the grey input value u_i considering the periodical resilience sequences of firms are developed based on Equations 6.150–6.154. The values of a_i and u_i for the considered three firms are built based on the first, second, and the third decision matrices, similar to as in the basic grey prediction model. The Excel calculations for the same are shown in Table 6.50 and the final values are shown in Table 6.51.

Step 4: The final whitenized scores are constructed based on the basic grey prediction model, where the whitenization equation for the same are built based on Equations 6.155–6.157. The construction of the simulated 1st AGO sequences and the simulated actual sequences are also shown in Tables 6.50 and 6.51.

Table 6.50 Excel formula: Prediction matrices and the simulated sequences

I55 =H55-H54

	A	B	C	D	E	F	G	H	I	J	K	L	M	N
33		inv (U T U)		U T Xn	inv (UTU)*UTXn		Year	predicted	predicted	x(0)^k				
34	Firm 1						2010	48						
35		7.6645E-06	0.0020009	-119389	-0.02865		2011	97.984	49.984	MINVERSE(MMULT(TRANSPOSE(G3:H10),(G3:H10)))				
36		0.00200092	0.6473652	443	47.89594		2012	149.42	51.436	MMULT(TRANSPOSE(G3:H10),(C3:C10))				
37							2013	202.351	52.931					
38							2014	256.821	54.47					
39							2015	312.873	56.052					
40							2016	370.555	57.682					
41							2017	429.913	59.358					
42							2018	490.996	61.083					
43							2019	553.854	62.858					
44	Firm 2						2010	28						
45		4.0459E-05	0.0048475	-26288.5	-0.07956		2011	46.808	18.808	MMULT(B45:C46,D45:D46)				
46		0.00484748	0.7057883	203	15.84213		2012	67.174	20.366	ROUND((($C$12-(E$46/E$45))*EXP(-E$45*(F14-1)))+(E$46/E$45),3)				
47							2013	89.227	22.053	H47-H46				
48							2014	113.105	23.878					
49							2015	138.962	25.857					
50							2016	166.959	27.997					
51							2017	197.276	30.317					
52							2018	230.103	32.827					
53							2019	265.648	35.545					
54	Firm 3						2010	55						
55		8.259E-06	0.0021876	-122988	-0.04446		2011	102.21	47.21					
56		0.00218761	0.704442	444	43.72303		2012	151.567	49.357					
57							2013	203.168	51.601					
58							2014	257.114	53.946					
59							2015	313.514	56.4					
60							2016	372.478	58.964					
61							2017	434.122	61.644					
62							2018	498.569	64.447					
63							2019	565.947	67.378					

Step 5: The data sequences are thus simulated and based on the simulated actual sequences, the resilience performance score predictions are made for the period 2019 for the three considered firms. This is also indicated in Tables 6.50 and 6.51.

Table 6.51 Prediction matrices and the simulated sequences

	A	B	C	D	E	F	G	H	I	J
33		inv (U T U)		U T Xn	inv (UTU)*UTXn		Year	predicted	predicted x(0)^k	
34	Firm 1						2010	48		
35		7.6645E-06	0.0020009	-119389	-0.02865		2011	97.984	49.984	
36		0.00200092	0.6473652	443	47.89594		2012	149.42	51.436	
37							2013	202.351	52.931	
38							2014	256.821	54.47	
39							2015	312.873	56.052	
40							2016	370.555	57.682	
41							2017	429.913	59.358	
42							2018	490.996	61.083	
43							2019	553.854	62.858	
44	Firm 2						2010	28		
45		4.0459E-05	0.0048475	-26288.5	-0.07956		2011	46.808	18.808	
46		0.00484748	0.7057883	203	15.84213		2012	67.174	20.366	
47							2013	89.227	22.053	
48							2014	113.105	23.878	
49							2015	138.962	25.857	
50							2016	166.959	27.997	
51							2017	197.276	30.317	
52							2018	230.103	32.827	
53							2019	265.648	35.545	
54	Firm 3						2010	55		
55		8.259E-06	0.0021876	-122988	-0.04446		2011	102.21	47.21	
56		0.00218761	0.704442	444	43.72303		2012	151.567	49.357	
57							2013	203.168	51.601	
58							2014	257.114	53.946	
59							2015	313.514	56.4	
60							2016	372.478	58.964	
61							2017	434.122	61.644	
62							2018	498.569	64.447	
63							2019	565.947	67.378	

Steps 6–9: The sequence of error measures, namely the residual sequences are constructed based on Equations 6.158–6.164. The Excel calculations for the sequences indicating residuals of prediction are shown in Table 6.52 and the final values are indicated in Table 6.53. This included the estimation of the coefficients of trigonometric residual prediction model; b_{0i}, b_{1i}, b_{2i}, and b_{3i} for the three considered firms and the residual sequences are built following Equations 6.155 and 6.156.

Table 6.52 Excel formula: Residual prediction and the simulated residual sequences

M86 | f_x | =L$86+(L$87*F22)+(L$88*SIN(2*PI()/8))+(L$89*COS(2*PI()/8))

	A	B	C	D	E	F	G	H	I	J	K	L	M	N	O	P	Q	R	S
65		Residuals		B'				inv(BTB)			BTRn	b0, b1, b2, b3	r0(k+1)	Xtr0(1)	Year				
66	Firm 1	0	1	1	0.707107	0.707107	1.503837	-0.30641	-0.73973	0.30640819	0.004	-3.823292335	-2.77526	48	2010	0			
67		-2.984	1	2	1	6.13E-17	-0.30641	0.068091	0.164386	-0.06809071	0.949	0.84973163	-1.92553	47.209	2011	SIN(4*PI()/8)			
68		0.564	1	3	0.707107	-0.707107	-0.73973	0.164386	0.646862	-0.16438551	2.303124638	2.627214785	-1.0758	49.51	2012	COS(6*PI()/8)			
69		2.069	1	4	1.23E-16	-1	0.306408	-0.06809	-0.16439	0.318090709	-5.988171678	-2.346774549	-0.22606	51.855	2013				
70		3.53	1	5	-0.70711	-0.707107							0.623667	54.244	2014	C6-I38			
71		-2.052	1	6	-1	-1.84E-16							1.473399	56.676	2015				
72		-0.682	1	7	-0.70711	0.707107							2.32313	59.155	2016				
73		-0.358	1	8	-2.5E-16	1							3.172862	61.681	2017				
74		-0.083											4.022594	64.256	2018				
75														66.881	2019				
76	Firm 2	0	1	1	0.707107	0.707107	1.503837	-0.30641	-0.73973	0.30640819	0.897	4.355153201	4.912835	28	2010	MINVERSE(MMULT(TRANSPOSE(C76:F83),C76:F83))			
77		7.192	1	2	1	6.13E-17	-0.30641	0.068091	0.164386	-0.06809071	-2.313	-0.942895156	3.96994	23.721	2011	MMULT(TRANSPOSE(C76:F83),B77:B84)			
78		-2.366	1	3	0.707107	-0.707107	-0.73973	0.164386	0.646862	-0.16438551	1.852324423	-1.813269167	3.027044	24.336	2012	L$76+(L$77*F14)+(L$78*SIN(2*PI()/8))+(L$79*COS(2*PI()/8))			
79		-3.053	1	4	1.23E-16	-1	0.306408	-0.06809	-0.16439	0.318090709	11.97003985	3.935405119	2.084149	25.08	2013	I47+M78			
80		-2.878	1	5	-0.70711	-0.707107							1.141254	25.962	2014				
81		2.143	1	6	-1	-1.84E-16							0.198359	26.998	2015				
82		-3.997	1	7	-0.70711	0.707107							-0.74454	28.195	2016				
83		1.683	1	8	-2.5E-16	1							-1.68743	29.572	2017				
84		2.173											-2.63033	31.14	2018				
85														32.915	2019				
86	Firm 3	0	1	1	0.707107	0.707107	1.503837	-0.30641	-0.73973	0.30640815	0.431	10.0690345	10.1412	55	2010				
87		10.79	1	2	1	6.13E-17	-0.30641	0.068091	0.164386	-0.06809071	-4.379	-2.225591	7.915607	57.351	2011				
88		-0.357	1	3	0.707107	-0.707107	-0.73973	0.164386	0.646862	-0.16438551	-0.22824412	-5.430113006	5.690016	57.273	2012				
89		-8.601	1	4	1.23E-16	-1	0.306408	-0.06809	-0.16439	0.318090709	25.81614813	8.679628033	3.464425	57.291	2013				
90		-3.946	1	5	-0.70711	-0.707107							1.238834	57.41	2014				
91		-4.4	1	6	-1	-1.84E-16							-0.98676	57.639	2015				
92		0.036	1	7	-0.70711	0.707107							-3.21235	57.977	2016				
93		6.356	1	8	-2.5E-16	1							-5.43794	58.432	2017				
94		0.553											-7.66353	59.009	2018				
95														59.714	2019				

Table 6.53 Residual prediction and the simulated residual sequences

	A	B	C	D	E	F	G	H	I	J	K	L	M	N	O
65		Residuals		B'				inv(BTB)			BTRn	b0, b1, b2, b3	r0(k+1)	Xtr0(1)	Year
66	Firm 1	0	1	1	0.707107	0.707107	1.503837	-0.30641	-0.73973	0.30640819	0.004	-3.823292335	-2.77526	48	2010
67		-2.984	1	2	1	6.13E-17	-0.30641	0.068091	0.164386	-0.06809071	0.949	0.84973163	-1.92553	47.209	2011
68		0.564	1	3	0.707107	-0.707107	-0.73973	0.164386	0.646862	-0.16438551	2.303124638	2.627214785	-1.0758	49.51	2012
69		2.069	1	4	1.23E-16	-1	0.306408	-0.06809	-0.16439	0.318090709	-5.988171678	-2.346774549	-0.22606	51.855	2013
70		3.53	1	5	-0.70711	-0.707107							0.623667	54.244	2014
71		-2.052	1	6	-1	-1.84E-16							1.473399	56.676	2015
72		-0.682	1	7	-0.70711	0.707107							2.32313	59.155	2016
73		-0.358	1	8	-2.5E-16	1							3.172862	61.681	2017
74		-0.083											4.022594	64.256	2018
75														66.881	2019
76	Firm 2	0	1	1	0.707107	0.707107	1.503837	-0.30641	-0.73973	0.30640819	0.897	4.355153201	4.912835	28	2010
77		7.192	1	2	1	6.13E-17	-0.30641	0.068091	0.164386	-0.06809071	-2.313	-0.942895156	3.96994	23.721	2011
78		-2.366	1	3	0.707107	-0.707107	-0.73973	0.164386	0.646862	-0.16438551	1.852324423	-1.813269167	3.027044	24.336	2012
79		-3.053	1	4	1.23E-16	-1	0.306408	-0.06809	-0.16439	0.318090709	11.97003985	3.935405119	2.084149	25.08	2013
80		-2.878	1	5	-0.70711	-0.707107							1.141254	25.962	2014
81		2.143	1	6	-1	-1.84E-16							0.198359	26.998	2015
82		-3.997	1	7	-0.70711	0.707107							-0.74454	28.195	2016
83		1.683	1	8	-2.5E-16	1							-1.68743	29.572	2017
84		2.173											-2.63033	31.14	2018
85														32.915	2019
86	Firm 3	0	1	1	0.707107	0.707107	1.503837	-0.30641	-0.73973	0.30640819	0.431	10.0690345	10.1412	55	2010
87		10.79	1	2	1	6.13E-17	-0.30641	0.068091	0.164386	-0.06809071	-4.379	-2.225591	7.915607	57.351	2011
88		-0.357	1	3	0.707107	-0.707107	-0.73973	0.164386	0.646862	-0.16438551	-0.22824412	-5.430113006	5.690016	57.273	2012
89		-8.601	1	4	1.23E-16	-1	0.306408	-0.06809	-0.16439	0.318090709	25.81614813	8.679628033	3.464425	57.291	2013
90		-3.946	1	5	-0.70711	-0.707107							1.238834	57.41	2014
91		-4.4	1	6	-1	-1.84E-16							-0.98676	57.639	2015
92		0.036	1	7	-0.70711	0.707107							-3.21235	57.977	2016
93		6.356	1	8	-2.5E-16	1							-5.43794	58.432	2017
94		0.553											-7.66353	59.009	2018
95														59.714	2019

Step 10: The predicted sequences generated through the GM (1, 1) model are corrected using the predicted value of residuals, which is obtained from the trigonometric residual prediction model and the predictions for future are made for the *three* considered firms. Here, for the case, the residual adjusted predicted value of resilience scores for 2019 are as follows: *Firm 1*: 66. 88, *Firm 2*: 32. 92, and *Firm 3*: 59. 71.

6.7 FIRST-ENTRY GREY PREDICTION MODEL

Grey prediction models are known for the prediction of small data, where the grey model of the first order and with one variable (GM (1, 1)) is considered to be most used and popular model. The grey prediction models can generate reliable prediction results, even with very small periodic data with *four* data points. First-entry grey prediction model is a modified GM (1, 1) model to overcome the limitation, as the first value is not used or extracted in a GM (1, 1) model. The first value can also be employed for prediction in the first-entry grey prediction model (FGM (1, 1)), where a random initial value is inserted into the sequences (Tien, 2009; 2012). As the first value do not make any significant difference in the prediction results of the GM (1, 1) model, FGM (1, 1) can produce better prediction results. The FGM (1, 1) model and its difference from the GM (1, 1) model is elaborated as follows:

6.7.1 The GM (1, 1) Model

Let us construct the basic grey prediction model for building initial model. The initial sequence for the same for the period $1 \le i \le n$ can be constructed as follows:

$$Y^{(0)} = \left(y^{(0)}(i)\right)_{i=1}^{n}, \tag{6.167}$$

Here, $Y_{(0)}$ is indicating the initial sequence representing the periodical performances of a typical attribute or a sequence indicating the periodical developmental tendencies of a system under consideration. The sequence can be elaborated as follows:

$$Y = \left(y(1), y(2), y(3), \ldots, y(n)\right). \tag{6.168}$$

6.7.1.1 Data conversion 1

As detailed prior, grey prediction uses different strengthening and weakening operators to reduce the interference of any shocks that can affect the developmental tendencies of data. These operators are performed on the sequences to improve the developmental tendencies of data. Suppose that ρ is a sequence operator applied on the sequence Y, which is represented as:

$$Y\rho = \left(y(1)\rho, y(2)\rho, y(3)\rho, \ldots, y(n)\rho\right). \tag{6.169}$$

Suppose for the *two* different cases, where Y is a monotonically increasing or decreasing sequence, Considering Y as a monotonically increasing sequence, ρ can indicate a *weakening* operator if,

$$y(k)\rho \ge y(k);\ k = 1, 2, 3, \ldots, n. \tag{6.170}$$

Similarly, we can categorize ρ as a strengthening operator for the monotonically increasing sequence Y, if

$$y(k)\rho \le y(k);\, k = 1, 2, 3, \ldots, n. \tag{6.171}$$

Similar to as mentioned prior for the case of monotonically decreasing sequences, the reverse of Equations 6.170 and 6.171 hold true. Here, the data will expand on the application of a weakening operator and will shrink on the application of a strengthening operator. Further, suppose that we are applying the second order weakening operator ρ^2 on the sequences as follows:

$$Y^{(0)}\rho = \left(y^{(0)}(1)\rho, y^{(0)}(2)\rho, y^{(0)}(3)\rho \ldots, y^{(0)}(n)\rho\right), \tag{6.172}$$

here $$y^{(0)}(k)\rho = \frac{1}{n-k+1}\left(y^{(0)}(k) + y^{(0)}(k+1) + y^{(0)}(k+2) \ldots, y^{(0)}(n)\right), \tag{6.173}$$

and $$Y^{(0)}\rho^2 = \left(y^{(0)}(1)\rho^2, y^{(0)}(2)\rho^2, y^{(0)}(3)\rho^2 \ldots, y^{(0)}(n)\rho^2\right), \tag{6.174}$$

here $$y^{(0)}(k)\rho^2 = \frac{1}{n-k+1}\left(y^{(0)}(k)\rho + y^{(0)}(k+1)\rho + y^{(0)}(k+2)\rho \ldots, y^{(0)}(n)\rho\right). \tag{6.175}$$

The sequence after application of the second order weakening operator ($Y^{(0)}\rho_2$), can be represented using $\tilde{Y}$, shown as follows:

$$Y^{(0)}\rho^2 = \tilde{Y} = \left(\tilde{y}^{(0)}(1), \tilde{y}^{(0)}(2), \tilde{y}^{(0)}(3) \ldots, \tilde{y}^{(0)}(n)\right). \tag{6.176}$$

6.7.1.2 Data conversion 2

Accumulated generating operator (1st AGO) is applied on the sequences, which can be presented ($\tilde{Y}$) as follows:

$$\tilde{Y}^{(1)} = \left(\tilde{y}^{(1)}(1), \tilde{y}^{(1)}(2), \tilde{y}^{(1)}(3), \ldots, \tilde{y}^{(1)}(n)\right), \tag{6.177}$$

here $$\tilde{y}^{(1)}(k) = \sum_{i=1}^{k} \tilde{y}^{(0)}(i);\; k = 1, 2, 3, \ldots, n, \tag{6.178}$$

Here, $\tilde{y}^{(1)}(k)$ is indicating the cumulative sum till k.

6.7.1.3 Data conversion 3

We further obtain the sequences $\dot{Y}^{(1)}$, after applying the mean generating operator and based on the neighborhood values of sequences $\widetilde{Y}^{(1)}$, as shown below:

$$\dot{Y}^{(1)} = \left(\dot{y}^{(1)}(2), \dot{y}^{(1)}(3), y^{(1)}(4), \ldots, \dot{y}^{(1)}(n)\right), \tag{6.179}$$

here $$\dot{y}^{(1)}(k) = \left(\left(0.5 \times \tilde{y}^{(1)}(k)\right) + \left(0.5 \times \tilde{y}^{(1)}(k-1)\right)\right);\, k = 2, 3, 4, \ldots, n. \tag{6.180}$$

6.7.1.4 Simulated sequences

Further, we predict the sequences based on the method of least squares, where the matrices β and B are constructed as follows:

$$\beta = \begin{bmatrix} \tilde{y}^{(0)}(2) \\ \tilde{y}^{(0)}(3) \\ \tilde{y}^{(0)}(4) \\ \vdots \\ \tilde{y}^{(0)}(n) \end{bmatrix}; \; B = \begin{bmatrix} -\dot{y}^{(1)}(2) & 1 \\ -\dot{y}^{(1)}(3) & 1 \\ -\dot{y}^{(1)}(4) & 1 \\ \vdots & \vdots \\ -\dot{y}^{(1)}(n) & 1 \end{bmatrix}. \tag{6.181}$$

The grey developmental coefficient a and the grey control parameter b are constructed as below:

$$\frac{d\tilde{y}^{(1)}}{dt} + a\tilde{y}^{(1)} = b, \tag{6.182}$$

here

$$\hat{a} = [a, b]^T, \tag{6.183}$$

We obtain the following expression for obtaining the grey developmental coefficient and the grey control parameter, as below:

$$\hat{a} = \left(\left[B^T B \right]^{-1} \times B^T \beta \right). \tag{6.184}$$

On expanding the terms, we obtain the below expression;

$$\hat{a} = \left[\begin{array}{c} \left(\dfrac{\left(\left(\frac{1}{n-1} \left(\sum_{k=2}^{n} \tilde{y}^{(0)}(k) \times \sum_{k=2}^{n} \dot{y}^{(1)}(k) \right) \right) - \left(\sum_{k=2}^{n} \left(\tilde{y}^{(0)}(k) \times \dot{y}^{(1)}(k) \right) \right) \right)}{\left(\sum_{k=2}^{n} \left[\dot{y}^{(1)}(k) \right]^2 - \frac{1}{n-1} \left[\sum_{k=2}^{n} \dot{y}^{(1)}(k) \right]^2 \right)} \right) \\ \left(\dfrac{1}{n-1} \left(\sum_{k=2}^{n} \tilde{y}^{(0)}(k) + a \sum_{k=2}^{n} \dot{y}^{(1)}(k) \right) \right) \end{array} \right]. \tag{6.185}$$

Further, the prediction is made based on the *GM* (1, 1) model based on the calculated values of the grey developmental coefficient and the grey control parameter as below:

$$\hat{y}^{(1)}(k+1) = \left(\left[\tilde{y}^{(0)}(1) - \left(\frac{b}{a} \right) \right] e^{-ak} + \left(\frac{b}{a} \right) \right); k = 0, 1, 2, 3, \ldots, n-1, \tag{6.186}$$

and

$$\hat{y}^{(0)}(k+1) = \hat{y}^{(1)}(k+1) - \hat{y}^{(1)}(k). \tag{6.187}$$

The sequences are simulated using Equations 6.186 and 6.187 and the predicted sequences for the future period can be constructed as follows:

$$\hat{Y} = \left(\hat{y}^{(0)}(k) \right)_{k=1}^{n}. \tag{6.188}$$

6.7.1.5 Error for prediction

The error sequences (residuals) are calculated for the simulated sequence and from this, we can check how far the predicted values differ from the actuals. The residual (error) sequences are obtained as follows:

$$\varepsilon^{(0)} = \left(\varepsilon^{(0)}(k)\right)_{k=1}^{n}, \tag{6.189}$$

here

$$\varepsilon^{(0)}(k) = \left(\tilde{z}^{(0)}(k) - \hat{z}^{(0)}(k)\right). \tag{6.190}$$

Based on the measures of errors, we ensure a *level one* prediction accuracy.

6.7.2 The FGM (1, 1) Model

After prediction of the values using the conventional GM (1, 1) model, a comparison of the results can be made with the first-entry grey prediction (FGM (1, 1)) model. Here, a random first value is inserted into the sequences.

Step 1: Construct the initial sequences

Suppose, that the initial sequences indicating the periodic performances be shown as follows:

$$Y'^{(0)} = \left(y^{(0)}(i)\right)_{i=0}^{n}, \tag{6.191}$$

here $y^{(0)}(0)$ is indicating the random first-entry value into the sequence and the sequence can be expanded as follows:

$$Y' = \left(y(0), y(1), y(2), \ldots, y(n)\right). \tag{6.192}$$

Step 2: Data conversion 1st, 2nd, and 3rd

The transformation operations of 1st, 2nd, and 3rd are applied on the initial $y^{(0)}$ sequences, similar to that of a GM (1, 1) model, consecutively. For this, a second order weakening operator is applied on the periodic sequences, indicated as follows:

$$Y'^{(0)}\rho = \left(y^{(0)}(0)\rho, y^{(0)}(1)\rho, y^{(0)}(2)\rho, \ldots, y^{(0)}(n)\rho\right), \tag{6.193}$$

here

$$y^{(0)}(k)\rho = \frac{1}{n-k+1}\left(y^{(0)}(k) + y^{(0)}(k+1) + y^{(0)}(k+2), \ldots, y^{(0)}(n)\right), \tag{6.194}$$

and

$$Y'^{(0)}\rho^2 = \left(y^{(0)}(0)\rho^2, y^{(0)}(1)\rho^2, y^{(0)}(2)\rho^2, \ldots, y^{(0)}(n)\rho^2\right), \tag{6.195}$$

here

$$y^{(0)}(k)\rho^2 = \frac{1}{n-k+1}\left(y^{(0)}(k)\rho + y^{(0)}(k+1)\rho + y^{(0)}(k+2)\rho, \ldots, y^{(0)}(n)\rho\right). \tag{6.196}$$

Thus, the transformation operation ($Y'^{(0)}\rho^2$) is applied and the sequences generated after that can be indicated using $\widetilde{Y}'$, which is presented as follows:

$$Y'^{(0)}\rho^2 = \widetilde{Y}' = \left(\tilde{y}^{(0)}(0), \tilde{y}^{(0)}(1), \tilde{y}^{(0)}(2), \ldots, \tilde{y}^{(0)}(n)\right). \tag{6.197}$$

Further to this, the first accumulating generator operator (1st AGO) can be applied on the sequence $\widetilde{Y}'$ and the same can be presented below:

$$\widetilde{Y}'^{(1)} = \left(\tilde{y}^{(1)}(0), \tilde{y}^{(1)}(1), \tilde{y}^{(1)}(2), \ldots, \tilde{y}^{(1)}(n)\right), \tag{6.198}$$

here $$\tilde{y}^{(1)}(k)=\sum_{i=1}^{k}\tilde{y}^{(0)}(i);\ k=0,1,2,\ldots,n. \tag{6.199}$$

Here, $\tilde{y}^{(1)}(k)$ is indicating a cumulative sum measure up to k.

Further to this, the mean generating operator is applied on the sequences $\widetilde{Y'}^{(1)}$ and the generated sequences can be further represented as $\dot{Y}'^{(1)}$ and is presented below:

$$\dot{Y}'^{(1)}=\left(\dot{y}^{(1)}(1),\dot{y}^{(1)}(2),y^{(1)}(3),\ldots,\dot{y}^{(1)}(n)\right), \tag{6.200}$$

here $$\dot{y}^{(1)}(k)=\left(\left(0.5\times\tilde{y}^{(1)}(k)\right)+\left(0.5\times\tilde{y}^{(1)}(k-1)\right)\right);\ k=1,2,3,\ldots,n. \tag{6.201}$$

Step 3: Simulate sequence of performance

The forecasted sequences are constructed based on the method of least squares as mentioned prior. For this, the matrices indicating β' and B' are shown below:

$$\beta'=\begin{bmatrix}\tilde{y}^{(0)}(1)\\ \tilde{y}^{(0)}(2)\\ \tilde{y}^{(0)}(3)\\ \vdots\\ \tilde{y}^{(0)}(n)\end{bmatrix};\ B=\begin{bmatrix}-\dot{y}^{(1)}(1) & 1\\ -\dot{y}^{(1)}(2) & 1\\ -\dot{y}^{(1)}(3) & 1\\ \vdots & \vdots\\ -\dot{y}^{(1)}(n) & 1\end{bmatrix}. \tag{6.202}$$

Further, the grey developmental coefficient a' and the grey control parameter b' are estimated similar to as that of the conventional GM (1, 1) model as follows:

$$\frac{d\tilde{y}^{(1)}}{dt}+a'\tilde{y}^{(1)}=b', \tag{6.203}$$

here $$\hat{b}=[a',b']^{T}, \tag{6.204}$$

The expression before and after expansion of the terms can be indicated below:

$$\hat{b}=\left(\left[B'^{T}B'\right]^{-1}\times B'^{T}B'\right), \tag{6.205}$$

or $$\hat{b}=\begin{bmatrix}\left(\dfrac{\left(\left(\dfrac{1}{n-1}\left(\sum_{k=1}^{n}\tilde{y}^{(0)}(k)\times\sum_{k=1}^{n}\dot{y}^{(1)}(k)\right)\right)-\left(\sum_{k=1}^{n}\left(\tilde{y}^{(0)}(k)\times\dot{y}^{(1)}(k)\right)\right)\right)}{\left(\sum_{k=1}^{n}\left[\dot{y}^{(1)}(k)\right]^{2}-\dfrac{1}{n-1}\left[\sum_{k=1}^{n}\dot{y}^{(1)}(k)\right]^{2}\right)}\right)\\ \left(\dfrac{1}{n-1}\left(\sum_{k=1}^{n}\tilde{y}^{(0)}(k)+a'\sum_{k=1}^{n}\dot{y}^{(1)}(k)\right)\right)\end{bmatrix}. \tag{6.206}$$

The predicted sequences using the FGM (1, 1) are constructed based on the estimated values of the grey developmental coefficient a and the grey control parameter b, which is represented as follows:

$$\hat{y}^{(1)}(k+1)=\left(\left[\tilde{y}^{(0)}(1)-\left(\frac{b'}{a'}\right)\right]e^{-a'k}+\left(\frac{b'}{a'}\right)\right);\ k=1,2,3,\ldots,n, \tag{6.207}$$

and

$$\hat{y}^{(0)}(k+1)=\hat{y}^{(1)}(k+1)-\hat{y}^{(1)}(k). \tag{6.208}$$

Thus, the simulated sequence for the future periods using the FGM (1, 1) model can be constructed based on Equations 6.207 and 6.208, which are presented as follows:

$$\hat{Y}'=\left(\hat{y}^{(0)}(k)\right)_{k=0}^{n}. \tag{6.209}$$

Step 4: Error estimation

The error indicators (residuals) of prediction using the FGM (1, 1) model can be calculated to ensure the accuracy of prediction at *level one*. The residual sequences are presented as follows:

$$\varepsilon^{(0)}=\left(\varepsilon^{(0)}(k)\right)_{k=0}^{n}, \tag{6.210}$$

here

$$\varepsilon^{(0)}(k)=\left(\tilde{y}^{(0)}(k)-\hat{y}^{(0)}(k)\right), \tag{6.211}$$

6.7.3 Sample Case Problem (First-Entry Grey Prediction Model)

The use of first-entry grey prediction models can also be seen in the management and social sciences literature (Rajesh, 2023c). We consider the same problem as discussed in Section 6.5.4. This is regarding the prediction of resilience performances of firms. As the previous periodical data had a cyclical trend in the developmental tendencies, we have used the trigonometric grey prediction model. Here, for the study, we consider the resilience performance data of *three* Indian manufacturing firms (the firms selected were different from those mentioned in Section 6.5.4, and the evaluation was for a period of *ten* years, where the performance data were extracted from the reported secondary data sources. As said prior, the resilience scores were generated based on multiple performance indicators and these scores can mirror their performances considering the indicators; *flexibility, responsiveness, quality, productivity*, and *accessibility*. Here, we aim to predict the resilience performances of the considered firms for immediate next periods. The forecasted resilience scores can help the firms to adjust their strategies for enhancing or maintaining the required level of resilience. As the considered firms are different from those mentioned prior, we name them as *Firm A, Firm B,* and *Firm C*, as the real names were masked due to privacy concerns. The initial sequences showing the resilience scores are shown in Table 6.54. The step-wise procedure for implementing the first-entry grey prediction model is elaborated as follows:

Step 1: The initial sequences of resilience performances of the *three* considered firms for a period of *eight* years (2011 – 2018) are shown in Table 6.54. A random first value for the year 2010 (*Firm A*: 60, *Firm B*: 55, and *Firm C*: 70) is inserted into the sequences to improve the prediction capability, which is as per the FGM (1, 1) model. The values are chosen seeing the sequence trends. These sequences are also shown in Table 6.54. These sequences are indicated as per Equations 6.191 and 6.192, respectively.

Table 6.54 The first-entry sequences of resilience scores

	A	B	C
1		Year	Resilience score
2	Firm A	2010	60
3		2011	67
4		2012	69
5		2013	75
6		2014	76
7		2015	77
8		2016	78
9		2017	80
10		2018	79
11			
12	Firm B	2010	55
13		2011	59
14		2012	63
15		2013	65
16		2014	67
17		2015	66
18		2016	71
19		2017	72
20		2018	72
21			
22	Firm C	2010	70
23		2011	73
24		2012	78
25		2013	79
26		2014	82
27		2015	80
28		2016	78
29		2017	84
30		2018	86
31			

Step 2: The transformational sequences are constructed based on applying the second order weakening operator, 1st aggregating generator operators and the mean generating operators, respectively. This is as per Equations 6.193–6.201. The Excel calculations for the same are shown in Table 6.55 and the transformed sequences are indicated in Table 6.56.

Table 6.55 Excel formula (Firm A): Sequence transformation operations

Q11 | f_x =O11-O10

	A	B	C	D	E	F	G	H	I	J	K	L	M	N	O	P	Q	R	S
1		Year	Resilience score	XD	XD2	1 AGO	Mean GS	k	B			B T B		Year	Simul. 1st AGO	Year	Predict Actual	Predict Errors	
2	Firm A	2010	60	73.444	77.373	77.373		0	-116.305	1	3.83E-06	0.0015		2010	77.373	2010	77.373	0	ROUND(((1/(9-1+1))*(SUM($C2:C$10))),3)
3		2011	67	75.125	77.864	155.237	116.305	1	-194.365	1	0.0015	0.712121		2011	155.496	2011	78.123	-0.259	ROUND(((1/(9-2+1))*(SUM($D3:D$10))),3)
4		2012	69	76.286	78.255	233.492	194.365	2	-272.784	1		B T Y		2012	233.794	2012	78.298	-0.043	ROUND(SUM(E2:E4),3)
5		2013	75	77.5	78.583	312.075	272.784	3	-351.475	1	-247138	-247138		2013	312.268	2013	78.474	0.109	ROUND((F4+F5)/2,3)
6		2014	76	78	78.8	390.875	351.475	4	-430.375	1	629.919	629.919		2014	390.918	2014	78.65	0.15	
7		2015	77	78.5	79	469.875	430.375	5	-509.459	1		inv (B T B)*B T Y		2015	469.745	2015	78.827	0.173	
8		2016	78	79	79.167	549.042	509.459	6	-588.667	1		-0.00225		2016	548.75	2016	79.005	0.162	
9		2017	80	79.5	79.25	628.292	588.667	7	-667.792	1		77.86117		2017	627.932	2017	79.182	0.068	
10		2018	79	79	79	707.292	667.792	8						2018	707.292	2018	79.36	-0.36	
11								9						2019	786.83	2019	79.538		

Table 6.56 Sequence transformation operations

	A	B	C	D	E	F	G
1		Year	Resilience score	XD	XD2	1 AGO	Mean GS
2	Firm A	2010	60	73.444	77.373	77.373	
3		2011	67	75.125	77.864	155.237	116.305
4		2012	69	76.286	78.255	233.492	194.365
5		2013	75	77.5	78.583	312.075	272.784
6		2014	76	78	78.8	390.875	351.475
7		2015	77	78.5	79	469.875	430.375
8		2016	78	79	79.167	549.042	509.459
9		2017	80	79.5	79.25	628.292	588.667
10		2018	79	79	79	707.292	667.792
11							
12	Firm B	2010	55	65.556	69.42	69.42	
13		2011	59	66.875	69.903	139.323	104.372
14		2012	63	68	70.336	209.659	174.491
15		2013	65	68.833	70.725	280.384	245.022
16		2014	67	69.6	71.103	351.487	315.936
17		2015	66	70.25	71.479	422.966	387.227
18		2016	71	71.667	71.889	494.855	458.911
19		2017	72	72	72	566.855	530.855
20		2018	72	72	72	638.855	602.855
21							
22	Firm C	2010	70	78.889	82.117	82.117	
23		2011	73	80	82.521	164.638	123.378
24		2012	78	81	82.881	247.519	206.079
25		2013	79	81.5	83.195	330.714	289.117
26		2014	82	82	83.533	414.247	372.481
27		2015	80	82	83.917	498.164	456.206
28		2016	78	82.667	84.556	582.72	540.442
29		2017	84	85	85.5	668.22	625.47
30		2018	86	86	86	754.22	711.22

Step 3: The prediction parameters including the grey developmental coefficient a' and the grey control parameter b' were estimated by constructing the first, second and the third decision matrices, similar to that of a basic GM (1, 1) model. Further, the sequences are simulated using the FGM (1, 1) model. The whole process follows Equations 6.202–6.209, where the Excel calculations for the same are shown in Table 6.57 and the final values are shown in Table 6.58.

Table 6.57 Excel formula (Firm B): Decision matrices and the simulated sequences

Q21 | =O21-O20

	A	B	C	D	E	F	G	H	I	J	K	L	M	N	O	P	Q	R	S	T	U	V	W
12	Firm B	2010	55	65.556	69.42	69.42		0	-104.372	1	4.69E-06	0.001653		2010	69.42	2010	69.42	0	-G13				
13		2011	59	66.875	69.903	139.323	104.372	1	-174.491	1	0.001653	0.707786		2011	139.487	2011	70.067	-0.164	MINVERSE(MMULT(TRANSPOSE(I12:J19),I12:J19))				
14		2012	63	68	70.336	209.659	174.491	2	-245.022	1		B T Y		2012	209.869	2012	70.382	-0.046					
15		2013	65	68.833	70.725	280.384	245.022	3	-315.936	1	-201658	-201658		2013	280.567	2013	70.698	0.027	MMULT(TRANSPOSE(I12:J19),E13:E20)				
16		2014	67	69.6	71.103	351.487	315.936	4	-387.227	1	569.435	569.435		2014	351.583	2014	71.016	0.087					
17		2015	66	70.25	71.479	422.966	387.227	5	-458.911	1		inv (B T B)*B T Y		2015	422.918	2015	71.335	0.144					
18		2016	71	71.667	71.889	494.855	458.911	6	-530.855	1		-0.00449		2016	494.574	2016	71.656	0.233	MMULT(K12:L13,K15:L16)				
19		2017	72	72	72	566.855	530.855	7	-602.855	1		69.59833		2017	566.552	2017	71.978	0.022					
20		2018	72	72	72	638.855	602.855	8						2018	638.854	2018	72.302	-0.302					
21								9						2019	711.481	2019	72.627						

Table 6.58 Decision matrices and the simulated sequences of data

	A	H	I	J	K	L	M	N	O	P	Q
1		k	B			BTB		Year	Simul. 1st AGO	Year	Predict Actual
2	Firm A	0	-116.305	1	3.83248E-06	0.0015		2010	77.373	2010	77.373
3		1	-194.365	1	0.001500044	0.712121		2011	155.496	2011	78.123
4		2	-272.784	1		BTY		2012	233.794	2012	78.298
5		3	-351.475	1	-247137.814	-247137.8		2013	312.268	2013	78.474
6		4	-430.375	1	629.919	629.919		2014	390.918	2014	78.65
7		5	-509.459	1		inv (B T B)*B T Y		2015	469.745	2015	78.827
8		6	-588.667	1		-0.002245		2016	548.75	2016	79.005
9		7	-667.792	1		77.86117		2017	627.932	2017	79.182
10		8						2018	707.292	2018	79.36
11		9				BTB		2019	786.83	2019	79.538
12	Firm B	0	-104.372	1	4.6913E-06	0.001653		2010	69.42	2010	69.42
13		1	-174.491	1	0.001653489	0.707786		2011	139.487	2011	70.067
14		2	-245.022	1		BTY		2012	209.869	2012	70.382
15		3	-315.936	1	-201658.465	-201658.5		2013	280.567	2013	70.698
16		4	-387.227	1	569.435	569.435		2014	351.583	2014	71.016
17		5	-458.911	1		inv (B T B)*B T Y		2015	422.918	2015	71.335
18		6	-530.855	1		-0.004486		2016	494.574	2016	71.656
19		7	-602.855	1		69.59833		2017	566.552	2017	71.978
20		8						2018	638.854	2018	72.302
21		9				BTB		2019	711.481	2019	72.627
22	Firm C	0	-123.378	1	3.38042E-06	0.001405		2010	82.117	2010	82.117
23		1	-206.079	1	0.001404732	0.708735		2011	164.39	2011	82.273
24		2	-289.117	1		BTY		2012	247.154	2012	82.764
25		3	-372.481	1	-281052.511	-281052.5		2013	330.412	2013	83.258
26		4	-456.206	1	672.103	672.103		2014	414.167	2014	83.755
27		5	-540.442	1		inv (B T B)*B T Y		2015	498.422	2015	84.255
28		6	-625.47	1		-0.005952		2016	583.181	2016	84.759
29		7	-711.22	1		81.53957		2017	668.445	2017	85.264
30		8						2018	754.218	2018	85.773
31		9						2019	840.503	2019	86.285

Step 4: The residual sequences of prediction are further built using Equations 6.210 and 6.211, where the basic errors are estimated to ensure a *level 1* prediction. If needed, the other error estimates as mentioned in Section 6.2.1 can be also estimated. Thus, after ensuring a *level 1* prediction, the prediction can be made for the next periods; here, the predicted resilience scores for the period 2019 is as follows: *Firm A*: 79.5, *Firm B*: 72.6, and *Firm C*: 86.3. The Excel calculations for the same are shown in Table 6.59 and the prediction results are presented in Table 6.60.

Table 6.59 Excel formula (Firm C): Estimation of residuals

Q31 | f_x =O31-O30

	A	B	C	D	E	F	G	H	I	J	K	L	M	N	O	P	Q	R	S	T	U	V	W	X
22	Firm C	2010	70	78.889	82.117	82.117		0	-123.378	1	3.38E-06	0.001405		2010	82.117	2010	82.117	0	ROUND((($E$22-($L$29/$L$28))*EXP(-$L$28*H22))+($L$29/$L$28),3)					
23		2011	73	80	82.521	164.638	123.378	1	-206.079	1	0.001405	0.708735		2011	164.39	2011	82.273	0.248	O23-O22					
24		2012	78	81	82.881	247.519	206.079	2	-289.117	1		B T Y		2012	247.154	2012	82.764	0.117	E24-Q24					
25		2013	79	81.5	83.195	330.714	289.117	3	-372.481	1	-281053	-281053		2013	330.412	2013	83.258	-0.063						
26		2014	82	82	83.533	414.247	372.481	4	-456.206	1	672.103	672.103		2014	414.167	2014	83.755	-0.222						
27		2015	80	82	83.917	498.164	456.206	5	-540.442	1		inv (B T B)*B T Y		2015	498.422	2015	84.255	-0.338						
28		2016	78	82.667	84.556	582.72	540.442	6	-625.47	1		-0.00595		2016	583.181	2016	84.759	-0.203						
29		2017	84	85	85.5	668.22	625.47	7	-711.22	1		81.53957		2017	668.445	2017	85.264	0.236						
30		2018	86	86	86	754.22	711.22	8						2018	754.218	2018	85.773	0.227						
31								9						2019	840.503	2019	86.285							

Table 6.60 Estimated residuals and future prediction

	A	H	P	Q	R
1		k	Year	Predict Actual	Predict Errors
2	Firm A	0	2010	77.373	0
3		1	2011	78.123	-0.259
4		2	2012	78.298	-0.043
5		3	2013	78.474	0.109
6		4	2014	78.65	0.15
7		5	2015	78.827	0.173
8		6	2016	79.005	0.162
9		7	2017	79.182	0.068
10		8	2018	79.36	-0.36
11		9	2019	79.538	
12	Firm B	0	2010	69.42	0
13		1	2011	70.067	-0.164
14		2	2012	70.382	-0.046
15		3	2013	70.698	0.027
16		4	2014	71.016	0.087
17		5	2015	71.335	0.144
18		6	2016	71.656	0.233
19		7	2017	71.978	0.022
20		8	2018	72.302	-0.302
21		9	2019	72.627	
22	Firm C	0	2010	82.117	0
23		1	2011	82.273	0.248
24		2	2012	82.764	0.117
25		3	2013	83.258	-0.063
26		4	2014	83.755	-0.222
27		5	2015	84.255	-0.338
28		6	2016	84.759	-0.203
29		7	2017	85.264	0.236
30		8	2018	85.773	0.227
31		9	2019	86.285	

6.8 CONCLUSION

The prediction models using grey theory were discussed in this chapter, where the basic idea is to forecast sequences and make reasonable prediction outcomes, when the datasets are small. Different modifications of the grey based prediction models are discussed, where the general model of grey prediction can be indicated as a *GM*(m, n); which indicates a grey prediction model of the order m and with n variables for prediction. GM (1, 1) is the most commonly used grey prediction model, where researchers can also explore other models, such as the grey disaster prediction models, Grey–Verhulst models, Grey–Markov models, trigonometric grey prediction models, and the first-entry grey prediction models. Step-by-step implementation, as well as the demonstration using practical cases are outlined in this chapter.

REFERENCES

Abhinav, P. and Rajesh, R. (2025). Forecasting sustainability performances of firms using grey theory and Markov models. *Benchmarking: An International Journal*, https://doi.org/10.1108/BIJ-12-2023-0856.

Elgharbi, S., Esghir, M., Ibrihich, O., Abarda, A., El Hajji, S. and Elbernoussi, S. (2020). Grey-Markov model for the prediction of the electricity production and consumption. In *Big Data and Networks Technologies* 3 (pp. 206–219). Springer International Publishing.

Liu, S. and Lin, Y. (2006). *Grey Prediction* (pp. 275–314). Springer London.

Liu, S., Yang, Y. J. and Forrest, J. (2022). *Grey Systems Analysis*. Springer-Verlag, Berlin.

Rajesh, R. (2016). Forecasting supply chain resilience performance using grey prediction. *Electronic Commerce Research and Applications*, 20, 42–58.

Rajesh, R. (2019). Social and environmental risk management in resilient supply chains: A periodical study by the Grey-Verhulst model. *International Journal of Production Research*, 57(11), 3748–3765.

Rajesh, R. (2022). Sustainability performance predictions in supply chains: Grey and rough set theoretical approaches. *Annals of Operations Research*, 310(1), 171–200.

Rajesh, R. (2023a). Grey–Markov models for predicting the social sustainability performances of firms. *Social Indicators Research*, 168(1), 297–351.

Rajesh, R. (2023b). Predicting environmental sustainability performances of firms using trigonometric grey prediction model. *Environmental Development*, 45, 100830.

Rajesh, R. (2023c). Performance predictions for sustainability governance of firms: implications to select Indian firms. *Benchmarking: An International Journal*, 31(5), 1492–1514.

Rajesh, R. and Rajendran, C. (2019). Grey-and rough-set-based seasonal disaster predictions: an analysis of flood data in India. *Natural Hazards*, 97, 395–435.

Rajesh, R., Agariya, A. K. and Rajendran, C. (2021). Predicting resilience in retailing using grey theory and moving probability based Markov models. *Journal of Retailing and Consumer Services*, 62, 102599.

Tien, T. L. (2009). A new grey prediction model FGM (1, 1). *Mathematical and Computer Modelling*, 49(7–8), 1416–1426.

Tien, T. L. (2012). A research on the grey prediction model GM (1, n). *Applied Mathematics and Computation*, 218(9), 4903–4916.

Wang, Q., Liu, S. and Yan, H. (2019). The application of trigonometric grey prediction model to average per capita natural gas consumption of households in China. *Grey Systems: Theory and Application*, 9(1), 19–30.

Zhan-Li, M. and Jin-Hua, S. (2011). Application of Grey-Markov model in forecasting fire accidents. *Procedia Engineering*, 11, 314–318.

Zhou, P. A. B. W., Ang, B. W. and Poh, K. L. (2006). A trigonometric grey prediction approach to forecasting electricity demand. *Energy*, 31(14), 2839–2847.

CHAPTER 7

Programming Models

7.1 INTRODUCTION

As discussed in previous chapters, grey theory and the related methodologies can be used to deal with uncertain and small datasets. Here, the uncertainty often refers to the information uncertainty considering the available data. Grey theory is used particularly to handle data with clear extensions and unclear intentions, whereas fuzzy set theory is often used to deal with the data having clear intensions and unclear extensions. Also, we have mentioned that rough set theory and probability theory are also used, where probability theory is used to handle stochastic uncertainty. This type of uncertainty mandates that the possible outcomes of an event are known. Also, rough set theory is employed to handle uncertainties with the approximation of data. Grey theory has also applications in formulating and solving programming models, where the flexibility of solutions is possible based on the construction of various optimistic and pessimistic models (Darvishi et al., 2021; Liu et al., 2022).

7.2 GREY PROGRAMMING

Grey programming models can be constructed for various problems including profit maximization and cost minimization problems (Huang and Dan Moore, 1993; Rajesh, 2020).

7.2.1 Profit Maximization Problem

A general grey programming model for profit maximization can be found in Liu and Lin (2010) and the same can be shown as follows:

$$\text{Max}\, S = C_1(\otimes) \times x_1 + C_2(\otimes) \times x_2 + \cdots + C_n(\otimes) \times x_n \tag{7.1}$$

$$\text{Sub to;}\begin{cases}\otimes_{11}x_1+\otimes_{12}x_2+\cdots+\otimes_{1n}x_n\le b_1(\otimes)\\ \otimes_{21}x_1+\otimes_{22}x_2+\cdots+\otimes_{2n}x_n\le b_2(\otimes)\\ \vdots\\ \otimes_{m1}x_1+\otimes_{m2}x_2+\cdots+\otimes_{mn}x_n\le b_m(\otimes)\\ x_1;x_2;\ldots,x_n\ge 0\end{cases}\tag{7.2}$$

This can be briefed as follows:

$$\text{Max}\,S=\sum_{j=1}^{n}C_j(\otimes)\times x_j\tag{7.3}$$

$$\text{Sub to;}\begin{cases}\sum_{j=1}^{n}\otimes_{ij}x_j\le b_i\,\forall 1\le i\le m\\ x_j\ge 0\,\forall 1\le j\le n\end{cases}\tag{7.4}$$

Further, the same can be summarized as follows:

$$\text{Max}\,S=C(\otimes)X\tag{7.5}$$

$$\text{Sub to;}\begin{cases}A(\otimes)X\le b(\otimes)\\ X\ge 0\end{cases}\tag{7.6}$$

Suppose, we can consider α_j, β_i, $\gamma_{ij}\in[0,1]$; $i=1,2,\ldots,m$; $j=1,2,\ldots,n$ as the whitenization weights, then the whitenized values can be represented as follows:

$$\tilde{C}_j(\otimes)=\alpha_j\bar{C}_j+(1-\alpha_j)\underline{C}_j\tag{7.7}$$

$$\tilde{b}_i(\otimes)=\beta_i\bar{b}_i+(1-\beta_i)\underline{b}_i\tag{7.8}$$

and

$$\tilde{a}_{ij}(\otimes)=\gamma_{ij}\bar{a}_{ij}+(1-\gamma_{ij})\underline{a}_{ij}\tag{7.9}$$

Suppose that we consider the mean value whitenization of the values, and then we assume that $\alpha_j=\beta_i=\gamma_{ij}=0.5\,\forall i=1,2,\ldots,n; j=1,2,3,\ldots,m$. Then, the positioned grey programming model can be indicated as follows:

$$\text{Max}\,S=\tilde{C}(\otimes)X\tag{7.10}$$

$$\text{Sub to;}\begin{cases}\tilde{A}(\otimes)X\le\tilde{b}(\otimes)\\ X\ge 0\end{cases},\tag{7.11}$$

Here let us assume that $\tilde{C}(\otimes)$, $\tilde{b}(\otimes)$, $\tilde{A}(\otimes)$ are indicating the whitenization vectors for price, resource constraints, and consumption, which are then represented below:

$$\tilde{C}=\left[\tilde{C}_1,\tilde{C}_2,\ldots,\tilde{C}_n\right],\tag{7.12}$$

$$\tilde{A}=\begin{bmatrix}\tilde{a}_{11} & \tilde{a}_{12} & \cdots & \tilde{a}_{1n}\\ \tilde{a}_{21} & \tilde{a}_{22} & \cdots & \tilde{a}_{2n}\\ \vdots & \vdots & \ddots & \vdots\\ \tilde{a}_{m1} & \tilde{a}_{m2} & \cdots & \tilde{a}_{mn}\end{bmatrix}, \tag{7.13}$$

$$\tilde{b}=\left[\tilde{b}_1, \tilde{b}_2, \ldots, \tilde{b}_m\right]. \tag{7.14}$$

Let us further assume that $\alpha_j (j = 1, 2, \ldots, n)$; $\beta_j (i = 1, 2, \ldots, m)$ and $\gamma_{ij} (i = 1, 2, \ldots, m;$ $j = 1, 2, \ldots, n)$ is indicating the positioned programming coefficient of price, resources, and the consumption vectors, respectively; then, various positioned programming models can be indicated as follows:

(i) Suppose that $\alpha = \beta = 1$ and $\gamma = 0$, then the positioned programming model can be indicated as the grey positioned programming model (GPPM *(1, 1, 0)*) and is referred to as the *ideal model* and the obtained value on solving can be represented as $\max\overline{S}$.

(ii) Let us assume that $\alpha = \beta = 0$ and $\gamma = 1$, then the positioned programming model can be indicated as the grey positioned programming model (GPPM *(0, 0, 1)*) and is referred to as the *critical model* and the obtained value on solving can be represented as $\max\underline{S}$.

(iii) Let us assume that $\alpha = \beta = \gamma = \theta$, then the positioned programming model can be indicated as the grey positioned programming model (GPPM (θ, θ, θ)) and is referred to as the *θ positioned programming model* and the obtained value on solving can be represented as $\max S(\theta)$.

(iv) Let us further assume that $\alpha = \beta = \gamma = \theta = 0.5$, then the positioned programming model can be indicated as the grey positioned programming model (GPPM (0.5)) and is referred to as *mean whitenization programming model* or the *most typical model* and the obtained value on solving can be represented as $\max S(0.5)$.

Further, the pleased degree of the programming model $GP(\alpha, \beta, \gamma)$ for $\alpha, \beta, \gamma \subset [0, 1]$, can be indicated as $\mu(\alpha, \beta, \gamma)$ as shown below:

$$\mu(\alpha,\beta,\gamma)=\left(\frac{1}{2}\left(1-\left(\frac{\max\underline{S}}{\max S(\alpha,\beta,\gamma)}\right)\right)+\frac{1}{2}\left(1-\left(\frac{\max S(\alpha,\beta,\gamma)}{\max\overline{S}}\right)\right)\right) \tag{7.15}$$

The relationship to the positioned optimal values, $\max\overline{S}$ indicating the critical model and $\max\overline{S}$ indicating the ideal model, can be shown using the pleased degree $\mu(\alpha, \beta, \gamma)$. If the pleased degree $\mu(\alpha, \beta, \gamma)$ is smaller, then the $\max S(\alpha, \beta, \gamma)$ value is closer to $\max\underline{S}$. Alternatively, if the pleased degree $\mu(\alpha, \beta, \gamma)$ is larger, then the value of $\max S(\alpha, \beta, \gamma)$ is closer to $\max\overline{S}$. Considering the case of θ positioned programming models, a higher value of pleased degree is preferable.

7.2.2 Sample Case Problem (Grey Programming)

The representative case problem is based on an electronic manufacturing firm in India, where the past data on the product mix problem are taken for estimating the parameters. The presented data is analyzed and the lowest and the highest scores are recorded and the limits for the parameter values are set accordingly. This data is used as the initial data for building grey programming models. We have used different models for whitenization of data in order to formulate the ideal, critical, and the most typical whitenization models. Thus, grey programming provides flexibility for managers in finding solutions when situations are most favorable and in cases where situations are most unfavorable. Also, the most likely solutions can also be observed. Considering the above, the first one corresponds to ideal solutions, the second one provides the critical solution, and the third one corresponds to the most typical solution, where the situations are neither favorable nor unfavorable. These solutions are classified in the positioned programming models, where managers can choose the environment they work to select the favorable, unfavorable, or the most likely models for grey programming. The product mix problem considered for the case is detailed below.

7.2.2.1 Problem Details 1

An aforementioned electronics manufacturing firm, *XYZ* is planning to release *three* new products, where one is in the smartphone segment, another is in the tablet segment and the third one belongs to laptop segment, focusing on the Indian market. The company is becoming popular due to its cheap and reliable products. The problem is to design the optimal product mix for the future period based on the past available and estimated data on average costs and resource constraints. The values indicating the lowest and highest are represented in intervals representing grey numbers for evaluations. The overall optimization problem is formulated as a profit maximization problem, so as to propose an optimal product mix for manufacturing.

The problem is summarized as follows: a smart phone needs 7~10 work days for production till dispatch, 8~12 skilled labors are required for production, 4~6 skilled laborers are required for ensuring quality and the product has a profit margin of ₹2000~2400 per item; considering a tablet, 10~12 work days are required to finish, where 9~13 skilled laborers are required for production, 2~4 skilled laborers are needed for ensuring quality and the item has a profit margin of ₹1500~2100; whereas a laptop can be finished in 13~16 work days by engaging 15~18 skilled laborers for production, 5~8 skilled laborers for quality assurance and is estimated to have a profit margin of ₹2500~3200. Considering availability, there are around 340~350 skilled laborers available for production, 200~210 skilled laborers available for quality testing and it is assumed that there are 300~315 working days in a year. We can consider the problem as a profit maximization problem, where we optimize the product mix for the same. Here, we formulate the problem as a grey programming model following Equations 7.1–7.14, and the same is given as follows:

$$\max S = C_1(\otimes)\times x_1 + C_2(\otimes)\times x_2 + C_3(\otimes)\times x_3 \tag{7.16}$$

$$Sub\,to;\begin{cases} \otimes_{11}x_1 + \otimes_{12}x_2 + \otimes_{13}x_3 \le b_1(\otimes) \\ \otimes_{21}x_1 + \otimes_{22}x_2 + \otimes_{23}x_3 \le b_2(\otimes) \\ \otimes_{31}x_1 + \otimes_{32}x_2 + \otimes_{33}x_3 \le b_3(\otimes) \\ x_1, x_2, x_3 \ge 0 \end{cases}, \tag{7.17}$$

here $$C_1(\otimes) \in [2000, 2400];\ C_2(\otimes) \in [1500, 2100];\ C_3(\otimes) \in [2500, 3200], \tag{7.18}$$

$$\left.\begin{array}{lll} \otimes_{11} \in [8, 12]; & \otimes_{12} \in [9, 13]; & \otimes_{13} \in [15, 18] \\ \otimes_{21} \in [4, 6]; & \otimes_{22} \in [2, 4]; & \otimes_{23} \in [5, 8] \\ \otimes_{31} \in [7, 10]; & \otimes_{32} \in [10, 12]; & \otimes_{33} \in [13, 16] \end{array}\right\}, \tag{7.19}$$

and $$b_1(\otimes) \in [340, 350];\ b_2(\otimes) \in [200, 210];\ b_3(\otimes) \in [300, 315]. \tag{7.20}$$

By varying values for α, β and γ, we can build different positioned programming models. The general form for the model can be presented as follows:

$$\max S_p = \tilde{C}_{1p}x_1 + \tilde{C}_{2p}x_2 + \tilde{C}_{3p}x_3 \tag{7.21}$$

$$\text{Sub to;} \begin{cases} \tilde{a}_{11p}x_1 + \tilde{a}_{12p}x_2 + \tilde{a}_{13p}x_3 \le \tilde{b}_{1p} \\ \tilde{a}_{21p}x_1 + \tilde{a}_{22p}x_2 + \tilde{a}_{23p}x_3 \le \tilde{b}_{2p} \\ \tilde{a}_{31p}x_1 + \tilde{a}_{32p}x_2 + \tilde{a}_{33p}x_3 \le \tilde{b}_{3p} \\ x_1, x_2, x_3 \ge 0 \end{cases}, \tag{7.22}$$

here p is showing the case number.

Case 1: While we consider $\alpha = \beta = 1$, $\gamma = 0$ and $p = 1$, the *ideal model* of the LGPM (LGPM (1, 1, 0)) can be constructed. The same can be denoted as $\max \overline{S}$, where the grey boundaries can be whitenized as follows.

$$\tilde{C}_{jp}(\otimes); p = 1 \text{ can be approximated to } C_{j1} = \overline{C}_{j1}\ \forall j \in (1, 2, 3) \tag{7.23}$$

$$\tilde{b}_{ip}(\otimes); p = 1 \text{ can be approximated to } \tilde{b}_{i1} = \overline{b}_{i1}\ \forall i \in (1, 2, 3) \tag{7.24}$$

$$\tilde{a}_{ijp}(\otimes); p = 1 \text{ can be approximated to } \tilde{a}_{ij1} = \underline{a}_{ij1}\ \forall i, j \in (1, 2, 3) \tag{7.25}$$

Thus, the model after whitenization using Equations 7.23–7.25 can be indicated as follows:

$$\max S_1 = 2400x_1 + 2100x_2 + 3200x_3 \tag{7.26}$$

$$\text{Sub to;} \begin{cases} 8x_1 + 9x_2 + 15x_3 \le 350 \\ 4x_1 + 2x_2 + 5x_3 \le 210 \\ 7x_1 + 10x_2 + 13x_3 \le 315 \\ x_1, x_2, x_3 \ge 0 \end{cases} \tag{7.27}$$

Thus, the *ideal model* of the LGPM is constructed and the same can be solved using Excel Solver. A solver Add-in can be activated in Excel by using the following path. File → Options → Add-ins → Excel Add-ins → Go → Solver Add-in → Ok. The Solver can be found under the data tab after activating. The formulation and the solver dialogue box for solution are presented in Table 7.1 and 7.2, respectively. The following results are obtained from the solver; $S_1 = 105000$; $x_1 = 43.75$; $x_2 = 0$; $x_3 = 0$. The values may be approximated to the lowest limits.

Table 7.1 Formulation of the model in Excel: Case 1

	A	B	C	D	E	F	G	H
1								
2	Case 1		X1	X2	X3			
3		Profits	2400	2100	3200			
4						Res. Used		
5		Constraint 1	8	9	15	32	<=	350
6		Constraint 2	4	2	5	11	<=	210
7		Constraint 3	7	10	13	30	<=	315
8								Objective fn.
9		Units	1	1	1			7700

Table 7.2 Excel formula and Solver dialogue box for solution: Case 1

	A	B	C	D	E	F	G	H	I
1									
2	Case 1		X1	X2	X3				
3		Profits	2400	2100	3200				
4						Res. Used			
5		Constraint 1	8	9	15	350	<=	350	SUMPRODUCT(C5:E5,C$9:E$9)
6		Constraint 2	4	2	5	175	<=	210	SUMPRODUCT(C6:E6,C$9:E$9)
7		Constraint 3	7	10	13	306.25	<=	315	SUMPRODUCT(C7:E7,C$9:E$9)
8								Objective fn.	
9		Units	43.75	0	0			105000	SUMPRODUCT(C3:E3,C9:E9)
10									
11	Case 2		X1	X2					
12		Profits	2000						
13									
14		Constraint 1	12						
15		Constraint 2	6						
16		Constraint 3	10						
17									
18		Units	1						
19									
20	Case 4		X1	X2					
21		Profits	2200						
22									
23		Constraint 1	10						
24		Constraint 2	5						
25		Constraint 3	8.5						
26									
27		Units	1						

Solver Parameters

Set Objective: $H$9

To: (•) Max ( ) Min ( ) Value Of: 0

By Changing Variable Cells: $C$9:$E$9

Subject to the Constraints:
$F$5:$F$7 <= $H$5:$H$7

Add | Change | Delete | Reset All | Load/Save

[x] Make Unconstrained Variables Non-Negative

Select a Solving Method: Simplex LP | Options

Solving Method

Select the GRG Nonlinear engine for Solver Problems that are smooth nonlinear. Select the LP Simplex engine for linear Solver Problems, and select the Evolutionary engine for Solver problems that are non-smooth.

Help | Solve | Close

Case 2: Let us further assume $\alpha = \beta = 0$, $\gamma = 1$ and $p = 2$, then the *critical model* of the LGPM (LGPM (0, 0, 1)) can be constructed and the optimum solution can be shown as $\max \underline{S}$. The values can be further whitenized and the following are obtained.

$$\tilde{C}_{jp}(\otimes); p = 2 \text{ can be approximated to } \tilde{C}_{j2} = \underline{C}_{j2}\ \forall j \in (1,2,3) \tag{7.28}$$

$$\tilde{b}_{ip}(\otimes); p = 2 \text{ can be approximated to } \tilde{b}_{i2} = \underline{b}_{i2}\ \forall i \in (1,2,3) \tag{7.29}$$

$$\tilde{a}_{ijp}(\otimes); p = 2 \text{ can be approximated to } \tilde{a}_{ij2} = \overline{a}_{ij2}\ \forall i,j \in (1,2,3) \tag{7.30}$$

The model constructed after whitenization is indicated below.

$$Max\, S_2 = 2000\,x_1 + 1500\,x_2 + 2500\,x_3 \tag{7.31}$$

$$\text{Sub to;} \begin{cases} 12x_1 + 13x_2 + 18x_3 \le 340 \\ 6x_1 + 4x_2 + 8x_3 \le 200 \\ 10x_1 + 12x_2 + 16x_3 \le 300 \\ x_1, x_2, x_3 \ge 0 \end{cases} \tag{7.32}$$

The model is constructed and solved using Excel solver. The model formulation and the dialogue box for solution are presented in Tables 7.3 and 7.4, respectively. The solution is obtained as follows:

$$S_2 = 56666.67;\ x_1 = 28.33;\ x_2 = 0;\ x_3 = 0\,.$$

Table 7.3 Formulation of the model in Excel: Case 2

	A	B	C	D	E	F	G	H
10								
11	**Case 2**		**X1**	**X2**	**X3**			
12		**Profits**	2000	1500	2500			
13						**Res. Used**		
14		**Constraint 1**	12	13	18	43	<=	340
15		**Constraint 2**	6	4	8	18	<=	200
16		**Constraint 3**	10	12	16	38	<=	300
17								**Objective fn.**
18		**Units**	1	1	1			6000

Case 3: For constructing different positioned programming models, we can consider $\alpha = \beta = \gamma = \theta$. Further, the solutions can be obtained for varying values of θ; say for example, $\theta \in \{0.2, 0.4, 0.6, 0.8\}$. Further, let us assume $\max S(\theta)$ shows the optimal values for each case. The final solutions for all these cases, as obtained from the results of solver are presented in Table 7.5. The individual calculations are not shown, but a special case of the positioned programming model with solution is shown as *Case 4*.

Table 7.4 Excel formula and Solver dialogue box for solution: Case 2

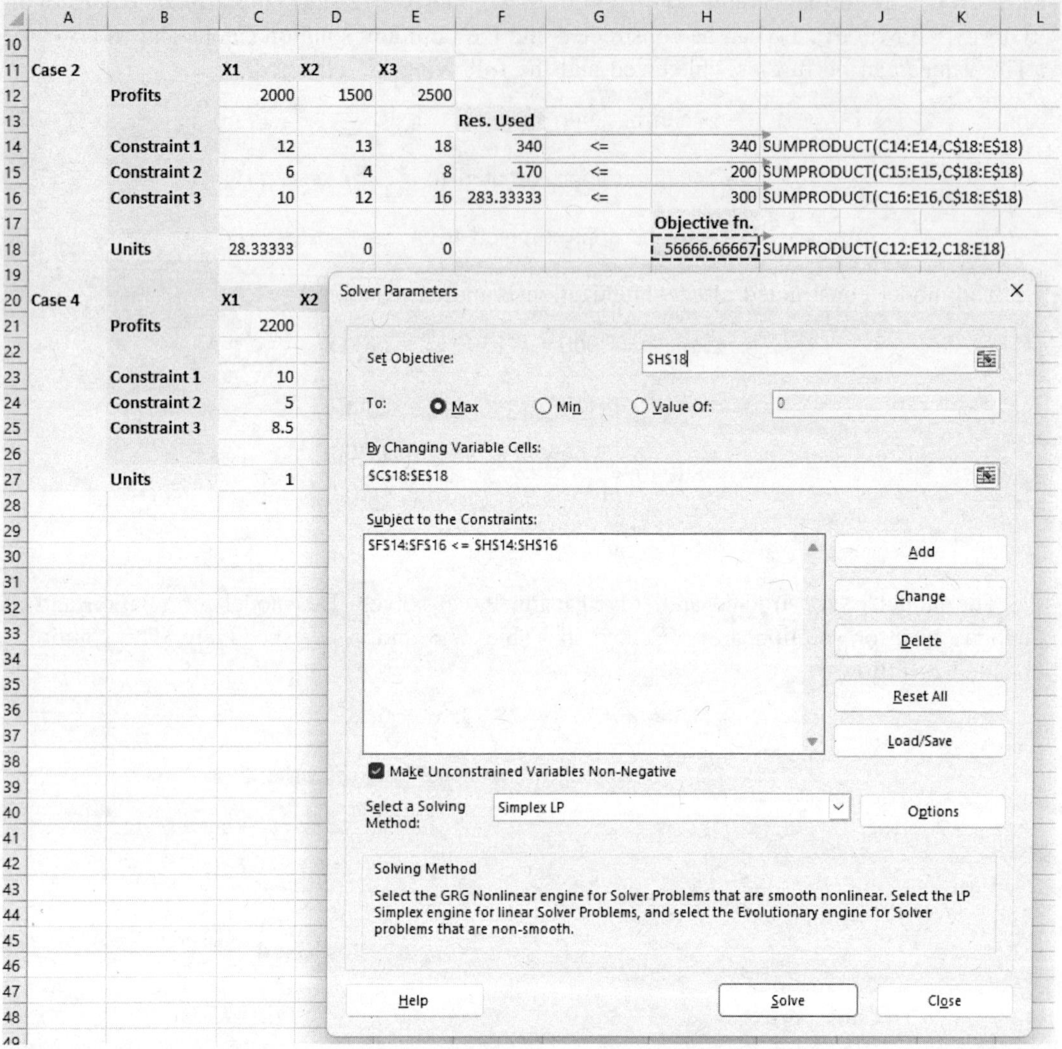

Table 7.5 Solutions for different positioned programming models

Cases 3 and 4	θ	x_1	x_2	x_3	max $S(\theta)$	Iterations in solver	Pleased degrees (μ)
Case 3.1	0.2	31.07	0	0	72085.71	1	0.45
Case 3.2	0.4	33.27	0	0	74523.08	2	0.475
Case 3.3	0.6	35.83	0	0	77400.00	4	0.503
Case 3.4	0.8	38.86	0	0	80836.36	1	0.534
Case 4	0.5	34.50	0	0	75900	1	0.488

(Contd.)

Table 7.5 Solutions for different positioned programming models (*Contd.*)

θ Values	Costs	Constraints	Resources			θ Values	Costs	Constraints	Resources		
θ = 0.2	$\tilde{c}_i$	$\tilde{b}_i$	$\tilde{a}_{i1}$	$\tilde{a}_{i2}$	$\tilde{a}_{i3}$	θ = 0.6	$\tilde{c}_i$	$\tilde{b}_i$	$\tilde{a}_{i1}$	$\tilde{a}_{i2}$	$\tilde{a}_{i3}$
i = 1	2320	348	1.2	12.2	17.4	i = 1	2160	344	9.6	10.6	16.2
i = 2	1980	208	5.6	3.6	7.4	i = 2	1740	204	4.8	2.8	6.2
i = 3	3060	312	9.4	11.6	15.4	i = 3	2780	306	8.2	10.8	14.2
θ = 0.4	$\tilde{c}_i$	$\tilde{b}_i$	$\tilde{a}_{i1}$	$\tilde{a}_{i2}$	$\tilde{a}_{i3}$	θ = 0.8	$\tilde{c}_i$	$\tilde{b}_i$	$\tilde{a}_{i1}$	$\tilde{a}_{i2}$	$\tilde{a}_{i3}$
i = 1	2240	346	10.4	11.4	16.8	i = 1	2080	342	8.8	9.8	15.6
i = 2	1860	206	5.2	3.2	6.8	i = 2	1620	202	4.4	2.4	5.6
i = 3	2920	309	8.8	11.2	14.8	i = 3	2640	303	7.6	10.4	13.6

Case 4: As said prior, this is a special occasion of Case 3 and is considered as the *most typical model*. The model is constructed by assuming $\alpha = \beta = \gamma = \theta = 0.5$, the corresponding solution is for the *mean whitenization programming model*, signified as $\max S(0.5)$. The whitenization model is constructed as follows.

$$\max S_4 = 2200x_1 + 1800x_2 + 2850x_3 \tag{7.33}$$

$$\text{Sub to;}\begin{cases} 10x_1 + 11x_2 + 16.5x_3 \le 345 \\ 5x_1 + 3x_2 + 6.5x_3 \le 205 \\ 8.5x_1 + 11x_2 + 14.5x_3 \le 307.5 \\ x_1, x_2, x_3 \ge 0 \end{cases} \tag{7.34}$$

The optimal values are obtained on solving this in Excel solver, where the formulation is shown in Table 7.6 and the dialogue box for solution is shown in Table 7.7. Also, we can calculate the *pleased degrees of the positioned programming model* $\mu(\alpha, \beta, \gamma)$ for varying values of θ as in Case 3 and 4, and the same is also shown in Table 7.5. The observed optimal solution is as follows:

$$S_4 = 75900;\ x_1 = 34.5;\ x_2 = 0;\ x_3 = 0.$$

Table 7.6 Formulation of the model in Excel: Case 4

	A	B	C	D	E	F	G	H
19								
20	Case 4		X1	X2	X3			
21		Profits	2200	1800	2850			
22						Res. Used		
23		Constraint 1	10	11	16.5	37.5	<=	345
24		Constraint 2	5	3	6.5	14.5	<=	205
25		Constraint 3	8.5	11	14.5	34	<=	307.5
26								Objective fn.
27		Units	1	1	1			6850

Table 7.7 Excel formula and Solver dialogue box for solution: Case 4

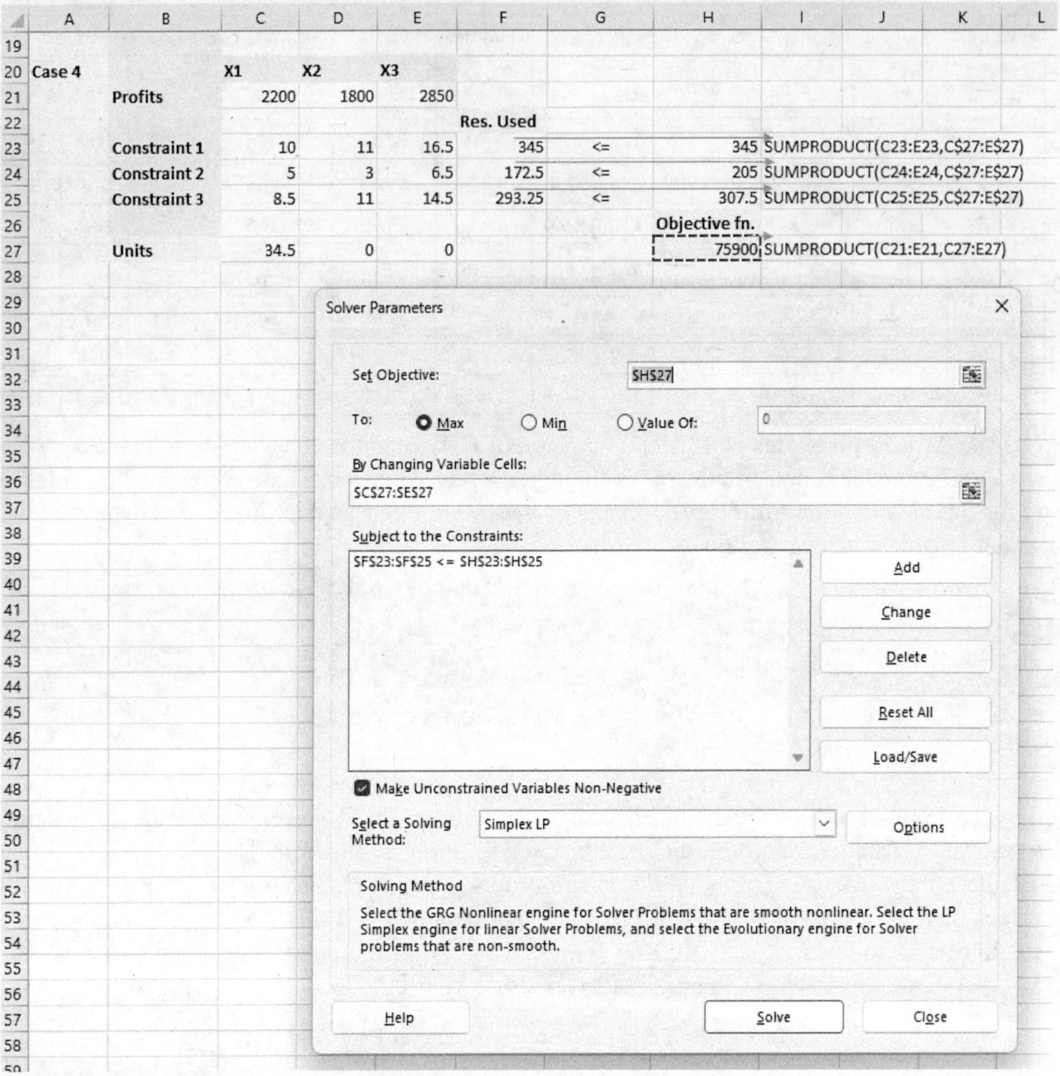

7.2.2.2 *Problem Details 2*

As there are *two* products for the considered firm in the smartphone segment. We consider the problem of introducing a *third* smartphone model, subject to constraints. These constraints are formulated well along. Prior to this, an initial check for the existing demands for the available products and the current profits are necessary. Hence, we assume that by modifying the problem in consideration of the existing products may lead to a better grey programming model. Further, we can carefully observe the solution to the ideal model, critical model, and the most typical model, and recommendations can be made for the introduction of the new product. Considering the introduction of a new smartphone model, we can consider three choices, where the first two are the existing products (smartphone models) and the third one is the model going to be introduced in the market.

The problem is solved for the ideal, critical, and the most typical models separately. Suppose that x_{11}, x_{12}, and x_{13} are indicating the number of units of the *two* existing smartphone models and the one going to be introduced, respectively. Also, the profit margins for the same are decided from the sales data and forecasts. The expected profit margins are indicated as follows:

$$C_{11}(\otimes)\in[2150, 2350];\ C_{12}(\otimes)\in[2100,2300];\ C_{13}(\otimes)\in[2000, 2400];$$
$$C_2(\otimes)\in[1500, 2100];\ C_3(\otimes)\in[2500,3200]$$

The optimization model is modified to include the *five* variables (x_{11}, x_{12}, x_{13}, x_2, and x_3) considered and the solution to the same is observed using Solver in Excel. As the formulation and execution in Solver is already shown for the Problem 7.1.2.1, the tables for calculation are not shown, but the model and the solved results from solver are presented below.

Case 5: Ideal model of the LGPM

The ideal model for the LGPM is solved and while observing the solutions, we can see that after the introduction of the new model, the profits can improve. That is when the situations appear favorable, the new product addition can be thought of a good choice. The solution for the same as obtained from Excel solver are as follows:

$$S_5 = 105000;\ x_{11} = 0;\ x_{12} = 0;\ x_{13} = 43.75;\ x_2 = 0;\ x_3 = 0.$$

Case 6: Critical model of the LGPM

The critical model for the LGPM was also constructed and solved, where we observe some interesting findings. We can perceive that when the market conditions are not favorable, it is suggested not to proceed with the introduction of the new product. The results also convey that the existing first smartphone model will yield more profits, when the critical values are assumed for the model. The optimum solution obtained from the Solver are shown as follows:

$$S_6 = 60916.67;\ x_{11} = 28.33;\ x_{12} = 0;\ x_{13} = 0;\ x_2 = 0;\ x_3 = 0.$$

Case 7: Most typical model of the LGPM

Further, the most typical model was also constructed and solved for the case, where the results were furthermore surprising. The results convey that under normal circumstances and market conditions, the introduction of the new model is not favorable. Also, the results favor production of the existing first model and the solved results from the Solver are shown below

$$S_7 = 77625;\ x_{11} = 34.5;\ x_{12} = 0;\ x_{13} = 0;\ x_2 = 0;\ x_3 = 0.$$

Hence, we may conclude that the introduction of a new model is only preferable in the ideal case and the same is not recommended for the most typical and the critical cases considered.

7.3 CONCLUSION

The programming applications of grey theory and the related models are discussed in this chapter. Grey theory provides flexibility in programming models to obtain results based on the *ideal*, the *critical*, and the *most typical* models by suitably employing the grey number operations. Researchers and practitioners can utilize the vast scope of grey programming models to build models for optimization that accommodate flexibility of decision-making.

REFERENCES

Darvishi, D., Liu, S. and Yi-Lin Forrest, J. (2021). Grey linear programming: a survey on solving approaches and applications. *Grey Systems: Theory and Application*, 11(1), 110–135.

Huang, G. and Dan Moore, R. (1993). Grey linear programming, its solving approach, and its application. *International Journal of Systems Science*, 24(1), 159–172.

Liu, S. F., Yang, Y. J. and Forrest, J. (2022). *Grey Systems Analysis*. Springer-Verlag, Berlin.

Rajesh, R. (2020). Group decision-making and grey programming approaches to optimal product mix in manufacturing supply chains. *Neural Computing and Applications*, 32(7), 2635–2649.

CHAPTER 8

Clustering Models

8.1 INTRODUCTION

In the last chapter of this book, we are discussing on the clustering applications of grey theory based models. Although several methods including neural networks and machine-learning based algorithms are available for clustering of data, most of these works good with large or bigdata. Clustering using grey theory can be found effective for classifying small to medium sized data groups, where most other methods may not work well. Grey clustering is another methodological approach using grey theory to deduct conclusions from relatively small set of data for categorizing and clustering of data (Liu and Yang, 2017; Liu et al., 2017). Suppose, if the grey classes are assigned based on importance, then *high*, *medium*, and *low* importance categories can be a classification for clustering.

8.2 GREY CLUSTERING

As indicated prior, grey clustering differs in its nature compared to other clustering methods that necessitate the mandate of having large datasets for execution of the clustering algorithm (Ke et al., 2012; Rajesh, 2018). The detailed implementation steps and the demonstration of implementation using a case problem are detailed further in the following sub-section.

8.2.1 Steps in Implementation

Let us learn the implementation steps.

Step 1: Identify the factors

The initial factors or attributes for clustering are identified first. Suppose that there are 'n' such identified factors or attributes. These attributes can be associated to a particular study and can be named as A_1, A_2, …, A_n, etc.

Step 2: Calculate the weights and impacts of the attributes

The importance weights and the actual performance of these attributes can be measured separately. This can be based on evaluation using a survey or expert response based study or through analysis of the secondary data. Suppose, that the weights assigned or obtained for n factors be $w_1, w_2, \ldots, w_n$. Also, the impact ratings for the factors are also collected. This can be based on the actual or measured level of performances of individual factors.

Step 3: Conversion to grey scales

Using a predetermined conversion scale, the linguistic measurements are converted to grey values. These grey values are represented by a lower and an upper bound of values. Suppose, that $\otimes a_i$ is indicating the rating of the ith factor and $\otimes w_i$ is indicating corresponding grey weighting assigned to the factor, where $1 \leq i \leq n$.

Step 4: Obtain the weighted impact rating

We can further obtain the weighted impact ratings $(\otimes \dot{a}_i)$ by multiplying the weights of factors with the impact ratings. As the weights and the impact ratings are indicated using grey numbers, the weighted impact ratings can be calculated following grey number multiplication.

$$\otimes \dot{a}_i = \left(\otimes w_i \times \otimes a_i\right) \tag{8.1}$$

Step 5: Conversion to crisp scores

We can use an enhanced CFCS (Conversion of Fuzzy to Crisp Scores) method for conversion of the grey values to corresponding crisp scores, following a *three* step procedure detailed as below:

(a) Normalization

$$\underline{\otimes}\tilde{a}_i = \left(\underline{\otimes}\dot{a}_i - \min_i \underline{\otimes}\,\dot{a}_i\right) / \Delta_{\min}^{\max}, \tag{8.2}$$

here $\underline{\otimes}\tilde{a}_i$ indicates the normalized lower bound of the grey number $\otimes\tilde{a}_i$

$$\overline{\otimes}\tilde{a}_i = \left(\overline{\otimes}\dot{a}_i - \max_i \overline{\otimes}\dot{a}_i\right) / \Delta_{\min}^{\max}, \tag{8.3}$$

here $\overline{\otimes}\tilde{a}_i$ indicates the normalized upper bound of the grey number $\otimes\tilde{a}_i$, and

$$\Delta_{\min}^{\max} = \max_i \overline{\otimes}\dot{a}_i - \max_i \underline{\otimes}\,\dot{a}_i \tag{8.4}$$

(b) Total normalized white scores

$$b_i = \left(\frac{\left(\underline{\otimes}\tilde{a}_i\left(1-\underline{\otimes}\tilde{a}_i\right)\right)+\left(\overline{\otimes}\tilde{a}_i \times \overline{\otimes}\tilde{a}_i\right)}{\left(1-\underline{\otimes}\tilde{a}_i+\overline{\otimes}\tilde{a}_i\right)}\right) \tag{8.5}$$

(c) Final white scores

$$b_i^* = \left(\min \underline{\otimes}\,\dot{a}_i + \left(b_i \times \Delta_{\min}^{\max}\right)\right) \tag{8.6}$$

and,

$$B = \left[b_i^*\right] \tag{8.7}$$

Step 6: Observe the grey clusters

The crisp ratings can be assigned to different grey classes for classification. Suppose that there are *three* grey classes indicating *high*, *medium*, and *low* importance. The whitenization grey weights are to be fixed first for classification. Suppose that there are *two* whitenization weight functions for evaluation. For the first set of factors, the whitenization weight function is indicated as follows:

$$f_2^1(x) = f_1^1(x) = \left\{ \begin{pmatrix} 0; \\ x/2; \\ 1; \end{pmatrix}; \begin{matrix} x < 0 \\ 0 \le x \le 2 \\ x > 2 \end{matrix} \right. \tag{8.8}$$

$$f_2^2(x) = f_1^2(x) = \begin{cases} 0; & x < 0 \text{ or } x > 2 \\ x; & 0 \le x \le 1 \\ (2-x); & 1 < x \le 2 \end{cases} \tag{8.9}$$

$$f_2^3(x) = f_1^3(x) = \begin{cases} 0; & x < 0 \text{ or } x > 1 \\ 1; & 0 \le x \le 0.5 \\ ((1-x)/0.5); & 0.5 < x \le 1 \end{cases} \tag{8.10}$$

Similarly, for the other set of factors, we can assign the whitenization weight functions as below:

$$f_4^1(x) = f_3^1(x) = \begin{cases} 0; & x < 0 \\ (x/1.5); & 0 \le x \le 1.5 \\ 1; & x > 1.5 \end{cases} \tag{8.11}$$

$$f_4^2(x) = f_3^2(x) = \begin{cases} 0; & x < 0 \text{ or } x > 1.5 \\ (x/0.75); & 0 \le x \le 0.75 \\ ((1.5-x)/0.75); & 0.75 < x \le 1.5 \end{cases} \tag{8.12}$$

$$f_4^3(x) = f_3^3(x) = \begin{cases} 0; & x < 0 \text{ or } x > 0.75 \\ 1; & 0 \le x \le 0.5 \\ ((0.75-x)/0.5); & 0.5 < x \le 0.75 \end{cases} \tag{8.13}$$

Step 7: Cluster coefficients of weights

Suppose that x_i (= b_i^*) is indicating the weighted impact rating of factor i, the whitenization weight function can be denoted using $f_i^k(\cdot)$, indicating the ith factor and the kth sub-class, where θ_i^k is indicating the weight for the ith factor considering the kth sub-class. Then the cluster coefficient of variable weights considering that i^{th} factor belong to the kth sub-class is represented as follows:

$$\sigma_i^k = \sum_{i=1}^{n} \left(f_i^k(x_i) \times \theta_i^k \right) \tag{8.14}$$

The vector of cluster coefficients of i factors can be indicated as follows:

$$\sigma_i = \left(\sigma_i^1, \sigma_i^1, \ldots, \sigma_i^s\right) \tag{8.15}$$

i.e.

$$\sigma_i = \left(\sum_{i=1}^{n} f_i^1(x_i) \times \theta_i^1, \sum_{i=1}^{n} f_i^2(x_i) \times \theta_i^2, \ldots, \sum_{i=1}^{n} f_i^s(x_i) \times \theta_i^s\right) \tag{8.16}$$

$[\sigma_i^k]_{n \times s}$ can be considered as the coefficient matrix. Suppose, if $\sigma_i^{k*} = \max_{1 \le k \le s} \{\sigma_i^k\}$, then we can assume that the factor i belongs to the grey class, k^*.

Step 8: Classify factors into grey classes

The n factors can be assigned to different grey classes. Say for example, we have used the grey classes indicating the importance into *high*, *medium*, and *low* importance categorizations.

Step 9: Observe factors of high importance

If the clustering is followed by a further critical qualitative or quantitative analysis of factors, we can consider only those factors in the category of *high* importance, so that the evaluation process can be simplified, based on the application and further results from grey clustering.

8.2.2 Sample Case Problem (Grey Clustering)

We have considered the case problem of the electronic manufacturing industry *ABC* in India. The firm is working on improving their resilience capabilities and are planning various measures to advance the same. The managerial team of the firm have identified that the primary step to improve the resilience capabilities is to identify the barriers to resilience for the firm and their supply chains. They have identified *thirty* barriers that hinder them from achieving and improving their resilience capabilities. The impact of the barriers and their respective ratings were decided by managers by objectively rating them in linguistic labels and were further converted to grey scales. Each of the barriers were noted using a two letter code *RB*, indicating a *Resilience Barrier* and a serial number has been assigned for identification purposes. The detailed *step-by-step* procedure for implementation of the grey clustering algorithm is shown below:

Step 1: The first step involves the identification of the barriers and *thirty* different barriers to achieving resilience were identified and were named as *RB 1, RB 2,…, RB 30*.

Step 2: Managers of the firm have evaluated the impact of each barrier on the supply chain processes on nine point linguistic labels varying between *extremely low (EL)* to *extremely high (EH)* (*extremely low (EL), very low (VL), moderately low (ML), low (L), medium (M), moderately high (MH), high (H), very high (VH),* and *extremely high (EH)*). Thus the managers have used nine point scales for both rating the impacts and the weightings assigned to each barriers. The linguistic labels showing the initial ratings and weightings for barriers are shown in Table 8.1.

Step 3: A conversion scale is used to convert the linguistic labels of ratings and impact weightings into grey values and the conversion scales are shown in Table 8.2.

Table 8.1 Linguistic ratings and weightings for barriers

	A	B	C	D	E	F	G
2	Sl No.	Barriers	Weighting of barriers	Impact on SRM	Impact on CRM	Impact on ISCM	Impact on MEE
3				(*Impact wt. = 0.3*)	(*Impact wt. = 0.3*)	(*Impact wt. = 0.2*)	(*Impact wt. = 0.2*)
4	1	RB 1	VH	H	H	VH	MH
5	2	RB 2	H	MH	MH	VH	H
6	3	RB 3	MH	H	MH	ML	L
7	4	RB 4	M	H	VH	EH	MH
8	5	RB 5	MH	VH	VH	H	MH
9	6	RB 6	VH	EH	EH	VH	H
10	7	RB 7	EH	VH	EH	H	H
11	8	RB 8	H	VH	H	EH	VL
12	9	RB 9	VH	L	EH	H	L
13	10	RB 10	VH	EH	L	H	L
14	11	RB 11	VH	H	H	VH	ML
15	12	RB 12	EH	VH	H	VH	EL
16	13	RB 13	EH	VH	VH	H	H
17	14	RB 14	MH	H	H	VH	H
18	15	RB 15	VH	MH	MH	H	VH
19	16	RB 16	H	H	MH	VH	EH
20	17	RB 17	VH	VH	VH	EH	EH
21	18	RB 18	EH	EH	EH	EH	VH
22	19	RB 19	ML	M	MH	M	ML
23	20	RB 20	ML	ML	MH	M	L
24	21	RB 21	MH	EH	VH	VH	H
25	22	RB 22	VH	EH	EH	VH	H
26	23	RB 23	EH	VH	H	MH	M
27	24	RB 24	M	M	ML	L	EL
28	25	RB 25	VH	EH	VH	EH	VH
29	26	RB 26	H	EH	M	M	ML
30	27	RB 27	ML	M	ML	MH	L
31	28	RB 28	H	VH	EH	H	VH
32	29	RB 29	ML	H	ML	L	L
33	30	RB 30	EH	EH	VH	EH	H

Table 8.2 Linguistic to grey scale conversion of ratings and weights

	I	J
2	Linguistic assessment of	Associated grey values
3	Extremely Low (EL)	[0.0, 0.2]
4	Very Low (VL)	[0.1, 0.3]
5	Low (L)	[0.2, 0.4]
6	Moderately Low (ML)	[0.3, 0.5]
7	Medium (M)	[0.4, 0.6]
8	Moderately High (MH)	[0.5, 0.7]
9	High (H)	[0.6, 0.8]
10	Very High (VH)	[0.7, 0.9]
11	Extremely High (EH)	[0.8, 1.0]
12	Linguistic	Associated grey
13	assessment of	weights
14	Extremely Low (EL)	[1 - 2]
15	Very Low (VL)	[2 - 3]
16	Low (L)	[3 - 4]
17	Moderately Low (ML)	[4 - 5]
18	Medium (M)	[5 - 6]
19	Moderately High (MH)	[6 - 7]
20	High (H)	[7 - 8]
21	Very High (VH)	[8 - 9]
22	Extremely High (EH)	[9 - 10]

Step 4: The impact on the supply chain processes were measured by classifying the supply chain processes into *four* stages indicating the supplier relations management *(SRM)*, customer relations management *(CRM)*, internal supply chain management *(ISCM)*, and managing external environments *(MEE)*. Subjective weightings for each of these processes (*SRM, CRM, ISCM* and *MEE*) are assigned, where *0.3, 0.3, 0.2* and *0.2*, indicates the weights assigned for these processes, respectively. We further calculate the weighted impact ratings ($\otimes \dot{a}_{ij}$) by multiplying the grey weights with corresponding grey ratings, as per Equation 8.1. The grey values indicating the ratings and weights (after conversion) are shown in Table 8.3. The Excel calculation for the weighted rating observations are shown in Table 8.4 and the final weighted ratings in grey values are presented in Table 8.5.

Table 8.3 Ratings and weights converted to grey values

	A	B	C	D	E	F	G
36–37	Sl No.	Barriers	Weighting of barriers	Impact on SRM (Impact wt. = 0.3)	Impact on CRM (Impact wt. = 0.3)	Impact on ISCM (Impact wt. = 0.2)	Impact on MEE (Impact wt. = 0.2)
38	1	RB 1	8	0.6	0.6	0.7	0.5
39			9	0.8	0.8	0.9	0.7
40	2	RB 2	7	0.5	0.5	0.7	0.6
41			8	0.7	0.7	0.9	0.8
42	3	RB 3	6	0.6	0.5	0.3	0.2
43			7	0.8	0.7	0.5	0.4
44	4	RB 4	5	0.6	0.7	0.8	0.5
45			6	0.8	0.9	1	0.7
46	5	RB 5	6	0.7	0.7	0.6	0.5
47			7	0.9	0.9	0.8	0.7
48	6	RB 6	8	0.8	0.8	0.7	0.6
49			9	1	1	0.9	0.8
50	7	RB 7	9	0.7	0.8	0.6	0.6
51			10	0.9	1	0.8	0.8
52	8	RB 8	7	0.7	0.6	0.8	0.1
53			8	0.9	0.8	1	0.3
54	9	RB 9	8	0.2	0.8	0.6	0.2
55			9	0.4	1	0.8	0.4
56	10	RB 10	8	0.8	0.2	0.6	0.2
57			9	1	0.4	0.8	0.4
58	11	RB 11	8	0.6	0.6	0.7	0.3
59			9	0.8	0.8	0.9	0.5
60	12	RB 12	9	0.7	0.6	0.7	0
61			10	0.9	0.8	0.9	0.2
62	13	RB 13	9	0.7	0.7	0.6	0.6
63			10	0.9	0.9	0.8	0.8
64	14	RB 14	6	0.6	0.6	0.7	0.6
65			7	0.8	0.8	0.9	0.8
66	15	RB 15	8	0.5	0.5	0.6	0.7
67			9	0.7	0.7	0.8	0.9
68	16	RB 16	7	0.6	0.5	0.7	0.8
69			8	0.8	0.7	0.9	1
70	17	RB 17	8	0.7	0.7	0.8	0.8
71			9	0.9	0.9	1	1
72	18	RB 18	9	0.8	0.8	0.8	0.7
73			10	1	1	1	0.9
74	19	RB 19	4	0.4	0.5	0.4	0.3
75			5	0.6	0.7	0.6	0.5
76	20	RB 20	4	0.3	0.5	0.4	0.2
77			5	0.5	0.7	0.6	0.4
78	21	RB 21	6	0.8	0.7	0.7	0.6
79			7	1	0.9	0.9	0.8
80	22	RB 22	8	0.8	0.8	0.7	0.6
81			9	1	1	0.9	0.8
82	23	RB 23	9	0.7	0.6	0.5	0.4
83			10	0.9	0.8	0.7	0.6
84	24	RB 24	5	0.4	0.3	0.2	0
85			6	0.6	0.5	0.4	0.2
86	25	RB 25	8	0.8	0.7	0.8	0.7
87			9	1	0.9	1	0.9
88	26	RB 26	7	0.8	0.4	0.4	0.3
89			8	1	0.6	0.6	0.5
90	27	RB 27	4	0.4	0.3	0.5	0.2
91			5	0.6	0.5	0.7	0.4
92	28	RB 28	7	0.7	0.8	0.6	0.7
93			8	0.9	1	0.8	0.9
94	29	RB 29	4	0.6	0.3	0.2	0.2
95			5	0.8	0.5	0.4	0.4
96	30	RB 30	9	0.8	0.7	0.8	0.6
97			10	1	0.9	1	0.8

Table 8.4 Excel formula: Grey weighted ratings of barriers

F161 | =MAX($C96*G96,$C96*G97,$C97*G96,$C97*G97)*0.2

	A	B	C	D	E	F	G
99			Weighted Impact				
100	Sl No.	Barriers	Impact on SRM	Impact on CRM	Impact on ISCM	Impact on MEE	
101			Impact wt. = 0.3	Impact wt. = 0.3	Impact wt. = 0.2	Impact wt. = 0.2	
102	1	RB 1	1.44	1.44	1.12	0.8	MIN($C38*D38,$C38*D39,$C39*D38,$C39*D39)*0.3
103			2.16	2.16	1.62	1.26	MAX($C38*D38,$C38*D39,$C39*D38,$C39*D39)*0.3
104	2	RB 2	1.05	1.05	0.98	0.84	
105			1.68	1.68	1.44	1.28	
106	3	RB 3	1.08	0.9	0.36	0.24	MIN($C42*F42,$C42*F43,$C43*F42,$C43*F43)*0.2
107			1.68	1.47	0.7	0.56	MAX($C42*F42,$C42*F43,$C43*F42,$C43*F43)*0.2
108	4	RB 4	0.9	1.05	0.8	0.5	
109			1.44	1.62	1.2	0.84	
110	5	RB 5	1.26	1.26	0.72	0.6	
111			1.89	1.89	1.12	0.98	
112	6	RB 6	1.92	1.92	1.12	0.96	
113			2.7	2.7	1.62	1.44	
114	7	RB 7	1.89	2.16	1.08	1.08	
115			2.7	3	1.6	1.6	
116	8	RB 8	1.47	1.26	1.12	0.14	
117			2.16	1.92	1.6	0.48	
118	9	RB 9	0.48	1.92	0.96	0.32	
119			1.08	2.7	1.44	0.72	
120	10	RB 10	1.92	0.48	0.96	0.32	
121			2.7	1.08	1.44	0.72	
122	11	RB 11	1.44	1.44	1.12	0.48	
123			2.16	2.16	1.62	0.9	
124	12	RB 12	1.89	1.62	1.26	0	
125			2.7	2.4	1.8	0.4	
126	13	RB 13	1.89	1.89	1.08	1.08	
127			2.7	2.7	1.6	1.6	
128	14	RB 14	1.08	1.08	0.84	0.72	
129			1.68	1.68	1.26	1.12	
130	15	RB 15	1.2	1.2	0.96	1.12	
131			1.89	1.89	1.44	1.62	
132	16	RB 16	1.26	1.05	0.98	1.12	
133			1.92	1.68	1.44	1.6	
134	17	RB 17	1.68	1.68	1.28	1.28	
135			2.43	2.43	1.8	1.8	
136	18	RB 18	2.16	2.16	1.44	1.26	
137			3	3	2	1.8	
138	19	RB 19	0.48	0.6	0.32	0.24	
139			0.9	1.05	0.6	0.5	
140	20	RB 20	0.36	0.6	0.32	0.16	
141			0.75	1.05	0.6	0.4	
142	21	RB 21	1.44	1.26	0.84	0.72	
143			2.1	1.89	1.26	1.12	
144	22	RB 22	1.92	1.92	1.12	0.96	
145			2.7	2.7	1.62	1.44	
146	23	RB 23	1.89	1.62	0.9	0.72	
147			2.7	2.4	1.4	1.2	
148	24	RB 24	0.6	0.45	0.2	0	
149			1.08	0.9	0.48	0.24	
150	25	RB 25	1.92	1.68	1.28	1.12	
151			2.7	2.43	1.8	1.62	
152	26	RB 26	1.68	0.84	0.56	0.42	
153			2.4	1.44	0.96	0.8	
154	27	RB 27	0.48	0.36	0.4	0.16	
155			0.9	0.75	0.7	0.4	
156	28	RB 28	1.47	1.68	0.84	0.98	
157			2.16	2.4	1.28	1.44	
158	29	RB 29	0.72	0.36	0.16	0.16	
159			1.2	0.75	0.4	0.4	
160	30	RB 30	2.16	1.89	1.44	1.08	
161			3	2.7	2	1.6	

Step 5: We use Equations 8.2–8.7 to whitenize these grey values, by employing the *three* step procedure. Before normalization, the minimum, maximum and delta values for the grey scores are calculated for impact on all the supply chain processes (SRM, CRM, ISCM, and MEE). The Excel calculations for the same are shown in Table 8.6. The Excel formula for the *three* step conversion are shown in Tables 8.7, 8.9, and 8.11 and the final values are presented in Tables 8.8, 8.10, and 8.12.

Table 8.5 Grey weighted ratings of barriers

	A	B	C	D	E	F
99			Weighted Impact			
100	Sl No.	Barriers	Impact on SRM	Impact on CRM	Impact on ISCM	Impact on MEE
101			(Impact wt. = 0.3)	(Impact wt. = 0.3)	(Impact wt. = 0.2)	(Impact wt. = 0.2)
102	1	RB 1	1.44	1.44	1.12	0.8
103			2.16	2.16	1.62	1.26
104	2	RB 2	1.05	1.05	0.98	0.84
105			1.68	1.68	1.44	1.28
106	3	RB 3	1.08	0.9	0.36	0.24
107			1.68	1.47	0.7	0.56
108	4	RB 4	0.9	1.05	0.8	0.5
109			1.44	1.62	1.2	0.84
110	5	RB 5	1.26	1.26	0.72	0.6
111			1.89	1.89	1.12	0.98
112	6	RB 6	1.92	1.92	1.12	0.96
113			2.7	2.7	1.62	1.44
114	7	RB 7	1.89	2.16	1.08	1.08
115			2.7	3	1.6	1.6
116	8	RB 8	1.47	1.26	1.12	0.14
117			2.16	1.92	1.6	0.48
118	9	RB 9	0.48	1.92	0.96	0.32
119			1.08	2.7	1.44	0.72
120	10	RB 10	1.92	0.48	0.96	0.32
121			2.7	1.08	1.44	0.72
122	11	RB 11	1.44	1.44	1.12	0.48
123			2.16	2.16	1.62	0.9
124	12	RB 12	1.89	1.62	1.26	0
125			2.7	2.4	1.8	0.4
126	13	RB 13	1.89	1.89	1.08	1.08
127			2.7	2.7	1.6	1.6
128	14	RB 14	1.08	1.08	0.84	0.72
129			1.68	1.68	1.26	1.12
130	15	RB 15	1.2	1.2	0.96	1.12
131			1.89	1.89	1.44	1.62
132	16	RB 16	1.26	1.05	0.98	1.12
133			1.92	1.68	1.44	1.6
134	17	RB 17	1.68	1.68	1.28	1.28
135			2.43	2.43	1.8	1.8
136	18	RB 18	2.16	2.16	1.44	1.26
137			3	3	2	1.8
138	19	RB 19	0.48	0.6	0.32	0.24
139			0.9	1.05	0.6	0.5
140	20	RB 20	0.36	0.6	0.32	0.16
141			0.75	1.05	0.6	0.4
142	21	RB 21	1.44	1.26	0.84	0.72
143			2.1	1.89	1.26	1.12
144	22	RB 22	1.92	1.92	1.12	0.96
145			2.7	2.7	1.62	1.44
146	23	RB 23	1.89	1.62	0.9	0.72
147			2.7	2.4	1.4	1.2
148	24	RB 24	0.6	0.45	0.2	0
149			1.08	0.9	0.48	0.24
150	25	RB 25	1.92	1.68	1.28	1.12
151			2.7	2.43	1.8	1.62
152	26	RB 26	1.68	0.84	0.56	0.42
153			2.4	1.44	0.96	0.8
154	27	RB 27	0.48	0.36	0.4	0.16
155			0.9	0.75	0.7	0.4
156	28	RB 28	1.47	1.68	0.84	0.98
157			2.16	2.4	1.28	1.44
158	29	RB 29	0.72	0.36	0.16	0.16
159			1.2	0.75	0.4	0.4
160	30	RB 30	2.16	1.89	1.44	1.08
161			3	2.7	2	1.6

Table 8.6 Excel formula: Minimum, maximum, and delta values

	B	C	D	E	F	G
163	min j lower xij	0.36	0.36	0.16	0	MIN(C102,C104,C106,C108,... ,C152,C154,C156,C158,C160)
164	min j upper xij	0.75	0.75	0.4	0.24	MIN(C103,C105,C107,C109,... ,C153,C155,C157,C159,C161)
165	max j upper xij	3	3	2	1.8	MAX(C103,C105,C107,C109,... ,C153,C155,C157,C159,C161)
166	del min max	2.64	2.64	1.84	1.8	C165-C163

Table 8.7 Excel formula: Grey to crisp conversion: Normalization

M161 | f_x | =ROUND(((F161-F$164)/F$166),3)

	H	I	J	K	L	M	N
99			Normalized Scores				
100	Sl No.	Barriers	Impact on SRM	Impact on CRM	Impact on ISCM	Impact on MEE	
101			(*Impact wt. = 0.3*)	(*Impact wt. = 0.3*)	(*Impact wt. = 0.2*)	(*Impact wt. = 0.2*)	
102	1	RB 1	0.409	0.409	0.522	0.444	ROUND(((C102-C$163)/C$166),3)
103			0.534	0.534	0.663	0.567	ROUND(((C103-C$164)/C$166),3)
104	2	RB 2	0.261	0.261	0.446	0.467	
105			0.352	0.352	0.565	0.578	
106	3	RB 3	0.273	0.205	0.109	0.133	ROUND(((E106-E$163)/E$166),3)
107			0.352	0.273	0.163	0.178	ROUND(((E107-E$164)/E$166),3)
108	4	RB 4	0.205	0.261	0.348	0.278	
109			0.261	0.33	0.435	0.333	
110	5	RB 5	0.341	0.341	0.304	0.333	
111			0.432	0.432	0.391	0.411	
112	6	RB 6	0.591	0.591	0.522	0.533	
113			0.739	0.739	0.663	0.667	
114	7	RB 7	0.58	0.682	0.5	0.6	
115			0.739	0.852	0.652	0.756	
116	8	RB 8	0.42	0.341	0.522	0.078	
117			0.534	0.443	0.652	0.133	
118	9	RB 9	0.045	0.591	0.435	0.178	
119			0.125	0.739	0.565	0.267	
120	10	RB 10	0.591	0.045	0.435	0.178	
121			0.739	0.125	0.565	0.267	
122	11	RB 11	0.409	0.409	0.522	0.267	
123			0.534	0.534	0.663	0.367	
124	12	RB 12	0.58	0.477	0.598	0	
125			0.739	0.625	0.761	0.089	
126	13	RB 13	0.58	0.58	0.5	0.6	
127			0.739	0.739	0.652	0.756	
128	14	RB 14	0.273	0.273	0.37	0.4	
129			0.352	0.352	0.467	0.489	
130	15	RB 15	0.318	0.318	0.435	0.622	
131			0.432	0.432	0.565	0.767	
132	16	RB 16	0.341	0.261	0.446	0.622	
133			0.443	0.352	0.565	0.756	
134	17	RB 17	0.5	0.5	0.609	0.711	
135			0.636	0.636	0.761	0.867	
136	18	RB 18	0.682	0.682	0.696	0.7	
137			0.852	0.852	0.87	0.867	
138	19	RB 19	0.045	0.091	0.087	0.133	
139			0.057	0.114	0.109	0.144	
140	20	RB 20	0	0.091	0.087	0.089	
141			0	0.114	0.109	0.089	
142	21	RB 21	0.409	0.341	0.37	0.4	
143			0.511	0.432	0.467	0.489	
144	22	RB 22	0.591	0.591	0.522	0.533	
145			0.739	0.739	0.663	0.667	
146	23	RB 23	0.58	0.477	0.402	0.4	
147			0.739	0.625	0.543	0.533	
148	24	RB 24	0.091	0.034	0.022	0	
149			0.125	0.057	0.043	0	
150	25	RB 25	0.591	0.5	0.609	0.622	
151			0.739	0.636	0.701	0.767	
152	26	RB 26	0.5	0.182	0.217	0.233	
153			0.625	0.261	0.304	0.311	
154	27	RB 27	0.045	0	0.13	0.089	
155			0.057	0	0.163	0.089	
156	28	RB 28	0.42	0.5	0.37	0.544	
157			0.534	0.625	0.478	0.667	
158	29	RB 29	0.136	0	0	0.089	
159			0.17	0	0	0.089	
160	30	RB 30	0.682	0.58	0.696	0.6	
161			0.852	0.739	0.87	0.756	

Table 8.8 Grey to crisp conversion: Normalization

	H	I	J	K	L	M
99			**Normalized Scores**			
100	**Sl No.**	**Barriers**	**Impact on SRM**	**Impact on CRM**	**Impact on ISCM**	**Impact on MEE**
101			*(Impact wt. = 0.3)*	*Impact wt. = 0.3*	*Impact wt. = 0.2*	*Impact wt. = 0.2)*
102	1	RB 1	0.409	0.409	0.522	0.444
103			0.534	0.534	0.663	0.567
104	2	RB 2	0.261	0.261	0.446	0.467
105			0.352	0.352	0.565	0.578
106	3	RB 3	0.273	0.205	0.109	0.133
107			0.352	0.273	0.163	0.178
108	4	RB 4	0.205	0.261	0.348	0.278
109			0.261	0.33	0.435	0.333
110	5	RB 5	0.341	0.341	0.304	0.333
111			0.432	0.432	0.391	0.411
112	6	RB 6	0.591	0.591	0.522	0.533
113			0.739	0.739	0.663	0.667
114	7	RB 7	0.58	0.682	0.5	0.6
115			0.739	0.852	0.652	0.756
116	8	RB 8	0.42	0.341	0.522	0.078
117			0.534	0.443	0.652	0.133
118	9	RB 9	0.045	0.591	0.435	0.178
119			0.125	0.739	0.565	0.267
120	10	RB 10	0.591	0.045	0.435	0.178
121			0.739	0.125	0.565	0.267
122	11	RB 11	0.409	0.409	0.522	0.267
123			0.534	0.534	0.663	0.367
124	12	RB 12	0.58	0.477	0.598	0
125			0.739	0.625	0.761	0.089
126	13	RB 13	0.58	0.58	0.5	0.6
127			0.739	0.739	0.652	0.756
128	14	RB 14	0.273	0.273	0.37	0.4
129			0.352	0.352	0.467	0.489
130	15	RB 15	0.318	0.318	0.435	0.622
131			0.432	0.432	0.565	0.767
132	16	RB 16	0.341	0.261	0.446	0.622
133			0.443	0.352	0.565	0.756
134	17	RB 17	0.5	0.5	0.609	0.711
135			0.636	0.636	0.761	0.867
136	18	RB 18	0.682	0.682	0.696	0.7
137			0.852	0.852	0.87	0.867
138	19	RB 19	0.045	0.091	0.087	0.133
139			0.057	0.114	0.109	0.144
140	20	RB 20	0	0.091	0.087	0.089
141			0	0.114	0.109	0.089
142	21	RB 21	0.409	0.341	0.37	0.4
143			0.511	0.432	0.467	0.489
144	22	RB 22	0.591	0.591	0.522	0.533
145			0.739	0.739	0.663	0.667
146	23	RB 23	0.58	0.477	0.402	0.4
147			0.739	0.625	0.543	0.533
148	24	RB 24	0.091	0.034	0.022	0
149			0.125	0.057	0.043	0
150	25	RB 25	0.591	0.5	0.609	0.622
151			0.739	0.636	0.761	0.767
152	26	RB 26	0.5	0.182	0.217	0.233
153			0.625	0.261	0.304	0.311
154	27	RB 27	0.045	0	0.13	0.089
155			0.057	0	0.163	0.089
156	28	RB 28	0.42	0.5	0.37	0.544
157			0.534	0.625	0.478	0.667
158	29	RB 29	0.136	0	0	0.089
159			0.17	0	0	0.089
160	30	RB 30	0.682	0.58	0.696	0.6
161			0.852	0.739	0.87	0.756

Table 8.9 Excel formula: Grey to crisp conversion: Crisp scores

T160 =ROUND(((M160*(1-M160)+(M161*M161))/(1-M160+M161)),3)

SI No.	Barriers	Crisp Scores Impact on SRM Impact wt. = 0.3	Impact on CRM Impact wt. = 0.3	Impact on ISCM Impact wt. = 0.2	Impact on MEE Impact wt. = 0.2)	
1	RB 1	0.468	0.468	0.604	0.506	ROUND(((J102*(1-J102)+(J103*J103))/(1-J102+J103)),3)
2	RB 2	0.29	0.29	0.506	0.525	ROUND(((K104*(1-K104)+(K105*K105))/(1-K104+K105)),3)
3	RB 3	0.299	0.222	0.117	0.141	ROUND(((L106*(1-L106)+(L107*L107))/(1-L106+L107)),3)
4	RB 4	0.219	0.282	0.383	0.295	ROUND(((M108*(1-M108)+(M109*M109))/(1-M108+M109)),3)
5	RB 5	0.377	0.377	0.335	0.363	
6	RB 6	0.686	0.686	0.604	0.612	
7	RB 7	0.681	0.806	0.586	0.702	
8	RB 8	0.475	0.382	0.597	0.085	
9	RB 9	0.054	0.686	0.5	0.2	
10	RB 10	0.686	0.054	0.5	0.2	
11	RB 11	0.468	0.468	0.604	0.3	
12	RB 12	0.681	0.558	0.705	0.007	
13	RB 13	0.681	0.681	0.586	0.702	
14	RB 14	0.299	0.299	0.411	0.44	
15	RB 15	0.362	0.362	0.5	0.719	
16	RB 16	0.382	0.29	0.500	0.711	
17	RB 17	0.576	0.576	0.709	0.828	
18	RB 18	0.806	0.806	0.825	0.824	
19	RB 19	0.046	0.094	0.089	0.135	
20	RB 20	0	0.094	0.089	0.089	
21	RB 21	0.456	0.377	0.411	0.44	
22	RB 22	0.686	0.686	0.604	0.612	
23	RB 23	0.681	0.558	0.469	0.463	
24	RB 24	0.095	0.035	0.023	0	
25	RB 25	0.686	0.576	0.709	0.719	
26	RB 26	0.569	0.201	0.241	0.256	
27	RB 27	0.046	0	0.135	0.089	
28	RB 28	0.475	0.569	0.417	0.617	
29	RB 29	0.142	0	0	0.089	
30	RB 30	0.806	0.681	0.825	0.702	

Table 8.10 Grey to crisp conversion: Crisp scores

Sl No.	Barriers	Crisp Scores			
		Impact on SRM	Impact on CRM	Impact on ISCM	Impact on MEE
		(Impact wt. = 0.3)	(Impact wt. = 0.3)	(Impact wt. = 0.2)	(Impact wt. = 0.2)
1	RB 1	0.468	0.468	0.604	0.506
2	RB 2	0.29	0.29	0.506	0.525
3	RB 3	0.299	0.222	0.117	0.141
4	RB 4	0.219	0.282	0.383	0.295
5	RB 5	0.377	0.377	0.335	0.363
6	RB 6	0.686	0.686	0.604	0.612
7	RB 7	0.681	0.806	0.586	0.702
8	RB 8	0.475	0.382	0.597	0.085
9	RB 9	0.054	0.686	0.5	0.2
10	RB 10	0.686	0.054	0.5	0.2
11	RB 11	0.468	0.468	0.604	0.3
12	RB 12	0.681	0.558	0.705	0.007
13	RB 13	0.681	0.681	0.586	0.702
14	RB 14	0.299	0.299	0.411	0.44
15	RB 15	0.362	0.362	0.5	0.719
16	RB 16	0.382	0.29	0.506	0.711
17	RB 17	0.576	0.576	0.709	0.828
18	RB 18	0.806	0.806	0.825	0.824
19	RB 19	0.046	0.094	0.089	0.135
20	RB 20	0	0.094	0.089	0.089
21	RB 21	0.456	0.377	0.411	0.44
22	RB 22	0.686	0.686	0.604	0.612
23	RB 23	0.681	0.558	0.469	0.463
24	RB 24	0.095	0.035	0.023	0
25	RB 25	0.686	0.576	0.709	0.719
26	RB 26	0.569	0.201	0.241	0.256
27	RB 27	0.046	0	0.135	0.089
28	RB 28	0.475	0.569	0.417	0.617
29	RB 29	0.142	0	0	0.089
30	RB 30	0.806	0.681	0.825	0.702

Table 8.11 Excel formula: Grey to crisp conversion: Final white scores

F200 | f_x =ROUND(F$163+(T160*F$166),3)

	B	C	D	E	F	G
168		Final Scores				
169	Barriers	Impact on SRM	Impact on CRM	Impact on ISCM	Impact on MEE	
170		*(Impact wt. = 0.3)*	*(Impact wt. = 0.3)*	*(Impact wt. = 0.2)*	*(Impact wt. = 0.2)*	
171	RB 1	1.596	1.596	1.271	0.911	ROUND(C$163+(Q102*C$166),3)
172	RB 2	1.126	1.126	1.091	0.945	ROUND(D$163+(R104*D$166),3)
173	RB 3	1.149	0.946	0.375	0.254	ROUND(E$163+(S106*E$166),3)
174	RB 4	0.938	1.104	0.865	0.531	ROUND(F$163+(T108*F$166),3)
175	RB 5	1.355	1.355	0.776	0.653	
176	RB 6	2.171	2.171	1.271	1.102	
177	RB 7	2.158	2.488	1.238	1.264	
178	RB 8	1.614	1.368	1.258	0.153	
179	RB 9	0.503	2.171	1.08	0.36	
180	RB 10	2.171	0.503	1.08	0.36	
181	RB 11	1.596	1.596	1.271	0.54	
182	RB 12	2.158	1.833	1.457	0.013	
183	RB 13	2.158	2.158	1.238	1.264	
184	RB 14	1.149	1.149	0.916	0.792	
185	RB 15	1.316	1.316	1.08	1.294	
186	RB 16	1.368	1.126	1.091	1.28	
187	RB 17	1.881	1.881	1.465	1.49	
188	RB 18	2.488	2.488	1.678	1.483	
189	RB 19	0.481	0.608	0.324	0.243	
190	RB 20	0.36	0.608	0.324	0.16	
191	RB 21	1.564	1.355	0.916	0.792	
192	RB 22	2.171	2.171	1.271	1.102	
193	RB 23	2.158	1.833	1.023	0.833	
194	RB 24	0.611	0.452	0.202	0	
195	RB 25	2.171	1.881	1.465	1.294	
196	RB 26	1.862	0.891	0.603	0.461	
197	RB 27	0.481	0.36	0.408	0.16	
198	RB 28	1.614	1.862	0.927	1.111	
199	RB 29	0.735	0.36	0.16	0.16	
200	RB 30	2.488	2.158	1.678	1.264	

Step 6: We have made a classification into grey classes of *high importance, medium importance* and *low importance*, based on the whitenization weight functions as shown in Figure 8.1. The weight functions for the impact on SRM and CRM were determined using Equations 8.8–8.10 and the weight functions for the impact on ISCM and MEE were obtained using Equations 8.11–8.13.

Step 7: Further, we determine the cluster coefficients of variable weightings for different *RB's* and the grey classes indicating the weighed impact ratings are presented. The Excel calculations for the same are shown in Table 8.13 and the final values are indicated in Table 8.14. The calculations are made following Equations 8.14–8.16.

Table 8.12 Grey to crisp conversion: Final white scores

	A	B	C	D	E	F
168			**Final Scores**			
169	**Sl No.**	**Barriers**	**Impact on SRM**	**Impact on CRM**	**Impact on ISCM**	**Impact on MEE**
170			*(Impact wt. = 0.3)*	*(Impact wt. = 0.3)*	*(Impact wt. = 0.2)*	*(Impact wt. = 0.2)*
171	1	RB 1	1.596	1.596	1.271	0.911
172	2	RB 2	1.126	1.126	1.091	0.945
173	3	RB 3	1.149	0.946	0.375	0.254
174	4	RB 4	0.938	1.104	0.865	0.531
175	5	RB 5	1.355	1.355	0.776	0.653
176	6	RB 6	2.171	2.171	1.271	1.102
177	7	RB 7	2.158	2.488	1.238	1.264
178	8	RB 8	1.614	1.368	1.258	0.153
179	9	RB 9	0.503	2.171	1.08	0.36
180	10	RB 10	2.171	0.503	1.08	0.36
181	11	RB 11	1.596	1.596	1.271	0.54
182	12	RB 12	2.158	1.833	1.457	0.013
183	13	RB 13	2.158	2.158	1.238	1.264
184	14	RB 14	1.149	1.149	0.916	0.792
185	15	RB 15	1.316	1.316	1.08	1.294
186	16	RB 16	1.368	1.126	1.091	1.28
187	17	RB 17	1.881	1.881	1.465	1.49
188	18	RB 18	2.488	2.488	1.678	1.483
189	19	RB 19	0.481	0.608	0.324	0.243
190	20	RB 20	0.36	0.608	0.324	0.16
191	21	RB 21	1.564	1.355	0.916	0.792
192	22	RB 22	2.171	2.171	1.271	1.102
193	23	RB 23	2.158	1.833	1.023	0.833
194	24	RB 24	0.611	0.452	0.202	0
195	25	RB 25	2.171	1.881	1.465	1.294
196	26	RB 26	1.862	0.891	0.603	0.461
197	27	RB 27	0.481	0.36	0.408	0.16
198	28	RB 28	1.614	1.862	0.927	1.111
199	29	RB 29	0.735	0.36	0.16	0.16
200	30	RB 30	2.488	2.158	1.678	1.264

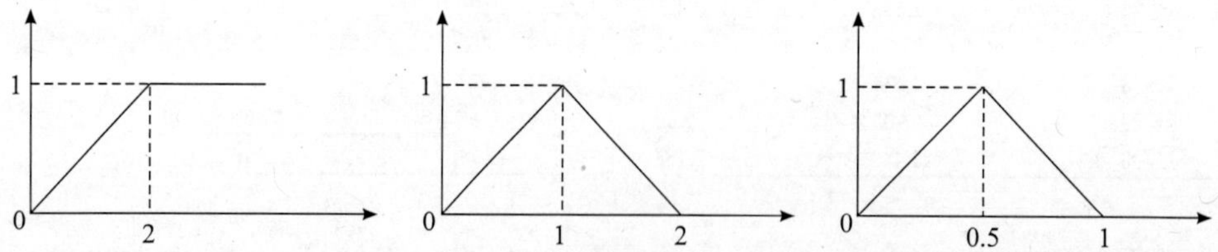

(I) High importance grey class (ii) Moderate importance grey class (iii) Low importance grey class

(a) Grey classes assigned for impact on SRM and CRM

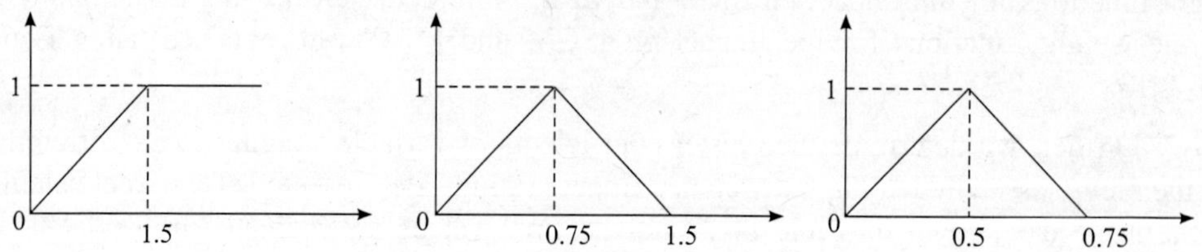

(I) High importance grey class (ii) Moderate importance grey class (iii) Low importance grey class

(b) Grey classes assigned for impact on ISCM and MEE

Figure 8.1 Whitenization weight functions

Table 8.13 Excel formula: Cluster coefficients of weights for RBs

T181 =ROUND((0.75-F181)/0.5,3)

	H	I	J	K	L	M	N	O	P	Q	R	S	T
168		Weights			Weights			Weights			Weights		
169	Barriers	0.3	0.3	0.3	0.3	0.3	0.3	0.2	0.2	0.2	0.2	0.2	0.2
170			*SRM*			*CRM*			*ISCM*			*MEE*	
171	RB 1	0.798	0.404	0	0.798	0.404	0	0.847	0.305	0	0.607	0.785	0
172	RB 2	0.563	0.874	0	0.563	0.874	0	0.727	0.545	0	0.63	0.74	0
173	RB 3	0.575	0.851	0	0.473	0.946	0.138	0.25	0.5	1	0.169	0.339	1
174	RB 4	0.469	0.938	0.124	0.552	0.896	0	0.577	0.847	0	0.354	0.708	0.438
175	RB 5	0.678	0.645	0	0.678	0.645	0	0.517	0.965	0	0.435	0.871	0.194
176	RB 6	1	0	0	1	0	0	0.847	0.305	0	0.735	0.531	0
177	RB 7	1	0	0	1	0	0	0.825	0.349	0	0.843	0.315	0
178	RB 8	0.807	0.386	0	0.684	0.632	0	0.839	0.323	0	0.102	0.204	1
179	RB 9	0.252	0.503	0.994	1	0	0	0.72	0.56	0	0.24	0.48	1
180	RB 10	1	0	0	0.252	0.503	0.594	0.72	0.56	0	0.24	0.48	1
181	RB 11	0.798	0.404	0	0.798	0.404	0	0.847	0.305	0	0.36	0.72	0.42
182	RB 12	1	0	0	0.917	0.167	0	0.971	0.057	0	0.009	0.017	1
183	RB 13	1	0	0	1	0	0	0.825	0.349	0	0.843	0.315	0
184	RB 14	0.575	0.851	0	0.575	0.851	0	0.611	0.779	0	0.528	0.944	0
185	RB 15	0.658	0.684	0	0.658	0.684	0	0.72	0.56	0	0.863	0.275	0
186	RB 16	0.684	0.632	0	0.563	0.874	0	0.727	0.545	0	0.853	0.293	0
187	RB 17	0.941	0.119	0	0.941	0.119	0	0.977	0.047	0	0.993	0.013	0
188	RB 18	1	0	0	1	0	0	1	0	0	0.989	0.023	0
189	RB 19	0.241	0.481	1	0.304	0.608	0.784	0.216	0.432	1	0.162	0.324	1
190	RB 20	0.18	0.36	1	0.304	0.608	0.784	0.216	0.432	1	0.107	0.213	1
191	RB 21	0.782	0.436	0	0.678	0.645	0	0.611	0.779	0	0.528	0.944	0
192	RB 22	1	0	0	1	0	0	0.847	0.305	0	0.735	0.531	0
193	RB 23	1	0	0	0.917	0.167	0	0.682	0.636	0	0.555	0.889	0
194	RB 24	0.306	0.611	0.778	0.226	0.452	1	0.135	0.269	1	0	0	1
195	RB 25	1	0	0	0.941	0.119	0	0.977	0.047	0	0.863	0.275	0
196	RB 26	0.931	0.138	0	0.446	0.891	0.218	0.402	0.804	0.294	0.307	0.615	1
197	RB 27	0.241	0.481	1	0.18	0.36	1	0.272	0.544	1	0.107	0.213	1
198	RB 28	0.807	0.386	0	0.931	0.138	0	0.618	0.764	0	0.741	0.519	0
199	RB 29	0.368	0.735	0.53	0.18	0.36	1	0.107	0.213	1	0.107	0.213	1
200	RB 30	1	0	0	1	0	0	1	0	0	0.843	0.315	0
201		ROUND(C171/2,3)	ROUND(2-C171,3)	ROUND((1-C174)/0.5,3)	ROUND(D171/2,3)	ROUND(2-D171,3)	ROUND((1-D173)/0.5,3)	ROUND(E171/1.5,3)		ROUND((0.75-E196)/0.5,3)		ROUND((1.5-F171)/0.75,3)	
202									ROUND((1.5-E171)/0.75,3)		ROUND(F171/1.5,3)		ROUND((0.75-F174)/0.5,3)

Table 8.14 Cluster coefficients of weights for RBs

	H	I	J	K	L	M	N	O	P	Q	R	S	T
168	Barriers		Weights			Weights			Weights			Weights	
169		0.3	0.3	0.3	0.3	0.3	0.3	0.2	0.2	0.2	0.2	0.2	0.2
170			SRM			CRM			ISCM			MEE	
171	RB 1	0.798	0.404	0	0.798	0.404	0	0.847	0.305	0	0.607	0.785	0
172	RB 2	0.563	0.874	0	0.563	0.874	0	0.727	0.545	0	0.63	0.74	0
173	RB 3	0.575	0.851	0	0.473	0.946	0.108	0.25	0.5	1	0.169	0.339	1
174	RB 4	0.469	0.938	0.124	0.552	0.896	0	0.577	0.847	0	0.354	0.708	0.438
175	RB 5	0.678	0.645	0	0.678	0.645	0	0.517	0.965	0	0.435	0.871	0.194
176	RB 6	1	0	0	1	0	0	0.847	0.305	0	0.735	0.531	0
177	RB 7	1	0	0	1	0	0	0.825	0.349	0	0.843	0.315	0
178	RB 8	0.807	0.386	0	0.684	0.632	0	0.839	0.323	0	0.102	0.204	1
179	RB 9	0.252	0.503	0.994	1	0	0	0.72	0.56	0	0.24	0.48	1
180	RB 10	1	0	0	0.252	0.503	0.994	0.72	0.56	0	0.24	0.48	1
181	RB 11	0.798	0.404	0	0.798	0.404	0	0.847	0.305	0	0.36	0.72	0.42
182	RB 12	1	0	0	0.917	0.167	0	0.971	0.057	0	0.009	0.017	1
183	RB 13	1	0	0	1	0	0	0.825	0.349	0	0.843	0.315	0
184	RB 14	0.575	0.851	0	0.575	0.851	0	0.611	0.779	0	0.528	0.944	0
185	RB 15	0.658	0.684	0	0.658	0.684	0	0.72	0.56	0	0.863	0.275	0
186	RB 16	0.684	0.632	0	0.563	0.874	0	0.727	0.545	0	0.853	0.293	0
187	RB 17	0.941	0.119	0	0.941	0.119	0	0.977	0.047	0	0.993	0.013	0
188	RB 18	1	0	0	1	0	0	1	0	0	0.989	0.023	0
189	RB 19	0.241	0.481	1	0.304	0.608	0.784	0.216	0.432	1	0.162	0.324	1
190	RB 20	0.18	0.36	1	0.304	0.608	0.784	0.216	0.432	1	0.107	0.213	1
191	RB 21	0.782	0.436	0	0.678	0.645	0	0.611	0.779	0	0.528	0.944	0
192	RB 22	1	0	0	1	0	0	0.847	0.305	0	0.735	0.531	0
193	RB 23	1	0	0	0.917	0.167	0	0.682	0.636	0	0.555	0.889	0
194	RB 24	0.306	0.611	0.778	0.226	0.452	1	0.135	0.269	1	0	0	1
195	RB 25	1	0	0	0.941	0.119	0	0.977	0.047	0	0.863	0.275	0
196	RB 26	0.931	0.138	0	0.446	0.891	0.218	0.402	0.804	0.294	0.307	0.615	1
197	RB 27	0.241	0.481	1	0.18	0.36	1	0.272	0.544	1	0.107	0.213	1
198	RB 28	0.807	0.386	0	0.931	0.138	0	0.618	0.764	0	0.741	0.519	0
199	RB 29	0.368	0.735	0.53	0.18	0.36	1	0.107	0.213	1	0.107	0.213	1
200	RB 30	1	0	0	1	0	0	1	0	0	0.843	0.315	0

Step 8: Following the class information in Table 8.14, the grey classes for the *thirty* barriers are assigned. The Excel calculations for the classification is shown in Table 8.15 and the final classification of barriers into categories is shown in Table 8.16.

Table 8.15 Excel formula: Classification of barriers (RBs)

AE199 | fx =IF(W199 = AD199, V199, (IF(Y199 = AD199, X199,(IF(AA199 = AD199, Z199,0)))))

	V	W	X	Y	Z	AA	AB	AC	AD	AE	AF	AG	AH	AI	AJ	AK	AL
169		Grey Classes						Barriers	Scores	Classes of RB							
170		*HI*		*MI*		*LI*											
171	1	0.77	2	0.46	3	0		RB 1	0.77	1	MAX(W171,Y171,AA171)						
172	1	0.609	2	0.781	3	0		RB 2	0.781	2							
173	1	0.398	2	0.707	3	0.432		RB 3	0.707	2							
174	1	0.493	2	0.861	3	0.125		RB 4	0.861	2							
175	1	0.597	2	0.754	3	0.039		RB 5	0.754	2							
176	1	0.916	2	0.167	3	0		RB 6	0.916	1	IF(W176 = AD176, V176, (IF(Y176 = AD176, X176,(IF(AA176 = AD176, Z176,0)))))						
177	1	0.934	2	0.133	3	0		RB 7	0.934	1							
178	1	0.636	2	0.411	3	0.2		RB 8	0.636	1							
179	1	0.568	2	0.359	3	0.498		RB 9	0.568	1							
180	1	0.568	2	0.359	3	0.498		RB 10	0.568	1							
181	1	0.72	2	0.447	3	0.084		RB 11	0.72	1							
182	1	0.771	2	0.065	3	0.2		RB 12	0.771	1							
183	1	0.934	2	0.133	3	0		RB 13	0.934	1							
184	1	0.573	2	0.855	3	0		RB 14	0.855	2							
185	1	0.711	2	0.577	3	0		RB 15	0.711	1							
186	1	0.69	2	0.619	3	0		RB 16	0.69	1							
187	1	0.959	2	0.083	3	0		RB 17	0.959	1							
188	1	0.998	2	0.005	3	0		RB 18	0.998	1							
189	1	0.239	2	0.478	3	0.935		RB 19	0.935	3							
190	1	0.21	2	0.419	3	0.935		RB 20	0.935	3							
191	1	0.666	2	0.669	3	0		RB 21	0.669	2							
192	1	0.916	2	0.167	3	0		RB 22	0.916	1							
193	1	0.823	2	0.355	3	0		RB 23	0.823	1							
194	1	0.187	2	0.373	3	0.933		RB 24	0.933	3							
195	1	0.95	2	0.1	3	0		RB 25	0.95	1							
196	1	0.555	2	0.593	3	0.324		RB 26	0.593	2							
197	1	0.202	2	0.404	3	1		RB 27	1	3							
198	1	0.793	2	0.414	3	0		RB 28	0.793	1							
199	1	0.207	2	0.414	3	0.859		RB 29	0.859	3							
200	1	0.969	2	0.063	3	0		RB 30	0.969	1							
201		ROUND((I171*I169+L171*L169+O171*O169+R171*R169),3)															
202				ROUND((J171*J169+M171*M169+P171*P169+S171*S169),3)													
203						ROUND((K171*K169+N171*N169+Q171*Q169+T171*T169),3)											

Table 8.16 Classification of barriers (RBs)

	V	W	X	Y	Z	AA	AB	AC	AD	AE
169			Grey Classes					Barriers	Scores	Classes of RB
170		*HI*		*MI*		*LI*				
171	1	0.77	2	0.46	3	0		RB 1	0.77	1
172	1	0.609	2	0.781	3	0		RB 2	0.781	2
173	1	0.398	2	0.707	3	0.432		RB 3	0.707	2
174	1	0.493	2	0.861	3	0.125		RB 4	0.861	2
175	1	0.597	2	0.754	3	0.039		RB 5	0.754	2
176	1	0.916	2	0.167	3	0		RB 6	0.916	1
177	1	0.934	2	0.133	3	0		RB 7	0.934	1
178	1	0.636	2	0.411	3	0.2		RB 8	0.636	1
179	1	0.568	2	0.359	3	0.498		RB 9	0.568	1
180	1	0.568	2	0.359	3	0.498		RB 10	0.568	1
181	1	0.72	2	0.447	3	0.084		RB 11	0.72	1
182	1	0.771	2	0.065	3	0.2		RB 12	0.771	1
183	1	0.934	2	0.133	3	0		RB 13	0.934	1
184	1	0.573	2	0.855	3	0		RB 14	0.855	2
185	1	0.711	2	0.577	3	0		RB 15	0.711	1
186	1	0.69	2	0.619	3	0		RB 16	0.69	1
187	1	0.959	2	0.083	3	0		RB 17	0.959	1
188	1	0.998	2	0.005	3	0		RB 18	0.998	1
189	1	0.239	2	0.478	3	0.935		RB 19	0.935	3
190	1	0.21	2	0.419	3	0.935		RB 20	0.935	3
191	1	0.666	2	0.669	3	0		RB 21	0.669	2
192	1	0.916	2	0.167	3	0		RB 22	0.916	1
193	1	0.823	2	0.355	3	0		RB 23	0.823	1
194	1	0.187	2	0.373	3	0.933		RB 24	0.933	3
195	1	0.95	2	0.1	3	0		RB 25	0.95	1
196	1	0.555	2	0.593	3	0.324		RB 26	0.593	2
197	1	0.202	2	0.404	3	1		RB 27	1	3
198	1	0.793	2	0.414	3	0		RB 28	0.793	1
199	1	0.207	2	0.414	3	0.859		RB 29	0.859	3
200	1	0.969	2	0.063	3	0		RB 30	0.969	1

Step 9: The absolute grey classes highlighting the barriers in the *high importance* category are presented in Table 8.16. This table is beneficial for managers, as they can assign top priority in dealing with those barriers falling in the high importance category for improving the resilience capabilities.

8.3 CONCLUSION

The application of grey theory in clustering the data is elaborated in this last chapter of the book. The detailed steps in the implementation process along with the implementation demonstration for a sample case problem are explained. Researchers and practitioners can find applications of the grey clustering based models to classify or to cluster, particularly small to medium sized datasets.

REFERENCES

Ke, L., Xiaoliu, S., Zhongfu, T. and Wenyan, G. (2012). Grey clustering analysis method for overseas energy project investment risk decision. *Systems Engineering Procedia*, 3, 55–62.

Liu, S. and Yang, Y. (2017). Explanation of terms of grey clustering evaluation models. *Grey Systems: Theory and Application*, 7(1), 129–135.

Liu, W., Zhang, J., Jin, M., Liu, S., Chang, X., Xie, N. and Wang, Y. (2017). Key indices of the remanufacturing industry in China using a combined method of grey incidence analysis and grey clustering. *Journal of Cleaner Production*, 168, 1348–1357.

Rajesh, R. (2018). Measuring the barriers to resilience in manufacturing supply chains using Grey Clustering and VIKOR approaches. *Measurement*, 126, 259–273.

Index